TESLA'   E

A NEW DIMENSION FOR POWER

Compiled by Jeffery A. Hayes

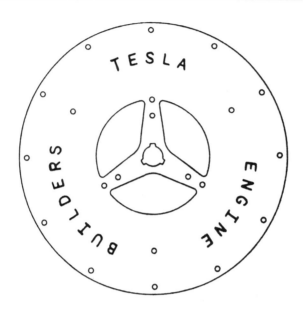

"The success of my propulsion scheme is about as certain as the law of gravity"

NIKOLA TESLA

Published by: **Tesla Engine Builders Association (TEBA)**
A Membership Organization (send S.A.S.E.)
5464 N. Port Washington Road, Suite 293
Milwaukee, Wisconsin 53217

ISBN 1-884917-33-X

Library of Congress Catalog Card Number **94-60502**
Includes Index
1.Turbines.   2.Geothermal power plants   3.Internal combustion engines.
4. Pumping machinery. 5. Electric vehicles. 6. Tesla, Nikola (1856-1943) I. Title.
TJ267.H39 1994   621.4'06 (QB I94-776)

About the Cover: Tesla's life size image glared out from a headline story announcing his new engine in the New York Herald Tribune, see p22.

A NEW DIMENSION FOR POWER

CONTENTS

CLASSIC WORKS

SUCCESSFUL COMMERCIALIZATION

SELECTED TESLA PATENTS

WAKE UP CALL

INTRODUCTION

Most people remember Nikola Tesla for his work and revelations in the field of electrical energy and the invention of radio. Most do not realize that he was a mechanical engineer by training and first love. He also had a life long passion for flight, envisioning himself as the first man that would fly, using an aircraft powered by electric motors. Tesla was, however, anticipated by men who successfully flew an aircraft using the reciprocating internal combustion engine. Though successful in achieving flight, aircraft using these engines were dangerous and unpredictable, due to the engine's lack of adequate power. Tesla turned his attention to revamping the internal combustion engine, so as to make flying safe for all and minimize its environmental impact. Documented in this text is the result of Tesla's endeavors and the resulting marvel of machines called the "Tesla Bladeless Turbine" or "Tesla Engine." Although Tesla's dream for his engines' application in aircraft was not realized in his lifetime, if used in aircraft today, it could provide a quiet, safe, simple and efficient alternative to our supposedly advanced, bladed turbine aircraft engines.

The application of this amazing engine was not to be limited to aircraft. Tesla was setting up plans to replace what he considered the wasteful, polluting, inefficient and complicated reciprocating piston engine, we continue to use today, in all of its applications, including the automobile. Tesla's, small but powerful, engine can run efficiently on any alternative fuel with little to no wear on the internal engine components.

Unlike most people of the time, Tesla was very concerned about the long range environmental damage that the reciprocating engines would create. He stressed over and over how we must take the long range view and not step out of harmony with our life support systems. Today the widening concern for *Spaceship* Earth and the renewal of an old ethic "We don't inherit the Earth from our ancestors, we borrow it from our children" is slowly beginning to awaken people to the concerns of Tesla.

Although the existence of the automobile on city streets dates back to the first years of the century, its role as a contributor to atmospheric contamination did not receive wide acceptance among scientists until the 60's. Factual evidence that urban area smog was chemically related to automobile emissions had been produced and acknowledge by scientific groups in the 1950's. Despite vehement disagreement which ensued between government and the automotive industry on this volatile issue, research and development programs were initiated by both groups in an effort to identify the reciprocating internal combustion engine's sources of pollution and determine what corrective action might be taken.

Obviously Tesla's pleas were not and are not being heeded. The basic issue of engine design continues to be ignored. Computers have instead been grafted to the piston engine, vastly increasing its complexity, but only marginally improving its performance. The only other major contender for engine design has been the Wankel, so called rotary engine. This engine is not a true rotary. It oscillates around the central axis with a complicated set of gears and seals. The Tesla machine is a true rotary engine and operates on an entirely different principle than the Wankel, it has no gears or wear prone seals. The Wankel has been a failure at increasing efficiency and in reducing emissions. Yet almost everyone has heard of the Wankel but few know of the Tesla.

If large scale commercial production was implemented, the Tesla rotary engine would be extremely affordable due to its simplicity of manufacture, longevity, almost total lack of maintenance with the added bonus that it requires no crank case oil.

Tesla insisted that the most efficient configuration for converting energy was not an engine mechanically connected to drive the wheels.   Although assailed by the experts at the time, he proposed that the engine should be coupled with an electric drive system. This involves driving an electric generator with an engine, which in turn powers an electric motor, the shaft of which drives the wheels. This configuration was announced by Tesla in 1900 and has become known as the "hybrid electric drive." It is currently the standard in railroad locomotives, which use a hybrid diesel/electric system. New electric motors have recently been developed, of unique design, using new materials, that can achieve unbelievable new gasoline consumption records when used in the hybrid gasoline/electric configuration. Tesla was convinced that it would only be a matter of time before a vehicle could drive coast to coast on a single tank of fuel.

Tesla is also responsible for the first commercial power generation of any magnitude, with the installation of his alternators at Niagara Falls. These Tesla "polyphase" alternators were coupled to bladed steam turbines and are the heart of our current power system. Unfortunately, power plants of today are only using half of Tesla's system.

The Record According to Guinness
Gasoline Consumption

At the Shell Mileage Marathon track at Silverstone, England, on July 1, 1988, Wasaki Oka of Japan drove an experimental Honda a distance of 6,409 miles on one imperial gallon (1$\frac{1}{8}$ US gallons) of gasoline.

Tesla's rotary engine or bladeless turbine, when used with steam, can easily exceed the performance of currently used bladed steam turbines. Tesla is well documented as stating that his engine, or thermal converter, could obtain a 95% efficiency if fully staged. Our best, fully staged, bladed steam turbines operate in the 60% range. Where is the rest of the energy going? Observe any large power plant and notice the huge amounts of steam being vented into the atmosphere.

The currently used steam turbines in coal, oil, gas and nuclear power plants must be periodically rebuilt, costing millions. The Tesla steam engine requires no such periodic rebuilding. It can even ingest solids. Multi-million dollar filtration systems must be used to prevent even the smallest solids from going through a conventional steam turbine. If solids do enter the conventional steam turbine it must be rebuilt.

Temperature regulation, something that is critical to a conventional steam turbine, is not a concern with the Tesla device.

Solar projects, such as the "Luz" in the Mojave desert of California, recently taken over by Southern California Edison, would also greatly benefit from application of this technology. They are currently using one of the latest bladed staged turbines but still must be concerned with temperature regulation and solids ingestion. On site at this latest 80 megawatt project you will see three huge heat exchangers venting off energy into the atmosphere. If Tesla's missing link was incorporated into our current power plants it would represent a great savings. It would also have the added bonus of drastically reduced maintenance.

Although Tesla's engine is referred to as a turbine in comparison to the devices it replaces, Tesla did not consider it a turbine in the strictest sense. A turbine operates as a result of impulse and reaction against lifting surfaces or blades with a resultant turbulent flow. The Tesla device has no lifting surfaces, using instead smooth flat disks. The driving fluid produces a laminar flow without turbulence, therefore extracting a larger percentage of the potential energy. Quoting Tesla:

"In this new invention we have a beautiful solution of many mechanical problems. We have a prime mover which is reversible, ideally simple, of enormous torque, incomparably greater than the turbine possesses, so I am looking for a revolution in mechanics from the application of this principle."

Tesla did, however, consider his engine to be in the category of turbo machinery. Turbo being Latin for "things that spin."

Tesla's engine is an easily understood device with especially fine and useful qualities. Not only is it the ideal prime mover, it can also be used as a pump in slightly modified form. And like its cousin the engine, it has Herculean power. Tesla's pumps are now in commercial production and are revolutionizing the pumping industry, garnering sales in the multi-millions. Conventional pumps are easily damaged by contaminants. The Bladeless Tesla Pump can handle particles and corrosives in stride as well as gases with no cavitation damage, factors that hasten the demise of conventional type pumps.

Due to the revolutionary concepts embodied in this engine, we can easily end the so called energy crisis and dramatically reduce pollution. Even the vested energy interests are beginning to understand that now is the time for change, realizing their future health and wealth is directly linked to that of the environment. We can't buy or hide our way out of a devastated planet. The Tesla Engine has valuable qualities that make it attractive to both the technological and evironmental communities alike. Nikola Tesla's crowning achievement can provide a simplified means by which the industrial plants of the future may be operated more economically, with cleaner and less environmentally intrusive equipment.

Tesla from his 1919 autobiography, My Inventions:

"My alternating system of power transmission came at a psychological moment, as a long-sought answer to pressing industrial questions, and altho considerable resistance had to be overcome and opposing interests reconciled, as usual, the commercial introduction could not be long delayed. Now, compare this situation with that confronting my turbine, for example. One should think that so simple and beautiful an invention, possessing many features of an ideal motor, should be adopted at once and, undoubtedly, it would under similar conditions. But the prospective effect of the rotating field was not to render worthless existing machinery; on the contrary, it was to give it additional value. The system lent itself to new enterprise as well as to improvement of the old. My turbine is an advance of a character entirely different. It is a radical departure in the sense that its success would mean the abandonment of the antiquated types of prime movers on which billions of dollars have been spent. Under such circumstances the progress must needs be slow and perhaps the greatest impediment is encountered in the prejudicial opinions created in the minds of experts by organized opposition." It has indeed been slow. Now is the time to bring this invention to fruition.

H. G. Wells once said that future history will be a race between education and catastrophe. This book is dedicated to the race for education.

Our Future Motive Power

By

Nikola

Tesla

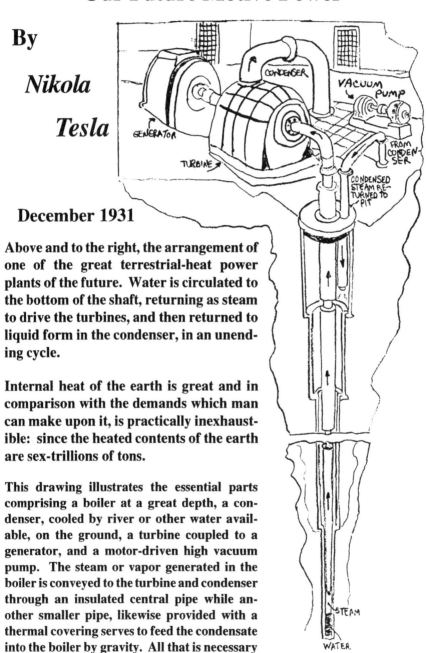

December 1931

Above and to the right, the arrangement of one of the great terrestrial-heat power plants of the future. Water is circulated to the bottom of the shaft, returning as steam to drive the turbines, and then returned to liquid form in the condenser, in an unending cycle.

Internal heat of the earth is great and in comparison with the demands which man can make upon it, is practically inexhaustible: since the heated contents of the earth are sex-trillions of tons.

This drawing illustrates the essential parts comprising a boiler at a great depth, a condenser, cooled by river or other water available, on the ground, a turbine coupled to a generator, and a motor-driven high vacuum pump. The steam or vapor generated in the boiler is conveyed to the turbine and condenser through an insulated central pipe while another smaller pipe, likewise provided with a thermal covering serves to feed the condensate into the boiler by gravity. All that is necessary to open up unlimited resources of power throughout the world is to find some economic and speedy way of sinking deep shafts.

Page **13**   **AMERICAN MAGAZINE**   April, 1921

MAKING YOUR IMAGINATION WORK FOR YOU

An interview with Nikola Tesla, great inventor, who tells the romantic story of his life. He also describes a method of work he has evolved, which will be of use to any imaginative man, whether he is an inventor, business man, or artist.

Interviewed by M.K. Wisehart

PHOTOGRAPH BY SARONY

NIKOLA TESLA

Born and educated in what was then Austria-Hungary, Tesla came to this country thirty-seven years ago when he was twenty-seven years old. His first invention, a telephone repeater, has been followed by other enormously valuable contributions to the science of telegraphy and telephony, especially in connection with the system of wireless transmission. He lives in New York City.

THERE were two inventions to my credit before I was six years old. The first was a hook for catching bullfrogs. A boy in our little village of Smiljan, JugoSlavia, had received a present of a hook and fishing tackle. This made a great stir among my playmates, and the next morning they all started out to catch frogs; but I was left alone because I'd had a quarrel with the boy who owned the tackle.

I never had seen a hook, and I imagined it to be a wonderful something with mysterious qualities; but, prompted by necessity, I got hold of a piece of soft iron wire, bent it, and sharpened it by means of two stones. Then I attached it to a strong string, cut a rod, gathered bait, and went to the brook, where the frogs were innumerable.

In vain I tried to capture the frogs in the water; and I was humiliated to think what a big catch my playmates would bring home with their fine tackle. But at last I dangled my empty hook in front of a frog sitting on a stump, and I can see now in my mind's eye what happened as vividly as though it were yesterday.

First, the fog collapsed, then his eyes bulged, and he swelled to twice his normal size, made a vicious snap at the hook—and I pulled him in. This method proved so infallible that I went home with a fine catch, whereas my playmates caught none. To this day I consider my frog-hook invention quite remarkable and very ambitious. It involved the invention both of an *apparatus* and a *method.* I may have been anticipated in the former, but I like to think that the latter was original.

My second invention was prompted by the very same desire that guides me in all I do today, the desire to harness the forces of nature to the service of man. This I did, at that time, through the medium of May bugs, or June bugs as we call them in America. These bugs were such a pest in our neighborhood that sometimes the sheer weight of their bodies brought down branches of trees.

Four of the bugs I attached to a crosspiece of wood, which was arranged so as to rotate on a thin spindle. The motion of the spindle was transmitted to a large disk, and in this way I derived my power, for, once started going the May bugs never knew when to stop; the hotter it was, the harder they worked. This invention gave me complete satisfaction until one day I saw the son of a retired officer of the Austrian army eating May bugs, and seeming to enjoy them. I never played with the bugs after that, and to this day I shrink from touching any kind of insect.

The memories of my youth and even of earliest childhood are very vivid, and it seems to me that my character began to develop a little sooner than is the case with most people. As a very small boy I was weak and vacillating, and made many childish resolves, only to break them. But when I was eight years old I read "The Son of Aba," a Serbian translation of a Hungarian writer, Josika, whose lessons are similar to those of Lew Wallace in Ben Hur. This book awakened my will power. I began to practice self-control, subdued many of my wishes, and resolved to keep every promise I ever made, whether to myself or to anyone else. The members of my family were not long in learning that if I promised a thing I would do it.

Long before I was twenty, I was smoking excessively—fifteen or twenty big black cigars every day. My health was threatened, and my family often tried to get me to promise to stop, but I would not.

One day I was standing in front of our house, when they told me the doctor had just said that my youngest sister, who had been very ill for some time, was dying. I went up to her room, carrying my lighted cigar, and before kneeling at her bedside I placed the cigar on a little table beside the bed.

"Niko." she said, so faintly that I could hardly hear her, "you are killing yourself with smoking. Promise me you will give it up."

"Yes," I said: "if you will get well, I promise to give up smoking."

"All right, Niko," she said feebly, "I will try."

She did get well, and I have never smoked since. It was very hard to give it up, but I was determined to keep my promise. Not only did I stop, but I finally destroyed every inclination for what had been such a great satisfaction. In this way I have freed myself of other habits and passions, and so have preserved my health and my zest for life. The satisfaction derived from demonstrating my own strength of will has always meant more to me in the end than the pleasurable habits I gave up. I believe that a man can and should stop any habit he recognizes to be "foolish."

When I was about twenty, I contracted a mania for gambling. We played for very high stakes; and more than one of my companions gambled away the full value of his home. My luck was generally bad, but on one occasion I won everything in sight. Still I was not satisfied, but must go on with the play. I lent my companions money so that we might continue, and before we left the table I had lost all that I had won and was in debt.

MY PARENTS were greatly worried by my gambling habits. My father especially was stern and often expressed his contempt at my wanton waste of time and money. However, I never would promise him to give up gambling, but instead defended myself with a bad philosophy that is very common. I told him that, of course, I could stop whenever I pleased, but that it was not worth while to give up gambling because the pleasure was more to me than the joys of Paradise.

My mother understood human nature better and never chided. She knew that a man cannot be saved from his own foolishness or vice by someone else's efforts or protests, but only by the use of his own will. One afternoon, when I had lost all my money, but still was craving to play, she came to me with a roll of bills in her hand—a large sum of money for those times and conditions—and said, "Here, Niko. Take these. They're all I have. But the sooner you lose everything we own, the better it will be. Then I know you will get over this."

She kissed me.

So blinded was I by my passion that I took the money, gambled the whole night, and lost everything, as usual. It was morning when I emerged from the den, and I went on a long walk through sunlit woods pondering my utter folly. The sight of nature had brought me to my senses, and my mother's act and faith came vividly to mind. Before I left the woods, I had conquered this passion. I went home to my mother and told her I never would gamble again. And there never has been the slightest danger of my breaking the promise.

My father was the son of an officer who served in the army of the Great Napoleon. He himself had received military training, and oddly enough, had subsequently embraced the clerical profession. A philosopher, poet, and writer, he achieved eminence as a preacher because of his learning and eloquence. But it is to my mother, I believe, that I trace my inventiveness. Her father and grandfather originated numerous implements for household and agricultural uses. My mother herself invented and constructed all kinds of tools and devices, and wove the finest designs from thread, spun by herself. I have always thought that my mother would have achieved great things if we had not lived so far from the opportunities of modern life.

Both my father and mother were very eager that I should become a preacher; but I had no leaning in that direction. From the age of ten I had been inventing all sorts of things in my mind: flying machines, a submarine tube for carrying letters and packages under the Atlantic, and means of getting power from the rotation of the planets; all fanciful, but even after I had gone to study at the gymnasium at Carlstadt, Croatia, where I became intensely interested in physics and electricity, my parents still wanted me to become a preacher.

Perhaps, if I had not become very ill, I should have given my promise. But because of overstudy, I had my first serious breakdown in health. Physicians absolutely gave me up. It was an American genius who saved my life.

During my illness I read books by the score from the public library, and one day I was handed a few volumes unlike anything I had ever read, and so interesting that I forgot my hopeless state. My recovery seemed miraculous.

The books I had been reading were the early works of Mark Twain— among them "Tom Sawyer," and "Huckleberry Finn." Twenty-five years later, when I met Mr. Clemens and we formed a lifelong friendship, I told him of this experience and of my belief that I owed my life to his books. I was deeply moved to see tears come to the eyes of this great man of laughter.

AFTER graduating from the Higher *Realschule* at Carlstadt, I went home to my parents, and on the very day of my arrival was stricken with cholera, which was then epidemic in those parts. Again I was near death. My father tried to cheer me with hopeful words.

"Perhaps," I said, "I might get well, if you would let me become an engineer instead of a clergyman."

He promised solemnly that I should go to the best technical institution in the world. This, literally, put new life into me; and, owing partly to my improved state of mind and partly to a wonderful medicine, I recovered. My father kept his word by sending me to the Polytechnic School in Gratz, Styria, one of the oldest institutions of Europe.

All during my first year there I started work at three A.M. and continued until eleven P.M., neither Sundays nor holidays being excepted. Such leisure as I allowed myself I spent in the library. It was during my second year that something happened that has determined the whole course of my life. To make this clear, I must tell you about an early experience.

During my boyhood I had suffered from a peculiar affliction due to the appearance of images, which were often accompanied by strong flashes of light. When a word was spoken, the image of the object designated would present itself so vividly to my vision that I could not tell whether what I saw was real or not. If I had witnessed a funeral, or perhaps come close to some animal while on a hunting trip, then inevitably in the stillness of night a vivid picture of the scene would thrust itself before my eyes and persist, despite all my efforts to banish it. Even though I reached out and passed my hand through it, the image would remain fixed in space.

IN TRYING to free myself from these tormenting appearances, I tried to concentrate my mind on some peaceful, quieting scene I had witnessed. This would give me momentary relief; but when I had done it two or three times the remedy would begin to lose its force. Then I began to take mental excursions beyond the small world of my actual knowledge. Day and night, in imagination, I went on journeys—saw new places, cities, countries, and all the time I tried very hard to make these imaginary things very sharp and clear in my mind. I imagined myself living in countries I never had seen, and I made imaginary friends, who were very dear to me and really seemed alive.

This I did constantly until I was about seventeen, when my thoughts turned seriously to invention. Then, to my delight, I found that I could *visualize* with the greatest facility. I needed no models, drawings, or experiments. I could picture them all in my mind.

During my second year at the Polytechnic Institute, we received a Gramme dynamo from Paris. It had a horseshoe form of field magnet and a wire-wound armature with a commutator—a type of machine that has since become antiquated. While the professor was demonstrating with this machine, the brushes sparked badly, and I suggested that it might be possible to operate a motor without such appliances. The professor declared that I could never create such a motor, because the idea was equivalent to a perpetual motion scheme.

This statement from such a high authority caused me to waver in my belief for some time. Then I took courage and began to think intently of the problem, trying to visualize the kind of machine I wanted to build, constructing all its parts in my imagination. These images were as clear and distinct as those I had conjured up to drive away the tormenting visions of my younger days. I conceived many schemes, changing them daily, but I did not at that time succeed in evolving a workable plan.

Four years later, in 1881, I was in Budapest, Hungary, studying the American telephone system, which was just being installed. But, during this interval, never for a day had I given up my attempt to visualize an electric motor without a commutator. In my anxiety to visualize one that would *work,* my health again broke down, just when I was feeling that the long sought solution was near; but after six months of careful nursing I recovered.

Then, one afternoon I was walking with a friend in the City Park and reciting poetry. At that time I knew entire books by heart, word for word. One of these was Goethe's "Faust;" and the setting sun reminded me of the passage:

The glow retreats, done is the day of toil;
It yonder hastes, new fields of life exploring;
Ah, that no wing can lift me from the soil,
Upon its track to follow, follow soaring!

Even while I was speaking these glorious words, the vision of my induction motor, complete, perfect, operable, came into my mind like a flash. I drew with a stick on the sand the vision I had seen. They were the same diagrams I was to show six years later before the American Institute of Electrical Engineers. My friend understood the drawings perfectly; and to me the images were so real that suddenly I cried. "Look! Watch me reverse my motor!" And I did it, demonstrating with my stick.

THIS discovery is known as the "rotating magnetic field." It is the principle on which my induction motor operates. In this invention I produced a sort of magnetic cyclone which grips the rotable part and *whirls* it—exactly what my professor had said could never be done.

After inventing this motor, I gave myself up more intensely than ever to the enjoyment of picturing in my mind new kinds of machines. It was my great delight to imagine motors constantly running. In less than two months, I had created *mentally* nearly all the types of motors and modifications of the system which are now identified with my name.

It was in 1888, after I had come to America, that arrangements were made with the Westinghouse Company for the manufacture of this motor and for the introduction on a large scale of my system, which has since then been universally adopted. It gave the first great impetus to the harnessing of water power, to the development of trolley lines, subway systems and electric railways. It is embodied in the electric drive on battleships, and used as a means of transmitting power for innumerable purposes all over the world.

By that faculty of *visualizing,* which I learned in my boyish effort to rid myself of annoying images, I have evolved what is, I believe, a new method of materializing inventive ideas and conceptions. It is a method which may be of great usefulness to any imaginative man, whether he is an inventor, business man, or artist.

Some people, the moment they have a device to construct or any piece of work to perform, rush at it without adequate preparation, and immediately become engrossed in *details,* instead of the central idea. They may get results, but they sacrifice quality.

Here, in brief, is my own method: After experiencing a desire to invent a particular thing, I may go on for months or years with the idea in the back of my head. Whenever I feel like it, I roam around in my imagination and think about the problem without any deliberate concentration. This is a period of incubation.

Then follows a period of direct effort. I choose carefully the possible solutions of the problem, I am considering, and gradually center my mind on a narrowed field of investigation. Now, when I am deliberately thinking of the problem in its specific features, I may begin to feel that I am going to get the solution. And the wonderful thing is that if I do feel this way, *then I know I have really solved the problem and shall get what I am after.*

This *feeling* is as convincing to me as though I already had solved it. I have come to the conclusion that at this stage the actual solution is in my mind *subconsciously,* though it may be a long time before I am aware of it *consciously.*

Before I put a sketch on paper, the whole idea is worked out mentally. In my mind, I change the construction , make improvements, and even operate the device.   Without ever having drawn a sketch, I can give the measurements of all parts to workmen, and when completed these parts will fit, just as certainly as though I had made accurate drawings. It is immaterial to me whether I run my machine in my mind or test it in my shop.

The inventions I have conceived in this way, have always worked. In thirty years there has not been a single exception. My first electric motor, the vacuum tube wireless light, my turbine engine, and many other devices have all been developed in exactly this way.

From Budapest I went to Paris, and there became associated with Mr. Charles Batchellor, an intimate friend and assistant of Mr. Edison. From Paris I made many trips throughout France and Germany, repairing the disorders of powerhouses; but I had no success in raising money for the development of my invention. I had already designed and constructed much improved electric machinery when Mr. Batchellor urged me to go to America and undertake the design of dynamos and motors for the Edison Company. So I decided to try my fortunes in this Land of Golden Promise.

On arriving here, I could see only the crudeness, in contrast with the gracefulness of Europe, and said, "America is twenty-five years behind Europe in civilization." But only five years later, I went abroad with new experience and became convinced that America is a century *ahead* of Europe in civilization. And that opinion I hold to this day.

ONE of the great events in my life was my first meeting with Edison. This wonderful man, who had received no scientific training, yet had accomplished so much, filled me with amazement. I felt that the time I had spent studying languages, literature and art was wasted; though later of course, I learned this was not so.

It was only a few weeks after first meeting Mr. Edison, that I knew I had won his confidence. The fastest steamship afloat at that time, the Oregon, had disabled both her lighting engines, so that her sailing was delayed. The machines could not be removed from the ship because of the character of the superstructure, and the difficulty annoyed Mr. Edison considerably, because it seemed that the ship would be held in port some length of time.

That evening I took the necessary instruments and went aboard the ship. The dynamos were in bad condition, with short circuits and breaks; but with the aid of the crew I put them in shape. At five that morning, on my way home, I met Mr. Edison on Fifth Avenue, with Mr. Batchellor and their assistants just going home from their own work. When Mr. Edison saw me, he laughed and said, "Here's our young man just over from Paris running around at all hours of the night." Then I told him I was coming from the "Oregon," and that I had repaired the machines. Without a word he turned away; but as they went on I heard him say, "Batchellor, this is a damn good man!"

Soon after I left Mr. Edison's employment a company was formed to develop my electric arc-light system. This system was adopted for street and factory lighting in 1886, but as yet I got no money—only a beautifully engraved stock certificate. Until April of the following year I had a hard financial struggle. Then a new company was formed, and provided me with a laboratory on Liberty Street, in New York City. Here I set to work to commercialize the inventions I had conceived in Europe.

AFTER returning from Pittsburgh, where I spent a year assisting the Westinghouse Company in the design and manufacture of my motors, I resumed work in New York in a little laboratory on Grand Street, where I experienced one of the greatest moments of my life—the first demonstration of the wireless light.

I had been constructing with my assistants the first high-frequency alternators (dynamos), of the kind now used for generating power for wireless telegraphy. At three o'clock in the morning I came to the conclusion that I had overcome all the difficulties and that the machine would operate, and I sent my men to get something to eat. While they were gone I finished getting the machine ready, and arranged things so that there was nothing to be done, except to throw in a switch.

When my assistants returned I took a position in the middle of the laboratory, without any connection whatever between me and the machine to be tested. In each hand I held a long glass tube from which the air had been exhausted. "If my theory is correct," I said, "when the switch is thrown in, these tubes will become swords of fire." I ordered the room darkened and the switch thrown in—and instantly the glass tubes became brilliant swords of fire.

Under the influence of great exultation I waved them in circles round and round my head. My men were actually scared, so new and wonderful was the spectacle. They had not known of my wireless light theory, and for a moment they thought I was some kind of a magician or hypnotizer. But the wireless light was a reality, and with that experiment I achieved fame overnight.

Following this success, people of influence began to take an interest in me. I went into "society." And I gave entertainments in return; some at home, some in my laboratory— expensive ones, too. For the one and only time in my life, I tried to roar a little bit like a lion.

But after two years of this, I said to myself, "What have I done in the past twenty-four months?" And the answer was, "Little or nothing." I recognized that accomplishment requires isolation. I learned that the man who wants to achieve must give up many things—society, diversion, even rest— and must find his sole recreation and happiness in work. He will live largely with his conceptions and enterprises; they will be as real to him as worldly possessions and friends.

In recent years I have devoted myself to the problem of the wireless transmission of power. Power can be, and at no distance date will be, transmitted without wires, for all commercial uses, such as the lighting of homes and the driving of aeroplanes. I have discovered the essential principles, and it only remains to develop them commercially. When this is done, you will be able to go anywhere in the world—to the mountain top overlooking your farm, to the arctic, or to the desert—and set up a little equipment that will give you heat to cook with, and light to read by. This equipment will be carried in a sachel not as big as the ordinary suit case. In years to come wireless lights will be as common on the farms as ordinary electric lights are nowadays in our cities.

The matter of transmitting power by wireless is so well in hand that I can say I am ready now to transmit 100,000 horsepower by wireless without a loss of more than five per cent in transmission. The plant required to transmit this amount will be much smaller than some of the wireless telegraph plants now existing, and will cost only $10,000,000, including water development and electrical apparatus. The effect will be the same whether the distance is one mile or ten thousand miles, and the power can be collected high in the air, underground, or on the ground.

A long time ago, I became possessed of a desire to produce an engine as simple as my induction motor; and my efforts have been rewarded. This engine has been perfected, is complete, and has been declared by the world's engineering experts to be a significant advance.

No mechanism could be simpler, and the beauty of it is that almost any amount of power can be obtained from it. In the induction motor I produced the rotation by setting up a magnetic whirl, while in the turbine I set up a whirl of steam or gas. The rotating part is nothing but a shaft with a few straight plates keyed to it. There are no buckets, blades nor veins. Machines of this kind can be produced that will develop ten horse-power for every pound of weight, while the lightest engines of the present day give only about one horse-power for each two pounds of weight, or one twentieth of the power developed by my turbine. I have no doubt that it is the engine of the future.

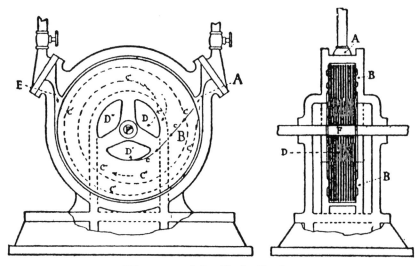

Diagram of the Tesla Engine

A–Steam Inlet. B–Disks. C–Path of Steam. **D,D'D''**–Exhaust.
E–Reverse Inlet. F–Shaft.

Page **1**   **NEW YORK HERALD TRIBUNE**   Oct. 15, 1911

WILL TESLA'S NEW MONARCH OF MACHINES REVOLUTIONIZE THE WORLD?

Noted Balkan Scientist claims to have perfected an engine that will develop ten horsepower to every pound of weight, and promises soon to give to the world a flying machine without wings, propeller, or gas bag. Characterizes aeroplanes of today as mere dangerous toys compared with the safe and stable appliance which will be used in a short time to dash through the air at a speed now unimagined.

Page **1**   **NEW YORK HERALD TRIBUNE**   Oct. 15, 1911

Latest Marvel of the Famous Inventor Nikola Tesla's Revolutionary Invention, *a Perfect Rotary Engine.*

By Frank Parker Stockbridge

Ten horse power from a tiny engine that a man could dangle from his little finger by a string!

Five hundred horse power in a package that a man could lift easily in one hand!

A thousand horse power motor occupying hardly more space than the cardboard box in which your hatter sent your new derby home!

Marvelous? *Wait until you hear the rest of it!*

Suppose some one should discover a new mechanical principle—something as fundamental as James Watt's discovery of the expansive power of steam—by the use of which it became possible to build a motor that would give ten horse power for every pound of the engine's weight, a motor so simple that the veriest novice in mechanics could construct it and so elemental that it could not possibly get out of repair. Then suppose that this motor could be run forward or backward at will, that it could be used as either an engine or a pump, that it cost almost nothing to build as compared with any other known form of engine, that it utilized a larger percentage of the available power than any existing machine, and, finally, that it would operate with gas, steam, compressed air or water, any one of them, as its driving power.

It does not take a mechanical expert to imagine the limitless possibilities of such an engine. It takes very little effort to conjure up a picture of a new world of industry and transportation made possible by the invention of such a device. "Revolutionary" seems a mild term to apply to it. That, however, is the word the inventor uses in describing it—Nikola Tesla, the scientist whose electrical discoveries underlie all modern electrical power development, whose experiments and deductions made the wireless telegraph possible, and who now, in the mechanical field, has achieved a triumph even more far reaching than anything he accomplished in electricity.

Tesla Engine with Upper Half of Casing Removed

This engine, whose rotor or "runner" consists simply of a set of flat disks 18 inches in diameter, developed a maximum of 330 brake horse-power on test. Because of safety considerations, involving the strength of the casing, it was conservatively rated at 200 HP. Half of the disks have been removed for better photographic resolution. See p. 34 for fully assembled unit, p. 94 for unit with all disks installed.

There is something of the romantic in this discovery of the famous explorer of the hidden realms of knowledge. The pursuit of an ideal is always romantic, and it was in the pursuit of an ideal which he has been seeking twenty years that Dr. Tesla made his great discovery. That ideal is the power to fly—to fly with certainty and absolute safety—not merely to go up in an aeroplane and take chances on weather conditions, "holes in the air," tornadoes, lightning and the thousand other perils the aviator of to-day faces, but to fly with the speed and certainty of a cannon ball, with power to overcome any of nature's aerial forces, to start when one pleases, go whither one pleases and alight where one pleases. That has been the aim of Dr. Tesla's life for nearly a quarter of a century. He believes that with the discovery of the principle of his new motor he has solved this problem and that incidentally he has laid the foundations for the most startling new achievements in other mechanical lines.

There was a time when men of science were skeptical—a time when they ridiculed the announcement of revolutionary discoveries. Those were the days when Nikola Tesla, the young scientist from the Balkans, was laughed at when he urged his theories on the engineering world. Times have changed since then, and the "practical" engineer is not so incredulous about "scientific" discoveries. The change came about when young Tesla showed the way by which the power of Niagara Falls could be utilized. The right to divert a portion of the waters of Niagara had been granted; then arose the question of how best to utilize the tremendous power thus made available—how to transmit it to the points where it could be commercially utilized. An international commission sat in London and listened to theories and practical plans for months.

Up to that time the only means of utilizing electric power was the direct current motor, and direct current dynamos big enough to be of practical utility for such a gigantic power development were not feasible.

Then came the announcement of young Tesla's discovery of the principle of the alternating current motor. Practical tests showed that it could be built—that it would work.

That discovery, at that opportune time, decided the commission. Electricity was determined upon as the means for the transmission of Niagara's power to industry and commerce. To-day a million horse power is developed on the brink of the great cataract, turning the wheels of Buffalo, Rochester, Syracuse and the intervening cities and villages operating close at hand the great new electro-chemical industries that the existence of this immense source of power has made possible, while all around the world a thousand waterfalls are working in the service of mankind, sending the power of their "white coal" into remote and almost inaccessible corners of the globe, all because of Nikola Tesla's first great epoch making discovery.

To-day the engineering world listens respectfully when Dr. Tesla speaks. The first announcement of the discovery of his new mechanical principle was made in a technical periodical in mid-September, 1911. Immediately it became the principal topic of discussions wherever engineers met.

"It is the greatest invention in a century," wrote one of the foremost American engineers, a man whose name stands close to the top of the list of those who have achieved scientific fame and greatness.

Tesla's 10,000 HP Steam Engine

"No invention of such importance in the automobile trade has yet been made," declared the editor of one of the leading engineering publications. Experts in other engineering lines pointed out other applications of the new principle and letters asking for further information poured in on Dr. Tesla from the four quarters of the globe.

"Oh, I've had too much publicity," he said, when I telephoned to him to ask for an interview in order to explain his new discovery to the non-technical public. It took a good deal of persuasion before he reluctantly fixed an hour when he would see me, and a good bit more after that before he talked at all freely. When he did speak, however, he opened up vistas of possible applications of the new engine that staggered the imagination of the interviewer.

Telling His Life Dream.

Looking out over the city from the windows of his office, on the twentieth floor of the Metropolitan Tower, his face lit up as he told of his life dream and its approaching realization, and the listener's fancy could almost see the air full of strange flying craft, while huge steamships propelled at unheard of speeds ploughed the waters of the North River, automobiles climbed the very face of the Palisades, locomotives of incredible power whisked wheeled palaces many miles a minute and all the discomforts of summer heat vanished as marvelous refrigerating plants reduced the temperature of the whole city to a comfortable maximum—for these were only a few of the suggestions of the limitless possibilities of the latest Tesla discovery.

"Just what is your new invention?" I asked.

"I have accomplished what mechanical engineers have been dreaming about ever since the invention of steam power," replied Dr. Tesla. "That is the perfect rotary engine. It happens that I have also produced an engine which will give at least twenty-five times as much power to a pound of weight as the lightest weight engine of any kind that has yet been produced.

"In doing this I have made use of two properties which have always been known to be possessed by all fluids, but which have not heretofore been utilized. These properties are adhesion and viscosity.

"Put a drop of water on a metal plate. The drop will roll off, but a certain amount of the water will remain on the plate until it evaporates or is removed by some absorptive means. The metal does not absorb any of the water, but the water adheres to it.

"The drop of water may change its shape, but until its particles are separated by some external power it remains intact. This tendency of all fluids to resist molecular separation is viscosity. It is especially noticeable in the heavier oils.

"It is these properties of adhesion and viscosity that cause the 'skin friction' that impedes a ship in its progress through the water or an aeroplane in going through the air. All fluids have these qualities—and you must keep in mind that air is a fluid, all gases are fluids, steam is fluid. Every known means of transmitting or developing mechanical power is through a fluid medium.

"Now, suppose we make this metal plate that I have spoken of circular in shape and mount it at its centre on a shaft so that it can be revolved. Apply power to rotate the shaft and what happens? Why, whatever fluid the disk happens to be revolving in is agitated and dragged along in the direction of rotation, because the fluid tends to adhere to the disk and the viscosity causes the motion given to the adhering particles of the fluid to be transmitted to the whole mass. Here, I can show you better than tell you."

Dr. Tesla led the way into an adjoining room. On a desk was a small electric motor and mounted on the shaft were half a dozen flat disks, separated by perhaps a sixteenth of an inch from one another, each disk being less than that in thickness. He turned a switch and the motor began to buzz. A wave of cool air was immediately felt.

"There we have a disk, or rather a series of disks, revolving in a fluid—the air," said the inventor. "You need no proof to tell you that the air is being agitated and propelled violently. If you will hold your hand over the centre of these disks—you see the centres have been cut away—you will feel the suction as air is drawn in to be expelled from the peripheries of the disks.

"Now, suppose these revolving disks were enclosed in an air tight case, so constructed that the air could enter only at one point and be expelled only at another—what would we have?"

"You'd have an air pump," I suggested.

"Exactly—an air pump or blower," said Dr. Tesla.

"There is one now in operation delivering ten thousand cubic feet of air a minute. "Now, come over here."

He stepped across the hall and into another room, where three or four draughtsmen were at work and various mechanical and electrical contrivances were scattered about. At one side of the room was what appeared to be a zinc or aluminum tank, divided into two sections, one above the other, while a pipe that ran along the wall above the upper division of the tank was connected with a little aluminum case about the size and shape of a small alarm clock. A tiny electric motor was attached to a shaft that protruded from one side of the aluminum case. The lower division of the tank was filled with water.

"Inside of this aluminum case are several disks mounted on a shaft and immersed in a fluid, water," said Dr. Tesla. "From this lower tank the water has free access to the case enclosing the disks. This pipe leads from the periphery of the case. I turn the current on, the motor turns the disks and as I open this valve in the pipe the water flows."

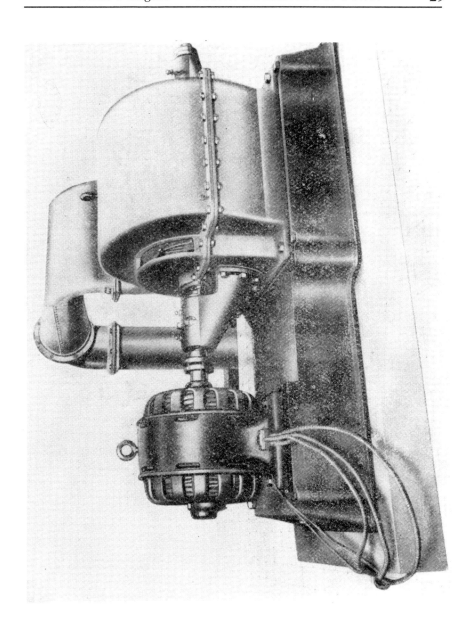

Tesla's Blower and Three-Phase Motor
10,000 Cubic Feet Per Minute

The Engine used as a Pump
This little pump, with a six inch volute housing, is driven by a motor of 1/12
horse-power. It is shown here delivering 40 gallons of water per minute.

He turned the valve and the water certainly did flow. Instantly a stream that
would have filled a barrel in a very few minutes began to run out of the pipe
into the upper part of the tank and thence into the lower tank.

"This is only a toy," said Dr. Tesla. "There are only half a dozen disks—
'runners,' I call them—each less than three inches in diameter, inside of that
case. They are just like the disks you saw on the first motor—no vanes,
blades or attachments of any kind. Just perfectly smooth, flat disks
revolving in their own planes and pumping water because of the viscosity
and adhesion of the fluid. One such pump now in operation, with eight
disks, eighteen inches in diameter, pumps four thousand gallons a minute
to a height of 360 feet."

We went back into the big, well lighted office. I was beginning to grasp the
new Tesla principle.

"Suppose now we reversed the operation," continued the inventor. "You
have seen the disks acting as a pump. Suppose we had water, or air under

The Tesla 110 Horsepower Engine, Conveying an Idea of the Size of the Machine   **The Runner of the 110 Horsepower Engine Measures 9 $3/_4$" in diameter and Weighs Twenty Pounds**

pressure, or steam under pressure, or gas under pressure, and let it run into the case in which the disks are contained—what would happen?"

"The disks would revolve and any machinery attached to the shaft would be operated—you would convert the pump into an engine," I suggested.

"That is exactly what would happen—what does happen," replied Dr. Tesla. "It is an engine that does all that engineers have ever dreamed of an engine doing, and more. Down at the Waterside power station of the New York Edison Company, through their courtesy, I have had a number of such engines in operation. In one of them the disks are only nine inches in diameter and the whole working part is two inches thick. With steam as the propulsive fluid it develops 110-horse power, and could do twice as much."

"You have got what Professor Langley was trying to evolve for his flying machine—an engine that will give a horse power for a pound of weight," I suggested.

Ten Horse Power to the Pound.

"I have got more than that," replied Dr. Tesla. "I have an engine that will give ten horse power to the pound of weight. That is twenty-five times as powerful as the lightest weight engine in use to-day. The lightest gas engine used on aeroplanes weighs two and one-half pounds to the horse power. With two and one-half pounds of weight I can develop twenty-five horse power."

"That means the solution of the problem of flying," I suggested.

"Yes, and many more," was the reply. "The applications of this principle, both for imparting power to fluids, as in pumps, and for deriving power from fluids, as in turbine, are boundless. It costs almost nothing to make, there is nothing about it to get out of order, it is reversible—simply have two ports for the gas or steam, to enter by, one on each side, and let it into one side or other. There are no blades or vanes to get out of order—the steam turbine is a delicate thing."

I remembered the bushels of broken blades that were gathered out of the turbine casings of the first turbine equipped steamship to cross the ocean, and realized the importance of this phase of the new engine.

"Then, too," Dr. Tesla went on, "there are no delicate adjustments to be made. The distance between the disks is not a matter of microscopic accuracy and there is no necessity for minute clearances between the disks and the case. All one needs is some disks mounted on a shaft, spaced a little distance apart and cased so that a fluid can enter at one point and go out at another. If the fluid enters at the centre and goes out at the periphery it is a pump. If it enters at the periphery and goes out at the centre it is a motor.

"Coupling these engines in series, one can do away with gearing in machinery. Factories can be equipped without shafting. The motor is especially adapted to automobiles, for it will run on gas explosions as well as on steam. The gas or steam can be let into a dozen ports all around the rim of the case if desired. It is possible to run it as a gas engine with a continuous flow of gas, gasoline and air being mixed and the continuous combustion causing expansion and pressure to operate the motor. The expansive power of steam, as well as its propulsive power, can be utilized as in a turbine or a reciprocating engine. By permitting the propelling fluid to move along the lines of least resistance a considerably larger proportion of the available power is utilized.

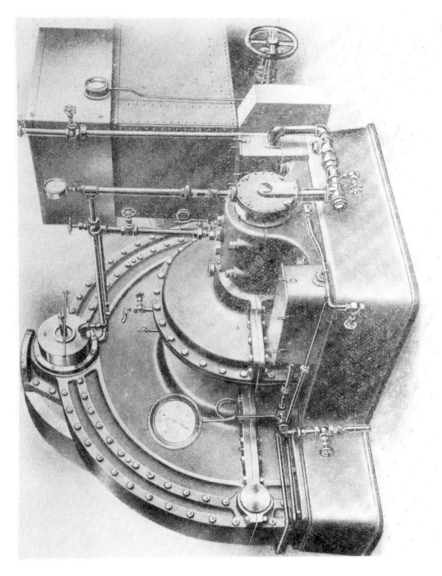

Tesla's Turbo Pump

"As an air compressor it is highly efficient. There is a large engine of this type now in practical operation as an air compressor and giving remarkable service. Refrigeration on a scale hitherto never attempted will be practical, through the use of this engine in compressing air, and the manufacture of liquid air commercially is now entirely feasible.

The 200-Horsepower, High-Pressure, Steam Engine
This view shows one complete high pressure unit with the steam throttle above, and below it the reversing valve and the compact engine. It stands on a base 20 by 35 inches and measures only five feet from the floor to the top of the steam inlet on the throttle housing.   Note the many gages used in the tests.

"With a thousand horse power engine, weighing only one hundred pounds, imagine the possibilities in automobiles, locomotives and steamships. In the space now occupied by the engines of the Lusitania twenty-five times her 80,000 horse power could be developed, were it possible to provide boiler capacity sufficient to furnish the necessary steam."

"And it makes the aeroplane practical," I suggested.

"Not the aeroplane, the flying machine," responded Dr. Tesla. "Now you have struck the point in which I am most deeply interested—the object toward which I have been devoting my energies for more than twenty years—the dream of my life. It was in seeking the means of making the perfect flying machine that I developed this engine.

"Twenty years ago I believed that I would be the first man to fly; that I was on the track of accomplishing what no one else was anywhere near reaching. I was working entirely in electricity then and did not realize that the gasoline engine was approaching a perfection that was going to make the aeroplane feasible. There is nothing new about the aeroplane but its engine, you know.

"What I was working on twenty years ago was the wireless transmission of electric power. My idea was a flying machine propelled by an electric motor, with power supplied from stations on the earth. I have not accomplished this as yet, but am confident that I will in time.

"When I found that I had been anticipated as to the flying machine, by men working in a different field I began to study the problem from other angles, to regard it as a mechanical rather than an electrical problem. I felt certain there must be some means of obtaining power that was better than any now in use, and by vigorous use of my gray matter for a number of years I grasped the possibilities of the principle of the viscosity and adhesion of fluids and conceived the mechanism of my engine. Now that I have it, my next step will be the perfect flying machine."

"An aeroplane driven by your engine?" I asked.

"Not at all," said Dr. Tesla. "The aeroplane is fatally defective. It is merely a toy—a sporting play-thing. It can never become commercially practical. It has fatal defects. One is the fact that when it encounters a downward current of air it is helpless. The 'hole in the air' of which aviators speak is simply a downward current, and unless the aeroplane is high enough above the earth to move laterally but can do nothing but fall.

"There is no way of detecting these downward currents, no way of avoiding them, and therefore the aeroplane must always be subject to chance and its operator to the risk of fatal accident. Sportsmen will always take these chances, but as a business proposition the risk is too great.

"The flying machine of the future—my flying machine—will be heavier than air, but it will not be an aeroplane. It will have no wings. It will be substantial, solid, stable. You cannot have a stable aeroplane. The gyroscope can never be successfully applied to the aeroplane, for it would give a stability that would result in the machine being torn to pieces by the wind, just as the unprotected aeroplane on the ground is torn to pieces by a high wind.

"My flying machine will have neither wings nor propellers. You might see it on the ground and you would never guess that it was a flying machine. Yet it will be able to move at will through the air in any direction with perfect safety, higher speeds than have yet been reached, regardless of weather and oblivious of 'holes in the air' or downward currents. It will ascend in such currents if desired. It can remain absolutely stationary in the air even in a wind for great length of time. Its lifting power will not depend upon any such delicate devices as the bird has to employ, but upon positive mechanical action."

"You will get stability through gyroscopes?" I asked.

"Through gyroscopic action of my engine, assisted by some devices I am not yet prepared to talk about," he replied.

"Powerful air currents that may be deflected at will, if produced by engines and compressors sufficiently light and powerful, might lift a heavy body off the ground and propel it through the air," I ventured, wondering if I had grasped the inventor's secret.

Dr. Tesla smiled an inscrutable smile.

"All I have to say on that point is that my airship will have neither gas bag, wings nor propellers," he said. "It is the child of my dreams, the product of years of intense and painful toil and research. I am not going to talk about it any further. But whatever my airship may be, here at least is an engine that will do things that no other engine ever has done, and that is something tangible."

Ed. note: see page 145 for Tesla's vision of a Tesla Engine powered flying machine.

The Tesla Rotary Steam Engine Testing Plant at the Edison Waterside Station, New York

The top half of the casing is removed, showing two rotors or "runners." Each runner consists of 25 disks, 18 inchs in diameter. The runner measures 3 $\frac{1}{8}$" across the face. The steam enters at the periphery, from the removed upper housing, and flows in spiral paths to exhaust at the center of the disks. The driving engine is to the left, the brake engine to the right. The steam inlets are on opposite sides of the upper housing and are fully reversible; the driving and brake engines can be switched during operation. The torsion of the spring is automatically shown by a beam of light, reflected from stationary and shaft end mounted mirrors. Horsepower is read from the reflected light position on a calibrated scale. At 9,000 revolutions per minute, with 125 pounds at the throttle and free exhaust, the rotary steam engine develops 200 horsepower. (See: photos and drawings featured on pages 24, 34, 92, 94, 128 and 146)

THE ELECTRICAL EXPERIMENTER

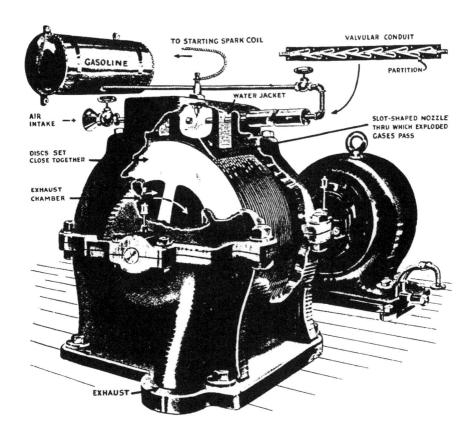

The Very Latest Invention In the Gasoline Engine Field Is the New *TESLA* "Valveless and Bucketless Gasoline Turbine," Here Illustrated. Two of the Main Features of This Remarkable Invention Are That the Usual Carburetor or Vaporizer is Done Away With and, Secondly, No Buckets Are Necessary on the Turbine Blades, the Latter Simply Comprising a Series of Flat Steel Discs, Placed a Short Distance Apart. The Successive Explosions of the Gaseous Vapor Are Projected Thru a Nozzle on to the Blades, Thus Causing the Rotation of the Blade Members and the Shaft to Which They Are Connected. A Dynamo Is Shown Connected to the Turbine at the Right of the Picture Herewith. This Article Was Prepared in Collaboration with Dr. Tesla.

Page **277**   **THE ELECTRICAL EXPERIMENTER**   July, 1920

The Tesla Gasoline Turbine

A Revolutionary Gas Engine That Requires No Spark Plug, No Carburetor, No Valves and No Pistons.

By Joseph H. Kraus

An immense amount of work has been done during the past fifteen or twenty years by engineers who have endeavored to produce a simple and practical explosive gas turbine, but the mechanical and thermal hindrances have been so great that up to the present time no signal success has been achieved. The turbine is an ideal prime mover; simple in principle, but the accessory apparatus for operating it explosively is very complex and liable to great wear. Thus the products of an explosion must affect the rotor, during which time a number of operations have to be performed.

Fuel and air must first be admitted thru separate channels into a combustion chamber; the mixture is then ignited, all inlets and outlets closed. The comprest gases thus exploded must be directed thru a nozzle to the rotor plates or buckets and the chamber cleaned and made ready for the admission of a fresh mixture.

All these operations are controlled by valves which must be opened and closed at precise moments and therefore are generally controlled by the motion of the turbine rotor itself. Irrespective of the difficulty of keeping the valves in good order at high temperatures, at which they must operate the apparatus taken as a whole, is so complicated that the ordinary form or reciprocating type gasoline engine more preferable.

Doctor Nikola Tesla, whom the readers of this publication know very well and whose amazing work in the various scientific fields is also universally recognized, again comes into the limelight with a very remarkable explosive gasoline turbine perfected by him recently which he describes in detail in a patent just granted. This remarkable turbine does away with all the troubles and complexity of the former attempted types. Stated briefly, the invention consists in the production of a peculiar shape conduit, thru which the gases are admitted into the turbine, and which has the singular property of permitting their passage in that direction only; in other words, uni-directionally.

This device when used in connection with his bucketless turbine produces an engine which may be explosively operated by gasoline, alcohol or other fuels and is absolutely devoid of all valves. It is the simplest internal combustion motor conceivable. Owing to the tremendous output of the Tesla turbine, one single disc being practically equivalent in performance to a whole bucket-wheel, a very small machine of this kind is capable of developing an astonishing amount of power. The principle of the operation will be clearly understood by the aid of the accompanying diagram.

Referring to the detailed view of the conduit, we first note a casing of metal or other suitable material which may be milled or prest from sheet metal into the desired form. From its side walls extend alternately projections terminating in buckets which in order to facilitate manufacture are congruent and spaced at equal distances.

In addition to these there are independent partitions, the purpose of which will presently be made clear. There is a nipple at each end provided for pipe connections. The bottom is solid and the upper or open side is closed by a close-fitting plate. When desired any number of such pieces may be joined in series, thus making up a valvular conduit of such length as the circumstances may require.

In elucidation of the mode of operation let it be assumed that the medium under pressure be admitted at the right. Evidently its approximate path will be as indicated by the dotted line, which is nearly straight, that is to say, if the channel be of adequate cross-section the fluid will encounter a very small resistance and pass thru, freely and undisturbed, at least to a degree. Not so if the entrance be at the opposite end.

In this case, the flow will be smooth and continuous, but intermittent, the fluid being quickly deflected and reversed in direction, set in whirling motion, brought to rest and again accelerated, these processes following one another in rapid succession. The partitions serve to direct the stream upon the buckets and to intensify the actions, causing violent surges and eddies which interfere very materially with the flow thru the conduit.

Examining more closely the mode of operation, it will be seen that in passing from one bucket to the next in the direction of disturbed flow the fluid undergoes two complete reversals or deflections upon itself thru 180 degrees, while it suffers only two small deviations of about 10 to 20 degrees when moving in the opposite sense. In each case the loss of head will be proportionate to a hydraulic coefficient dependent on the angle of deflection, from which it follows that, for the same velocity, the ratio of the two resistances will be as that of two coefficients. The theoretical value of this ratio may be 200 or more, but must be taken as appreciably less altho the surface friction too is greater in the direction of disturbed flow. In order to keep it as large as possible, sharp bends should be avoided.

The illustration shows in perspective cross-section a turbine which may be of any type but is in this instance one invented and described by Dr. Tesla, and familiar to engineers. Suffice it to state that the rotor of the same is composed of flat plates which are set in motion thru the same and viscous action of the working fluid, entering the system tangentially at the periphery or outer circumference, and leaving it at the center.

Such a machine is a thermodynamic transformer of an activity surpassing by far that of any other prime mover, it having been demonstrated in practice that each single disk of the rotor is capable of performing as much work as a whole bucket-wheel of the ordinary type. Besides, a number of other advantages, equally important, make it especially adapted for operation as an internal combustion motor.

The upper part of the turbine casing has bolted to it, a separate casting, the central cavity of which forms the combustion chamber. To prevent injury thru excessive heating a cooling jacket may be used, or else water injected, and when these means are objectionable recourse may be had to air cooling, this all the more readily as very high temperatures are practicable. The top of the casting is closed by a plate with a spark-plug inserted and in its sides are screwed two of the new Tesla valvular conduits communicating with the central chamber. One of these is, normally, open to the atmosphere while the other connects to a source of fuel supply.

The bottom of the combustion chamber terminates in a suitable nozzle which consists of separate member of heat-resisting material. To regulate the influx of the explosion constituents and secure the proper mixture the air and gas conduits are equipt, respectively, with regulating valves. The exhaust openings of the rotor should be in communication with a ventilator, of any suitable construction. Its use, however, while advantageous, is not indispensable, the suction produced by the turbine rotor itself being, in some cases at least, sufficient to insure proper working.

But a few words will be needed to make clear the mode of operation. The air valve being open and sparking establisht across the gap, the gas is turned on slowly until the mixture in the explosion chamber reaches the critical state and is ignited. Both the conduits behaving with respect to efflux, as closed valves, the products of combustion rush out thru the nozzle acquiring still greater velocity by expansion and, imparting their momentum to the rotor, start it from rest. Upon the subsidence of the explosion the pressure in the chamber sinks below the atmospheric, owing to the pumping action of the rotor or ventilator and new air and gas are permitted to enter, cleaning the cavity and channels and making up a fresh mixture which is detonated as before, and so on; the successive impulses of the working fluid producing an almost continuous rotary effort. After a short lapse of time, the chamber becomes heated to such a degree that the ignition device may be shut off without disturbing the establisht regime.

The turbine thus shown presents the advantages of extreme simplicity, cheapness and reliability, there being no compressor, buckets or troublesome valve mechanism. It also permits, with the addition of certain well-known accessories, the use of any kind of fuel and thus meets the pressing necessity of a self- contained, powerful, light and compact internal combustion motor for general work. When the attainment of the highest efficiency is the chief object, as in machines of large size, the explosive constituents will be supplied under high pressure and provision made for maintaining a vacuum at the exhaust. Such arrangements are quite familiar and an enlargement on this subject is deemed unnecessary.

In speaking about the rapidity of explosions. Dr. Tesla says, "I have been able to speed up the rate of such explosions until the sound of exploding gases produced a musical note. The device is by far the simplest I have ever seen and I consider myself indeed fortunate in perfecting it at this time. I have also used this valvular conduit to great effect in rarifaction of air or the compression of gases when operated by my oscillator."

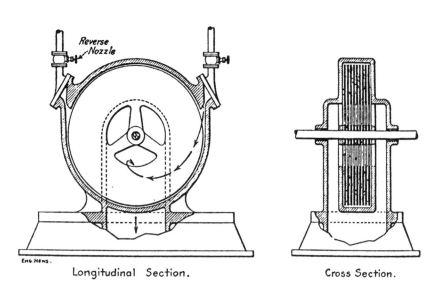

Longitudinal Section.   Cross Section.

THE TESLA DISK WHEEL IN A STEAM TURBINE

Page **1**   **NEW YORK TIMES**   Nov. 8, 1931

SEA POWER PLANT
DESIGNED BY TESLA

He Holds Steam Can Be Made Economically by Using
Different Temperatures of Ocean
Plans Land Device, Too
Both Embody Improvements in Wollaston's Toy, Says Scientist
Tests To Be Made Soon.

Designs of two new power plants, one to utilize the heat below the surface of the earth, the other to take advantage of the difference in temperature between upper and lower levels of the ocean, are announced by Dr. Nikola Tesla, the inventor, in an article in the December issue of Everyday Science and Mechanics, out tomorrow.

While many attempts have been made in the past fifty years to devise ways to utilize the heat energy of the ocean and the interior of the earth, Dr. Tesla said his design embodied improvements which would make it possible to supply power from ocean and terrestrial sources on an economical basis in competition with other sources of power.

Only last year Professor Georges Claude of Paris constructed at Matanzas Bay, Cuba, an experimental plant for the purpose of harnessing the temperature differences in the tropical seas for power purposes. Several engineers, Dr. Tesla among them, are of the opinion, however, that the Claude plant, while workable, is too expensive to produce power on an economical basis. Dr. Tesla said his own designs do away with the most expensive and objectionable features of former experiments.

Temperatures in Tropical Seas

"It is well known," Dr. Tesla writes, "that there exists, in tropical seas, a difference of 50 degrees F. between the surface water and that three miles below. The temperature of the former, being subject to variations, averages 82 F., while that of the latter is normally at least 32 degrees F., or nearly so, as the result of the slow influx of the ice-cold polar stream.

"In solid land these relations are reversed, the temperature increasing about one degree F. for every 64 feet descent. But while all this was common knowledge for at least 75 years and the utilization of the heat of the earth for

See page 10 for illustration of terrestrial heat plant; Also see page 51

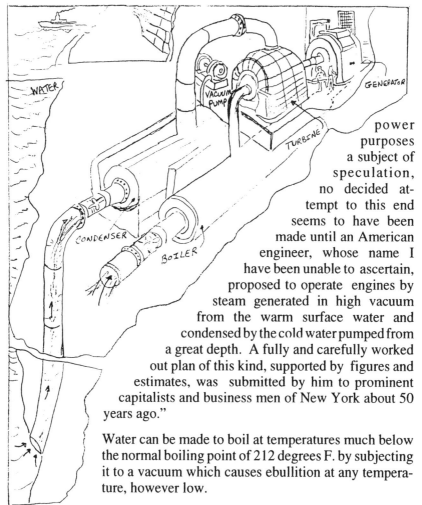

power
purposes
a subject of
speculation,
no decided at-
tempt to this end
seems to have been
made until an American
engineer, whose name I
have been unable to ascertain,
proposed to operate engines by
steam generated in high vacuum
from the warm surface water and
condensed by the cold water pumped from
a great depth. A fully and carefully worked
out plan of this kind, supported by figures and
estimates, was submitted by him to prominent
capitalists and business men of New York about 50
years ago."

Water can be made to boil at temperatures much below
the normal boiling point of 212 degrees F. by subjecting
it to a vacuum which causes ebullition at any temperature, however low.

"This behavior of water, or liquids in general," says Dr.
Tesla, "was long before beautifully exemplified in the classical device called
"cryophoros," consisting of two communicating and exhausted bulbs
partially filled with a liquid, which is evaporated in one and condensed in the
other. It was invented by W. H. Wollaston, a great English scientific man
and investigator (1766-1828) who first commercialized platinum, and was
credited by some to have anticipated Faraday in the discovery of electromagnetic rotation.

"The original instrument brought out at the beginning of the nineteenth
century had one of the bulbs packed in ice with the result of the freezing water
in the other. In conformity with the views of that time it was thought that the

cold of the ice was carried to the water, and so the Greek name, meaning "cold-carrier," was given to the device. But now we know that the process is of the opposite character, the freezing being brought about by the transport of the latent heat of evaporation from the warm to the cold bulb. One would naturally infer that the operation would cease as soon as the water is frozen at the surface, but curiously enough the ice itself continues to yield steam, and it is only because of this that all of the water is solidified."

A Toy on a Huge Scale

The ocean plant originally proposed by the French engineer, Professor Claude, and Dr. Tesla is no more than Wollaston's scientific toy on a huge scale, Dr. Tesla points out, adapted for continuous operation and having an engine interposed between the two communicating vessels.

The principal parts of Dr. Tesla's designs consist of a vacuum pump, a turbine, a condenser and a generator. The plan for the ocean plant has as one of the novel features a tunnel dug to the level of the cold waters, which in the design for the terrestrial plant is substituted by a heat-insulated shaft, extending a mile or less below the surface.

The vacuum pump starts the sea water boiling at surface temperature. The steam thus generated is directed against the turbine, which it turns, and passes on to the condenser. By an ingenious arrangement the cold water from the depths is made to come to the surface through the tunnel and to the condenser, thus condensing the steam exhausted by the turbine. The turbine is connected with the shaft of a generator, in this manner transforming heat energy into mechanical and electrical energy.

In the terrestrial power plant water is circulated to the bottom of the shaft, returning as steam to drive the turbine, and then returned to liquid form in the condenser, in an unending cycle.

Asked what constituted the chief improvement in his designs over those of his predecessors, Dr. Tesla said:

"First of all I do away with the necessity of lifting the water, which has heretofore involved the expenditure of a very large portion of the power developed. I attain this by submerging the two elements of the plant, the boiler and the condenser, so that the work to be performed is only that of circulation, notwithstanding the changing level of the ocean owing to ebb and tide. The quantity of water necessary is so enormous that it cannot be supplied with sufficient economy by centrifugal pumps, which had been heretofore proposed.

"The second improvement consists in employing screw propellers which, being rotated in solid water, can operate with an efficiency of 87 per cent. Thirdly, I do away with pipelines, which are limited in size and are otherwise objectionable, and bring the cold water up from the depths through a tunnel which is permanent and reduces greatly resistance to flow.

"A fourth improvement is the adoption of a form of apparatus which lends itself to very large units, 100,000 or 200,000 horsepower if desired, and thus effect all those savings which are secured in this manner, and with which power engineers are thoroughly familiar.

"In embodying these improvements in my system I also dispense with other drawbacks and difficulties, such as degasification of the water and the excessive moisture in the steam. I may mention, furthermore, that I secure a perfect automatic control of the power without the usual complex appliances, by placing the condenser a little higher than the boiler, so that the condensate flows up into the latter automatically through a pipe connection, without the employment of a pump.

"Yet even with all these economies the power obtainable is still too dear under the present exceptionally low prices of oil. However, a plant embodying all these improvements can, I believe, successfully compete with fuel under normal conditions. It must be borne in mind, however, that the ocean power plant is not perfectly constant in it's performance as there are seasonal and also casual variations.

The Terrestrial Power Plant

"For these, and other reasons, the utilization of terrestrial heat on solid land is very superior. After thirty years I have developed a plan which enables me to derive by means of a shaft of given depth many times the amount of power obtainable according to plans heretofore proposed either by myself or others, including Sir Charles Parsons.

"Instead of placing the boiler at the bottom of the shaft, and so limiting the influx of heat, I utilize the heat flowing into the whole shaft, which is many times greater, of course, to generate steam. The arrangement is of ideal simplicity. The steam is drawn in from the bottom of the shaft through a heavily insulated pipe to a turbine on level ground. From the turbine the steam is discharged into the condenser and the condensed water flows by gravity through another insulated pipe reaching to a depth at which the temperature of the ground exceeds that of the condensate.

"By circulating the steam in great volume through the turbine and condenser I am able to maintain a considerable temperature difference between the ground and the interior of the shaft, so that a very great quantity of heat flows into the same continually; to be transformed into mechanical work. The only requisite is a sufficient volume of condensing water, and this problem is the more easily satisfied the colder the climate.

"With my improved method it is practicable to supply all the power which a small community may require from a shaft of moderate depth, certainly less than a mile. And for isolated dwellings a few hundred feet depth would be ample, particularly if such a fluid as ether is employed for running the turbine.

"The power obtained by this method is ideal on account of its perfect constancy and the elementary simplicity of the whole plant. I have been for some time engaged in making estimates of costs of installation, and I find that it would not be prohibitive by comparison with other sources of power."

Dr. Tesla made it clear that neither of the two proposed power plants has anything to do with the work he is conducting on a new source of power, about which he told the New York Times on the occasion of his seventy-fifth birthday, July 10, 1931. (Ed. Cosmic Ray Power, see TEBA Membership Manual) He confessed rather reluctantly that he is taking steps for making practical tests for both the terrestrial and ocean power plants in the near future.

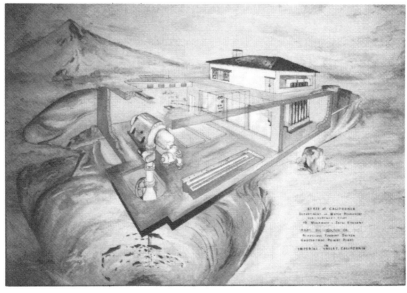

Artist's Conception of a Modern, Tesla Terrestrial, Heat Plant

The 110 HP Tesla Steam Engine Driving a 50KW Tesla Alternator

RECOVERING THE LATENT HEAT OF VAPORIZATION
What does this mean?

Latent Heat of Vaporization. -- *The quantity of heat necessary to change a given quantity of liquid to vapor without change of temperature.*

For the first time in history, a turbine, the bladeless variety, can recover the tremendous potential energy contained in steam called the **latent heat of vaporization**. Conventional bladed type turbines would be quickly destroyed in any attempt to directly recover this energy. The Tesla steam engine, however, can recover this energy with absolutely no damage or reduction in operating life.

Although water when heated to the boiling point stabilizes at 212° F (100° C) before it turns to steam, it absorbs a large amount of heat in undergoing this change. For example, approximately 180 BTUs of heat must be absorbed to raise 1 pound of water from room temperature 72° F (22°C) to the just under the boiling point 212°F or 100°C (Saturated Liquid). To further change the same pound of water into steam (Phase Change) takes approximateley 970 BTUs of heat. That's over five times the energy! The amount of heat absorbed before boiling the 212° water into steam is called the **heat of vaporization**. So, as you can see, just before water boils and turns to steam, it becomes an energy sponge. This latent or stored energy is *released* when the steam condenses and changes back into liquid water. In the bladeless steam turbine, steam can go through a phase state change, condensing directly back to water, *inside of the turbine*, thereby capturing this potential energy. Vacuum can also be applied to the bladeless turbine to lower the atmospheric pressure and therefore the boiling point, allowing this effect to occur with low temperature geothermal heat sources. This would destroy a bladed type turbine which can tolerate no water and uses a separate condenser and heat exchange system outside the turbine, thereby throwing most of this energy off as waste heat. Power plants of today are obviously very inefficient. Tesla is documented as stating that, in theory, his bladeless turbine or engine could achieve upwards of 97% efficiency with steam operation if properly staged. This extra energy would be made available from the stored latent energy released from the steam as it phase changes back to water inside the turbine.

Freon (CFC), a common class of phase change material that has extremely low boiling or phase change temperatures is frequently used in our refrigerators and air conditioning systems as well as heat pumps. Low boiling points can also be achieved with vacuum pumps, a technique proposed by Tesla for use with his turbine that would eliminate the need for freon or other exotic phase change materials (See pages 10 and 44).

The illustration below shows the various conditions of water in its liquid and vapor states labeled **A-E**. Conventional bladed type turbines can only operate in region **E**, (Superheated Vapor). The Bladeless Turbine can operate in all five liquid/vapor states **A-E**. To recover the latent heat of vaporization it is required that the turbine be operated in region **C & D**, the two-phase region of condensing water, thereby immediately surrendering the tremendous latent or stored energy of vaporization directly *back* to the turbine. If you told a bladed turbine manufacturer you were going to run one of their turbines in just the **D** range (saturated vapor) they would tear up their guarantee on the turbine before they sold it to you. Obviously the time for implementation of the incredible bladeless steam turbine system is long overdue

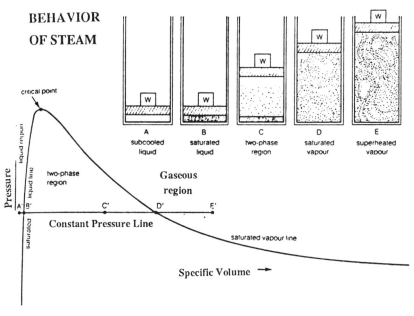

The stages in the transition of a given amount of water from a liquid to a superheated vapor, at a contant pressure, correspond to the points along the constant-pressure line in the diagram. The critical point is the pressure temperature point beyond which a designation of the water as either liquid or vapor becomes arbitrary.

Tesla wrote about recovering the latent heat of vaporization from terrestrial heat sources in the previously quoted article (page 10) entitled 'Our Future Motive Power' published in *Everyday Science and Mechanics,* December, 1931. The following is a further excerpt from this article with Tesla explaining the history of the methods discovery. (Also see page 43)

"Undoubtedly, the essential conditions required to operate a steam or other thermodynamic engine could be fulfilled, a considerable temperature difference being available at all times. No proof had to be furnished that heat would flow from a higher to a lower level and could be transformed into mechanical work. Nor was it necessary to show that the surface water, although much below its normal boiling point of 212 F., can be readily converted into steam by subjecting it to a vacuum which causes ebullition at any temperature however low. It is of common knowledge that, due to this same effect, beans cannot be cooked or eggs hard-boiled on high mountains. Also, for a like reason turbines have been wrecked in steam power plants with the boilers completely shut off, the slightly warm water in the system of connecting pipes being evaporated under a high vacuum inadvertently applied. This behavior of water, or liquids in general, was long before beautifully exemplified in the classical device called "cryophoros" consisting of two communicating and exhausted bulbs partially filled with liquid, which is evaporated in one and condensed in the other. It was invented by W.H. Wollaston, a great English scientific man and investigator (1766-1828), who first commercialized platinum and was credited by some to have anticipated Faraday in the discovery of electromagnetic rotation. The original instrument brought out at the beginning of the nineteenth century had one of the bulbs packed in ice with the result of freezing water in the other. Conformably to the views of that time it was thought that the cold of the ice was carried to the water and so the Greek name, meaning "cold-carrier," was given to the device. But now we know that the process is of opposite character, the freezing being brought about by the transport of the latent heat of evaporation from the warm to the cold bulb. One would naturally infer that the operation would cease as soon as the water is frozen at the surface, but curiously enough the ice itself continues to yield steam and it is only because of this that all of the water is solidified. We may imagine how puzzling this phenomenon appeared more than one century ago!"

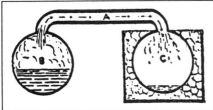

The "cryophoros" is well known as a scientific toy, exemplifying also the principle of refrigerating machinery.

Tesla's thermodynamic system with Bladeless Turbine **D**, driving generator. Also note motor driven vacuum pump **E**.

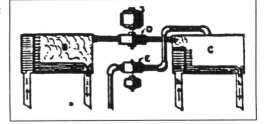

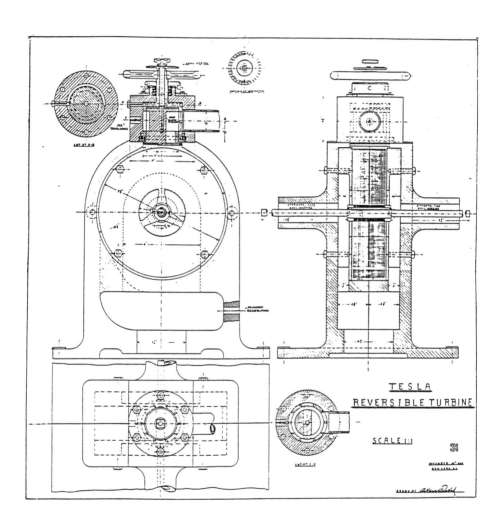

Tesla Reversible Rotary Steam Engine

Tesla's New System of Fluid Propulsion

by Nikola Tesla

In subduing the forces of Nature to his service man must invariably avail himself of some process in which a fluid acts as carrier of energy, this being an essential step in any industrial undertaking dependent on mechanical power. Evidently then, a discovery or radical departure in that domain must be of extreme importance and far-reaching influence on the existing conditions and phases of modern life.

Fluid propulsion is now effected by means of pistons, vanes or blades, which entail complexity of construction and impose many limitations on the propelling as well as propelled mechanism and its performance. Tesla has dispensed with these devices and produced machines of extraordinary simplicity which, moreover, are in many other respects superior to the old types universally employed. A few words will be sufficient to convey a clear idea of his invention.

Every fluid, as water or air, possesses two salient properties: adhesion and viscosity. Owing to the first it is attracted and clings to a metallic surface; by virtue of the second it resists the separation of its own particles. As an inevitable consequence a certain amount of fluid is dragged along by a body propelled through it; conversely, if a body be placed in a fluid in motion it is impelled in the direction of movement. The practical forms of Tesla's apparatus consist of flat, circular disks, with central openings, mounted on a shaft and enclosed in a casing provided with ports at the peripheral and central portions, when deriving energy from any kind of fluid it is admitted at the periphery and escapes at the center; when, on the contrary, the fluid is to be energized, it enters in the center and is expelled at the periphery. In either case it traverses the interstices between the disks in a spiral path, power being derived from, or imparted to it, by purely molecular action. In this novel manner the heat energy of steam or explosive mixtures can be transformed with high economy into mechanical effort; motion transmitted from one shaft to another without solid connection; vessels may be propelled with great speed; water raised or air compressed; an almost perfect vacuum can be attained, substances frozen and gases liquefied.

While this improvement has the broadness and applicability of a fundamental mechanical concept, the widest field for its commercial exploitation is, obviously, the thermodynamic conversion of energy.

The commercial value of a prime mover is determined by its efficiency, specific performance relative to weight and space occupied, cheapness of manufacture, safety and reliability of operation, adaptability to construction in large units, capability of running at high peripheral velocity, reversibility, and a number of other features of lesser importance. In the majority of these a machine, operating on the new principle, excels. But there is one quality which is most desirable in a thermo-dynamic transformer from the economic point of view, and that is great resistance to deterioration and impairment of efficiency by heat.

The employment of high temperature is of such vital bearing on the efficiency of prime movers that it is of paramount importance to extend the thermal range as far as practicable. In the present state of the art radical progress towards more economical transformation of the energy of fuel can only be achieved in that direction. Such being the case, the capability of the machine to withstand deteriorating effects of great heat is the controlling factor in determining its commercial value. In that most desired quality the Tesla turbine surpasses all the older types of heat motors. The Diesel and other internal combustion engines are fatally limited in this respect by their complete dependence on closely fitting sliding joints and unfailing supply of clean lubricant; while in the present forms of turbine buckets, blades and inherent mechanical deficiencies impose similar restrictions. These parts are too delicate and perishable to serve as elements of a gas turbine and this has been the main obstacle in the way of its successful realization. The rotor of the Tesla turbine presents a relatively enormous active area and the wear is quite insignificant as the fluid, instead of striking against the propelling organs in the usual destructive manner, flows parallel with the same, imparting its momentum by adhesion and viscosity instead of impact. Moreover, it has been shown that the efficiency of this form of rotor is not impaired to any appreciable degree by a roughening of the disks and that it operates satisfactorily even if the working medium is corrosive to an extent.

The universal adoption of steam as motive power under certain standard conditions, settled upon in the course of time, gradually forced upon the minds of engineers the Rankine Cycle Efficiency as criterion of performance and long continued endeavors to improve the same have finally resulted in complex multistage constructions entirely unsuitable for high temperatures. The Tesla turbine, by virtue of its exceptional heat-resisting and other unique properties, makes possible the attainment of great fuel economy with but a single stage, incidentally offering the additional advantages of an extremely simple, small, compact, and reliable mechanism. But perhaps the chief commercial value of this new prime mover will be found in the fact that it can be operated with the cheapest grade of crude oil, colloidal fuel, or powdered coal, containing considerable quantities of grit, sulphur and other impurities, thus enabling vast sums of money to be saved annually in the production of power from fuel.

The Tesla turbine also lends itself to use in conjunction with other types, especially with the Parsons with which it forms an ideal combination. Although its practical introduction has been delayed by the force of circumstances, a number of years have been spent in exhaustive investigations and experiments on the basis of which the performance in any given case can be closely calculated. The first public tests were made before the outbreak of the war at the Waterside Station of the New York Edison Company where several machines, ranging from 100 to 5000 h.p., were installed and operated with satisfactory results. That the invention was appreciated by the technical profession may be seen from the excerpts of statements by experts and periodicals printed on the annexed page.

The salient advantages of the Tesla turbine may be summed up as follows:

Efficiency: The most economical of the present prime movers is the Diesel engine. But, quite apart of many practical and commercial drawbacks, inseparable from this type, it is entirely dependent on comparatively expensive oil, so that the Tesla Gas Turbine, working with much cheaper fuel, would have the better in competition even if its efficiency as a thermodynamic transformer were appreciably lower, all the more so in view of its greater mechanical perfection.

Referring to turbines, all of which are surpassed by the Parsons in economy as well as extent of use, definite limits have already been reached and the only possibilities of saving fuel exist in the employment of steam at very high super-heat and utilization of gas or oil as motive fuel. But none of the prime movers mentioned is adapted for such operation and although every effort has been made in this direction, no signal success has been achieved. The super-heat is at most 250° F, this being considered the maximum permissible. All attempts to considerably extend the thermal range have failed chiefly because of the inability of bucket structures to withstand the action of intense heat. The Tesla Turbine can operate quite satisfactorily with the motive agent at very high temperature and, owing to this quality, lends itself exceedingly well to these purposes.

Specific Performance: In this particular it is superior to all other forms. Each disk is virtually the equivalent of a whole bucket wheel, and as many of them take up but a small width the output of the machine, considering its weight and size, is surprisingly great. This, while not being a measure of efficiency, is nevertheless a feature of considerable importance in many instances.

Cheapness of Manufacture: The new turbine can be produced without a single machined part except the shaft, all the disks being punched and the casing pressed. By this method, with proper machinery installed on a large scale, the cost of production may be reduced to a figure never deemed possible in the construction of an engine. What is more, this can be done without material sacrifice of efficiency as small clearances are not essentially required.

Safety and Reliability of Operation: There is an ever present danger in the running of high speed machines. A bucket turbine may at any moment run away and wreck the plant. Such accidents have happened again and again and this peril has often proved to be a deterrent to investment. A remarkable quality of this turbine is its complete safety. As regards the wear and tear of the propelling organs it is insignificant and, in any event, of no consequence on the performance.

Adaptability to Construction in Large Units: In all the present machines there is a distinct limit to capacity, for although large units can be manufactured, they are very costly and difficult to manage. The new turbine is so simple and the output so large that the limits in this direction can be greatly extended.

Resistance to Deterioration by Heat and Other Agents: In this feature it has an overwhelming advantage over the old type in which the maintenance of smooth surfaces and sharp edges is indispensable to efficient working. In the Tesla turbine, for the reasons already stated, the destructive actions of heat and corrosive agents are much less pronounced and of relatively negligible effect. This fact has a most important bearing on the saving of fuel.

Capability of Running at High Peripheral Speed: In this respect also it is superior to others. The rotating structure carries no load and is excellently adapted to withstand tensile stresses. Judging from the most recent turbine practice this quality should be of special value.

Reversibility: The present turbines are greatly handicapped by their incapability of reversal which is a very serious defect in certain applications, as the propulsion of vessels, necessitating the employment of auxiliary turbines which detracts from the propulsive power and adds materially to the cost of production and maintenance of the equipment. The Tesla turbine has the unique property of being reversible; not only this but it operates with the same efficiency in either direction. For marine purposes it therefore constitutes an ideal motor whether used alone or in conjunction with older types.

Besides the above it possesses other desirable features, constructive and operative, which will add to its value and adaptability to many industrial and commercial uses as, railroading, marine navigation, aerial propulsion, generation of electricity, refrigeration, operation of trucks and automobiles, hydraulic gearing, agriculture, irrigation, mining and similar purposes.

Expressions of Opinion on the Tesla Turbine

C.B. Richards, Professor Emeritus of Mechanics, Yale University: *"I am amazed at the development of power given by the turbine and stunned by the exhibit."*

F. Sargent, Chief Engineer and Turbine Expert: *"I am impressed with the newness and novelty of the underlying principle of this invention. It is such as will claim the attention and admiration of anyone of a scientific turn of mind in a mechanical direction."*

Reynold Janney, Chief Engineer, Universal Transmission Co.: *"It is a great invention."*

Brigadier Allen of the War Department: *"Something new in the world. Officers are greatly impressed with it."*

Miller Reese Hutchinson, Chief Engineer: *"It is the greatest invention of the age."*

Arnold Trinyi, Chief Engineer, Oelfeurungs-Gesellschaft, Germany: *"The ideal of the turbine engine."*

B.R.T. Colline (power plant economist): *"It is a wonderful turbine."*

The Motor World: *"The new principle unquestionably is a great contribution to science and engineering, great in its simplicity and breadth of application."*

Scientific American: *"Considered from the mechanical standpoint, the turbine is astonishingly simple and economical in construction, should prove to possess such a durability and freedom from wear and breakdown as to place it, in these respects, far in advance of any type of steam or gas motor of the present day."*

Engineering Magazine: *"An entirely new form of prime mover with interesting possibilities."*

Technical World Magazine: *"The Tesla Turbine is the apotheosis of simplicity. It is so violently opposed to all precedent that it seems unbelievable."*

From Numerous Articles and Comments

"The turbine is different in principle to any heretofore in use and one which will take less room and less coal than the best engine now running..." "Turbine of revolutionary design..." "Improvement in dynamics which promises revolutionary results..." "Results seem revolutionary to the point of staggering the imagination..." "This motor will revolutionize the turbine industry..." "Wonderful motor. Extraordinary mechanical principle..." etc., etc.

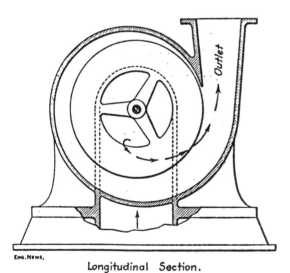

Longitudinal Section.

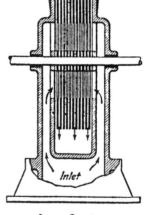

Cross Section.

THE TESLA DISK-IMPELLER PUMP

A LIGHTING MACHINE

February 7, 1918

OF

NOVEL PRINCIPLES

by **Nikola Tesla**

A machine built on novel and original lines is about to be placed on the market. It consists of a turbine and electric generator, both employing basically new principles in construction as well as operation, and intimately associated to constitute a unit. The former has been pronounced revolutionary in its design and performance. It is simplicity itself, being devoid of buckets, deflecting blades, guide passages, vanes and the like, and presents many other decisive advantages over the ordinary prime mover.

In the first place there is no windage, which is the cause of a most serious loss of power in bucket turbines, often amounting to a large percentage of the integral mechanical effort. What is still more important, the new turbine is capable of taking up the whole velocity of the motive fluid in one continuous process, thus saving the expense and avoiding the complication incident to "staging." Furthermore, it has the precious quality of transforming into useful work frictional energy irretrievably spent in other heat motors.

The corrosion and erosion of buckets and vanes in the present turbines is the cause of another great and irremediable waste of energy, the water rate frequently increasing 30% to 40% after but a few months of use. No such hurtful actions exist in the new turbine, and if they did, they would not impair the performance to any appreciable degree. Again, the former are subject to considerable loss owing to unpreventable wear and deterioration of the nozzles. It is essential that the high velocity streams of fluid issuing from them be directed upon the curved blades with great precision, as a failure of this is fatal to good results. To such an extent is this the case that even a slight roughening of the polished surfaces will reduce the useful energy as much as 25%. The new turbine is entirely free from this defect. However the nozzle may be used up, the fluid is made to flow through the wheel smoothly and evenly in natural stream lines, transmitting power to the same with undiminished efficiency. Another feature of superiority is found in its adaptability to high temperatures far beyond those practicable in bucket turbines. For every hundred degrees of increase in temperature, the steam consumption is reduced from 10% to 12%. Great economies are thus made possible by the use of the new prime mover.

In every turbine the device regulating the speed of rotation and controlling the admission of the working fluid to the nozzles is of vital importance. With scarcely an exception it is of the centrifugal type driven from the shaft in some or other way and constituting an assemblage of gears, flying weights, links, levers, sleeves, thrust bearings and other parts. It is an apparatus complex and delicate, expensive to construct and easily deranged, often with disastrous consequences. All this has been done away in the new turbine which is controlled in a novel and striking manner. The regulator is elementary in its construction, positive and unfailing in its action, and yet so sensitive as to respond to variations of load amounting to less than 1% of the normal. This simple device is rendered still more valuable by the fact that it adjusts itself instantaneously to pressure changes so that the effects of these on the lamps are inappreciable. To illustrate, the steam gauge on the boiler may indicate fluctuations from 100 to 200 pounds or more and following each other however rapidly without the slightest observable change in the intensity of the light. This remarkable action of the device is independent of its function as regulator of speed.

Another advantage deserving the most careful consideration of the user is the perfect safety of the new turbine. There is an ever present danger in a machine of the old type, that the wheel might burst and destroy life and property. Such a deplorable accident is absolutely impossible with the new turbine rotor, composed of thin discs which expand slightly and come to rest, invariably without damage, as has been shown in exhaustive experiments.

The one feature, however, which has most amazed experts, is the extraordinary power of this form of prime mover. Owing to the great effectiveness of the underlying principle and peculiar construction, ten times more power can be produced than with any other machine known. For example, a rotor of 9" in diameter, weighing less than 20 pounds, can readily develop 200 brake horsepower, and this is by no means the limit of performance.

But the merits of this lighting outfit do not rest on the turbine alone. The dynamo associated with the same is perhaps equally noteworthy by its simplicity of construction, high efficiency and rare and valuable properties it possesses. It consists of a smooth cylindrical body mounted on the turbine shaft and arranged to rotate within a magnetic field of novel form. There is no brush or sliding contact whatever, the current being taken from stationary terminals to which the ends of the generating coils are connected. By employing the best materials and workmanship and resorting to artifices of design, a most economical electrical generator is produced, the efficiency being over 90% even in machines of very small size having rotors of not more than $2 \frac{1}{2}$" in diameter. This generator possesses extraordinary qualities, especially desirable in electric lighting. It is capable of furnishing a current constant within a minute fraction of 1% through a very wide range of speed variation, and as such is ideally suited for running arc lamps or kindred electrical devices in series. More surprising still and also of greater commercial import is its capability of maintaining a constant potential. Such results as are obtainable with it are wholly impossible with other types of electrical generators. It has been found in practice that all lamps but one can be turned off suddenly without the slightest perceptible flicker and even without any observable effect on the needle of a delicate instrument indicating the voltage.

That an apparatus of such simplicity and presenting so many salient advantages should find an extensive use in electric lighting might be naturally expected, but its overwhelming superiority will be better appreciated when it is stated that it occupies hardly more than one-tenth of the space of apparatus of the usual forms and weighs less in proportion. A machine capable of developing 1-kilowatt, for instance, goes into a space of 8 x 8 x 10" and weighs but 40 pounds. It takes not more than one-third of the steam consumed in other turbo-generators of that size.

The guiding idea in the development of this new machine was to evolve a mechanism approximating a static transformer of energy in simplicity, efficiency and reliability of operation. Every detail has been worked out with this object in view. There is no exciter, no commutator, brush or sliding contact whatever, no centrifugal regulator, voltage controller or any such complicated and hazardous device. The machine consists of but a stationary solid frame and two smooth cylindrical steel bodies mounted on a strong shaft arranged to rotate in bearings virtually frictionless. No oiling is required, although a small quantity of lubricant is provided rather as a precaution than necessity. A perfect dynamic balance is secured in a novel manner and insures a steady and quiet running without tremor and vibration. The whole apparatus can be boxed up and depended upon to operate uninterruptedly through long periods of time. The outfit can be constructed in various sizes up to 100-kilowatt or more, and should meet more satisfactorily than any yet devised the varied requirements of electric lighting on railroads, boats, in public buildings, factories and mines, and may also be advantageously utilized in connection with existing plants for replacing belt driven dynamos and storage batteries, and relieving larger engines through the night and hours of small load.

A modern corrosion resistant, non-metalic, Tesla Pump
manufactured by Begemann Pompen

"It was perfectly well known that a fluid would be dragged by rotating surfaces, but somehow nobody realized the conditions for economic working, nor has any one properly grasped the principles which could be applied to propulsion. So it happens again that it is my good fortune to come to the rescue, and I have produced a highly economical way of compressing or pumping fluids."

Nikola Tesla

From an address before the New York section of the
National Electric Light Association May 15, 1911

TESTIMONIAL OF A FIRE FIGHTER

by Ray Russell   May 1990

I was first introduced to the boundary layer pump quite by accident. I was attending a demonstration of a fire retarding agent called Flame Out. The demonstration was to show how this product could protect the grass and wild-land. An area of dry grass was to be completely surrounded by the flame out material.

A small pump and a 55 gallon drum was used to apply the flame out material. When we were filling the 55 gallon drum from the fire truck the pump was started up. *This is absolutely unheard of* in the centrifugal pumping industry. You *never ever* run a centrifugal pump without water in it. My first thought was that the pump was going to burn up. The operator said; "No I want the motor to warm up." I thought: go ahead but you'll burn the thing up. After it was started he hooked the water suction hose to it. The operator then hooked up 50 feet of the $1\,^1/_2$ inch output hose. My men had also noticed that the pump was now running with no water input. They commented that the pump was going to blow up when water hit it. Its going to steam like crazy. Everyone twinged when the operator opened up the valve. As the

A motorized Tesla Pump manufactured by Hybrid Pump

water came into the pump, to my surprise, the pump didn't explode or even labor as a centrifugal pump would. Water came out the nozzle and we sprayed down the area. When we were done there was water left in the suction hose. I hollered you better shut it off. In the pumps I was familiar with, if you leave a pump running with water in it and the output shut off, it will become very hot and explode and possibly hurt someone. So I ran down to shut it off. Before I shut it off I touched the back of the pump with my finger and it was ice cold. I walked over to the operator and said; "what kind of centrifugal pump is that." He said; "It's not a centrifugal pump it's a boundary layer drag pump." Of course I said; "I need that." Suddenly I didn't care about the Flame Out material, I was thinking of nothing but the possibilities of these pumps in fire fighting. It is my belief that this technology will revolutionize pumping in the fire service in the 90's.

This is probably the most progressive thing that has happened to fire pumps. Unfortunately the fire service is noted for being 200 years of tradition unhampered by progress. The main drawback of the conventional fire pump is cavitation and its weight and its tendency to heat up. If small particles or air bubbles hit the lifting surfaces of a conventional centrifugal pump it creates about 23,000 pounds PSI of energy hitting the lifting surface. This does not happen with the boundary layer pump. I am totally convinced that this is the pump to go into the future fire fighting equipment and that it will totally eliminate centrifugal pumping. This is more than a fly by night thing that will be around for a few years and then disappear. This technology has been around since Tesla.

A cutaway view of a bladeless Tesla Pump manufactured by U.S. Pump & Turbine

A QUANTUM LEAP
TESLA PUMPING TECHNOLOGY

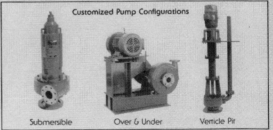
Tesla Pumps manufactured by the Discflo Corporation

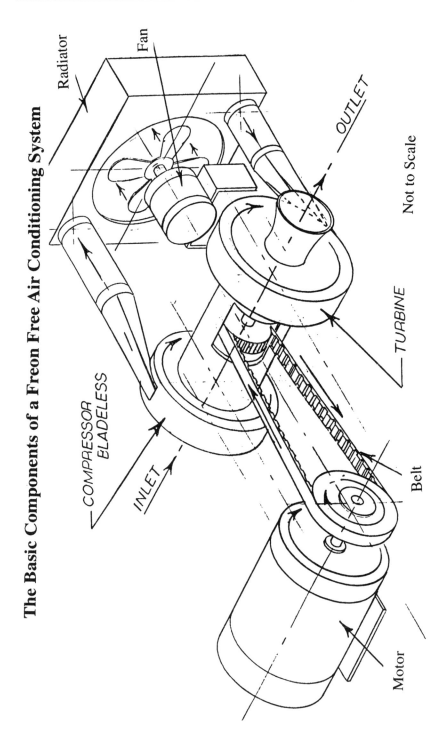

The Basic Components of a Freon Free Air Conditioning System

Freon Free Air-Conditioning

Because of the tremendous compression and expansion possible with the Tesla Compressor and Engine, air conditioning can be accomplished without the use of freon or other expensive refrigerants. The use of freon or its substitutes is entirely unnecessary.

Tesla stated: *"As an air compressor it is highly efficient... Refrigeration on a scale hitherto never attempted will be practical through the use of this engine in compressing air."* (see page 33)

An air to air refrigeration system is conceptualized on the opposite page. A Tesla Compressor and Tesla Engine are mounted on a common shaft driven by an electric motor via a belt. As the shaft turns it drives both compressor on one end of the shaft and the engine on the other. Air is drawn into the compressor, concentrating heat at its output, which is then fed to a radiator removing the excess heat. The high pressure output of the radiator is then fed to the input of the engine. The air is greatly expanded, giving up its heat energy as it preforms work through the shaft of the engine. This is an extremely efficient configuration, energy being returned and recycled through the shaft back to the compressor.

Above is pictured an electric motor with a bladeless cooling fan installed. Another "runner" of the Tesla fan or blower is displayed next to the bladed version it has replaced.

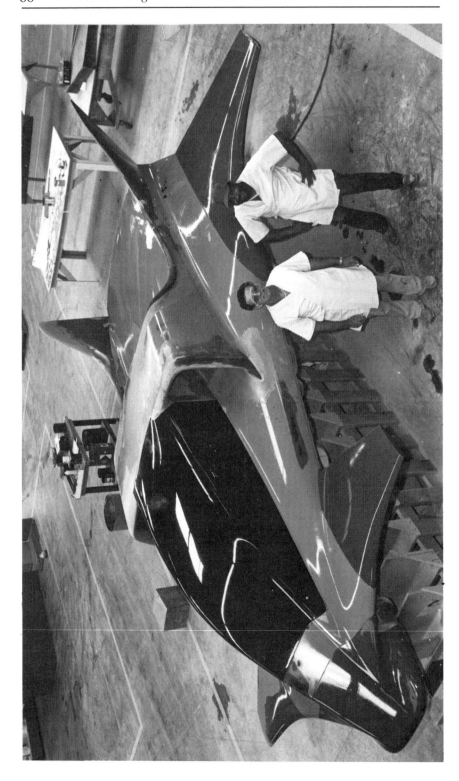

A NEW DIMENSION FOR FLIGHT

Tesla's main objective in developing the bladeless engine was for use in aircraft. He conceived aircraft that would not require airports or runways, with an ability to rise vertically. The photo on the opposite page is the airframe of a revolutionary new device developed by All American Aircraft in Long Beach, California. It is fabricated from high strength composite materials and was intended to ascend and descend vertically. This aircraft called the Phalanx was never fully developed due to lack of funding. The intention was to ultimately power the Phalanx device with the Tesla Engine operating at high compression and temperature.

If engine inlet temperatures are raised only a few hundred degrees fahrenheit, substantial increases in power are developed. It is very significant if power can be doubled or tripled for a given size and weight of aircraft engine. Today conventional bladed turbines are limited to a turbine inlet temperature of around 2,000 degrees F. Yet fossil fuels, in use today, can burn at temperatures as high as 3,400 to 3,500 degrees F. These temperatures dare not be applied to the blades of a conventional turbine engine. It would be too hot, resulting in the blades coming apart with the catastrophic demise of that particular turbine engine. Another disadvantage of the conventional bladed turbine aircraft engine is the tremendous noise created. This is one of biggest negative aspects of these engines. The noise is an unwanted parasitic energy that is largely reduced with the Tesla Engine.

The Tesla Engine offers tremendous advantages. The conventional bladed turbine engine operates under the most difficult stress levels imaginable, called combined bending, occurring at the root of each blade. The impulse or reaction, applied to which, causes this very severe stress and can result in the destruction of a conventional engine. The Tesla Engine has a tremendous advantage in this case. The stress level is entirely different on a Tesla Engine than on the bladed turbine engine. There is no combined bending in the Tesla Engine. The *bladeless* Tesla Engine can survive operating under conditions that a bladed turbine engine cannot. It is possible today to build a Tesla Engine that can operate at much higher power outputs than the present state of the art bladed turbines. The overall thrust and efficiency can also be increased by raising the compression ratio of the compressor. That is true of almost any engine including the internal combustion engine of an automobile. By staging, the compression ratio is raised and the efficiency and power of the engine is increased significantly. If the compression ratio is raised in a Tesla Engine from simple cycle (around five to one compression ratio) to twelve to one or as high as twenty five to one, with an increase in the engine inlet temperature at the same time, an unusually powerful and light-weight engine will result.

TESLA'S PLAN FOR PRIME MOVERS

Tesla believed that the future for prime movers should be an engine coupled to an electric drive system (Hybrid) as he is publicly on record as stating in 1904(see page 75). He insisted that this was the most efficient way to convert energy. Tesla was proven correct with this hybrid system being implemented and proven in our present day rail system with diesel electric locomotion becoming the standard.

Quoting Tesla:

"During many years the scheme was declared to be impracticable and I was assailed in a manner as vicious as incompetent. In 1900, when an article from me advocating the electric drive appeared in the Century Magazine, Marine Engineering pronounced the plan to be the "climax of asininity," and such was the fury aroused by my proposals that the editor of another technical periodical resigned and severed his connection rather than to allow the publication of some attacks. A similar reception was accorded to my wireless boat repeatedly described in the Herald of 1898. The patents on these inventions have since expired and they are now common property. Meanwhile insane antagonism and ignorance have been replaced by helpful interest and appreciation of their value."

Volvo has recently introduced a concept car that uses just this principle but is using a conventional bladed turbine engine. This engine is coupled to a Tesla high frequency alternator which feeds an electronic "drive" control. The electronic motor control is used to adjust the supply frequency, and therefore the speed, of a Tesla polyphase induction motor. This full size concept car by Volvo is reported to perform very nicely while at the same time attaining 45 miles per gallon at 55 miles per hour. Volvo has coined this vehicle as "The Environmental Concept Car" or ECC. The only mechanical part of the system that is not Tesla's is the turbine engine.

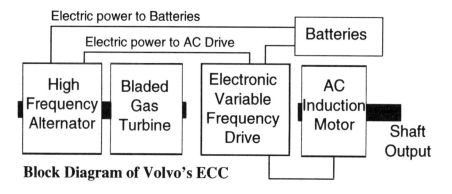

Block Diagram of Volvo's ECC

Tesla did, however, provide plans for this part of the system. Tesla's Engine is much simpler than conventional bladed turbine engines and can operate at much higher temperatures. Our prime movers have been allowed to languish, with the basic piston motor design and efficiencies not much different than that of 100 years ago. In an attempt to control emissions and increase efficiency, computers have been grafted to today's piston engines drastically increasing their complexity but only marginally improving their operation. Although the heart of the electrical system of all of today's automobiles is a Tesla polyphase alternator, little else from Tesla's realm has been permitted to manifest in today's engines.

While it is obvious that a very similar car to the ECC could have been built 50 years ago, it still remains to be seen whether Volvo will actually make their new "concept" car commercially available.

Tesla claimed efficiencies for his engine, without benefit of the electric drive intermediary, operating alone, that would match the performance of the Volvo ECC . Tesla made claims, based on actual test results, that his engine would achieve an efficiency of 60% when used with gasoline. This is almost three times greater than what typical piston engines of today are capable. The automobile would be entirely gearless, using a variation of the engine as a gearless transmission or speed/torque converter (see page 176). The engine would require almost no maintenance, require no crankcase oil and would operate for millions of miles if high quality main bearings are employed which, along with the combustion chamber nozzles, are the only wear prone component. The gearless transmission would provide performance as has never been known in an automobile and would eliminate the electronic drive control used in the ECC. The Tesla transmission's smooth and effortless acceleration with no shifting, would, alone, be a revolution. The current standard for prime movers pales in comparison (see page 76).

In 1987 Chevrolet developed and tested a gas turbine powered automobile, called the Express. It was never put into production. This was not a hybrid but derived power directly from the gas turbine. The engine used was rated at 120 horse power and developed 350 pound-feet of torque and could operate at 150 miles per hour continuously at 20 miles per gallon.

What is the main problem with this engine? Quoting GM executive engineer Albert H. Bell; "The problem is the temperature ratio between the inlet and exhaust at ground level. Airplanes fly at minus sixty-five degrees. We have to raise the operating temperature to get the same ratio for a car and that means more ceramics." It is very difficult to fabricate conventional turbine engines from high temperature materials.

Quoting Tesla:

"It is the lightest prime mover ever produced and can be operated without trouble at red heat, thereby obtaining a very high economy in the transformation of heat energy."

The problem GM encountered with their engine is very considerable when you understand that temperature differential from inlet to exhaust has dramatic effects on fuel consumption and power. This is why a temperature difference of just over 100°F could be so critical to a jet engine's performance. Conventional jet engines are limited to about 2,000°F. If high temperature materials were used in the Tesla Engine, it could easily operate continuously at 2,500°F, vastly exceeding the performance, at ground level, of a bladed turbine at altitude. Fuel efficiency is increased by about 10% for each increase in temperature of several hundred degrees fahrenheit. It would be possible to operate the Tesla Engine at upwards of 3,000°F for short periods, allowing unheard of power from a dwarf of a device. Nitrogen oxide is formed in large amounts above 2,400°F, however, presenting a pollution problem. Water injection can be used with the Tesla Engine preventing nitrogen oxide formation. This would eliminate the need for exotic high temperature materials while still extracting the full energy from the fuel (adiabatic expansion). A conventional turbine would not long survive water injection. Tesla also talked of the fuel savings possible with steam operation stating:

"Two hundred degrees superheat will usually effect a savings of about twenty-three percent of steam and ten percent of fuel."

The main problem Tesla encountered in increasing power output was in twisting the output shaft, it being the only limitation to torque!

Tesla said it would only be a matter of time before it would be possible for an automobile to travel across the country on a single tank of fuel. With his chief engineer on the turbine project stating: "He always talked of traveling from coast to coast on a tank full of gasoline." This was considered to be "against the laws of physics" by the orthodoxy, until only recently. It is now being admitted that Tesla's hybrid electric system can, even without benefit of the Tesla Engine, achieve upwards of 300 MPG in a family type sedan. These new vehicles have been coined "Super Cars." (See TEBA Membership Manual)

The current world record for gasoline consumption of 5,127 miles per gallon, achieved in 1988 with a modified Honda at the Shell Mileage Marathon, is testament to an even greater reality. (Documented by Guinness: see p. 8)

When Tesla's Engine / Transmission is coupled to new technologies in Pulse Resonant Electric Motors, it would provide a practical way to substantially improve mileage in automobiles.

Tesla's electrical achievements were largely based on his understanding of resonance. His electric motors use alternating currents and mechanically resonate to the frequency applied which determines their operating speed and torque.

Tesla's designs are still the most efficient available for using electrically generated magnetic flux. However, the best new motors use powerful magnetic materials which provide stored, so called permanent, magnetic flux that is leveraged with very little input power. In this case resonance is raised to a new level with input energy properly timed being the only requirement to stimulate substantial output power. (see page 74)

The Tesla Engine can be coupled with these new Magnetic Pulse Motors to provide unprecedented performance, with full low end torque, while still allowing for tremendous mileage at highway speeds. As the speed of an automobile increases its need for torque decreases (Power = Torque X Speed). This allows a relatively small pulse motor (10 HP), electrically and mechanically coupled to the Tesla Engine, the ability to provide almost all the energy required at speed. (see diagram page 76)

Since the pulse motor was announced in 1979, there has been a significant improvement in magnetic materials making these motors even more attractive. New magnets have been introduced possessing extremely high tesla ratings, unheard of when these motors were first announced. (The **tesla**, symbol **T**, is the only official Standard International [**SI**] term quantifying magnetic flux density.)

In one possible combination, the Tesla Engine is coupled to a high frequency alternator, providing power for the vehicle's electrical system and pulse motor. The alternator and Tesla Engine are on the same shaft and are coupled thru a Tesla Hydrostatic Transmission to the pulse motor. The engine operates at a fixed high speed in the tens of thousands rpm range for highest efficiency. The unique gearless transmission, which is a variation of the Tesla Engine design, converts this high speed to controllable lower speeds with high torque and provides power beyond the rating of the pulse motor. After the pulse motor is started, the transmission is disengaged and only electrical power is provided unless heavy loads require direct engine assistance. This allows a fuel sipping, economy miser, conversion to a monster horse power, muscle machine, almost instantly, on command! (See page 76)

REVOLUTIONARY ELECTRIC MOTORS
Powered by Magnets and Electric Resonance

Illustrated here is a diagram of an electric pulse motor announced by the Japanese engineering firm, Kure Tekko, in 1979. Its unique design requires only a pulse of energy when the permanent magnet rotor is in proximity to the electromagnet. The motors have been fully tested and have the reported ability to substantially reduce the amount of power required in electric or hybrid drive vehicles. A 45 HP motor documented in 1979 weighed less than half that of a conventional DC motor. Both the rotor and stator have like poles facing each other. The expanding scroll of

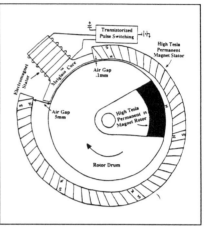

the permanent magnet stator provides geometrically expanding field intensities resulting in a continuous attractive force for the permanent magnet rotor. After the rotor is turning above 200 rpm, all that is required to propell it back into the magnetic region of the stator is a short burst of propeily timed power from the electromagnet. Once the rotor has entered the field, it is attracted to the area of lower flux density represented by the mechanically expanding scroll of permanent magnet material. As the distance of the magnetic scroll is increased, the magnetic lines of flux decrease. This represents an area of lower magnetic density and the rotor is literally squeezed out of the magnetic region bringing it full circle when another pulse of electrically generated flux is applied. This forces the motor's rotor, which is attached to the output shaft, back into the magnetic region and the procéss repeats itself. The only input energy required is short duration pulses. Since the pulse motor was announced in 1979 there has been a significant improvement in magnetic materials, making this device even more attractive. New high tesla magnets have been introduced, possessing power unheard of when these motors were first announced. (The **tesla**, symbol **T**, is the only official Standard International [**SI**] term quantifying magnetic flux density). There is also a new metal available, developed by Allied Signal called Metglass, it has no magnetic permeability or memory. This can be used in the electromagnet to eliminate saturation effects and reactive losses that occur in high speed pulse switching. The core of the electromagnet does not retain magnetic charge, allowing the induced field to immediately collapse after excitation current is removed. The collapsing field can then be recovered and stored in a capacitor, using simple steering diodes, for use on the next switching cycle, further reducing input power requirements. Simple high speed power switching is also now available with a new generation of power transistors, replacing the mechanical distributor used originally in the motor. See the June 1979 Popular Science article "Magnetic Wankel" announcing this device to the public. *The author and publisher disclaim any liability for infringement, by the construction use or sales of this device, possibly protected by US and foreign patents.*

p. 583   **Manufacturers' Record**   Dec. 29, 1904

ELECTRIC AUTOS
Nikola Tesla's View of the Future in Motive Power

In view of the great interest which is being taken in the articles published by the Manufacturers' Record and some of the magazines on the development of new power-producers, through the internal-combustion engine, for use for transportation purposes both by land and sea, the following signed statement, made by Mr. Nikola Tesla after a discussion of a new type of autobus designed by Mr. Charles A. Lieb, mechanical engineer of the Manhattan Transit Co., will doubtless be read with much general interest:

December 17, 1904; To Mr. Albert Phenis, Special Correspondent Manufacturers' Record, New York:

Dear Sir - Replying to your inquiry of yesterday, the application of electricity to the propulsion of automobiles is certainly a rational idea. I am glad to know that Mr. Lieb has undertaken to put it into practice. His long experience with the General Electric Co. and other concerns must have excellently fitted him for the task.

There is no doubt that a highly-successful machine can be produced on these lines. The field is inexhaustible, and this new type of automobile, introducing electricity between the prime mover and the wheels, has, in my opinion, a great future.

I have myself for many years advocated this principle. You will find in numerous technical publications statements made by me to this effect. In my article in the Century, June, 1900, I said, in dealing with the subject: "Steamers and trains are still being propelled by the direct application of steam power to shafts or axles. A much greater percentage of the heat energy of the fuel could be transformed in motive energy by using, in place of the adopted marine engines and locomotives, dynamos driven by specially designed high-pressure steam or gas engines, by utilizing the electricity generated for the propulsion. A gain of 50 to 100 percent, in the effective energy derived from the fuel could be secured in this manner. It is difficult to understand why a fact so plain and obvious is not receiving more attention from engineers.

At first glance it may appear that to generate electricity by an engine and then apply the current to turn a wheel, instead of turning it by means of some mechanical connection with the engine, is a complicated and more or less wasteful process. But it is no so; on the contrary, the use of electricity in this manner secures great practical advantages. It is but a question of time when this idea will be extensively applied to railways and also to ocean liners, though in the latter case the conditions are not quite so favorable. How the railroad companies can persist in using the ordinary locomotive is a mystery. By providing an engine generating electricity and operating with the current motors under the cars a train can be propelled with greater speed and more economically. In France this has already been done by Heilman, and although his machinery was not the best, the results he obtained were creditable and encouraging. I have calculated that a notable gain in speed and economy can also be secured in ocean liners, on which the improvement is particularly desirable for many reasons. It is very likely that in the near future oil will be adopted as fuel, and that will make the new method of propulsion all the more commendable. The electric manufacturing companies will scarcely be able to meet this new demand for generators and motors.

In automobiles practically nothing has been done in this direction, and yet it would seem they offer the greatest opportunities for application of this principle. The question, however, is which motor to employ - the direct-current or my induction motor. The former has certain preferences as regards the starting and regulation, but the commutators and brushes are very objectionable on an automobile. In view of this I would advocate the use of the induction motor as an ideally simple machine which can never get out of order. The conditions are excellent, inasmuch as a very low frequency is practicable and more than three phases can be used. The regulation should offer little difficulty, and once an automobile on this novel plan is produced its advantages will be readily appreciated.

Yours very truly,
NIKOLA TESLA

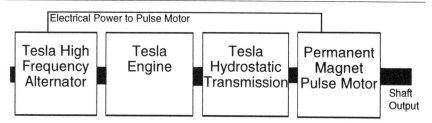

In one possible combination, the Tesla Engine is coupled to a high frequency alternator, providing power for the vehicle's electrical system and pulse motor. The alternator and Tesla Engine are on the same shaft and are coupled thru a Tesla Transmission to the pulse motor. The engine operates at a fixed high speed in the tens of thousands rpm range for highest efficiency. The unique gearless transmission, which is a variation of the Tesla Engine design, converts this high speed to controllable lower speeds with high torque and can provide power beyond the rating of the pulse motor. After the engine is started and up to speed, fluid is introduced into the transmission, turning the pulse motor which requires 200 rpm to start. After the pulse motor is started, the transmission is disengaged and only electrical power is provided, unless heavy loads require direct engine assistance. This allows a fuel sipping, economy miser, conversion to a monster horse power, muscle machine, almost instantly, on command!

page 986   **ELECTRICAL REVIEW & WESTERN ELECTRICIAN** May 20, 1911

NEW INVENTIONS BY TESLA

ADDRESS AT MEETING OF NEW YORK SECTION OF NATIONAL ELECTRIC LIGHT ASSOCIATION.

The meeting of the New York section of the National Electric Light Association was held at the Engineering Societies Building, New York City, on Monday evening, May 15, 1911. Chairman Williams presided.

T. C. Martin introduced Nikola Tesla, preceding the introduction by a statement that the membership of the N. E. L. A. on May 15 was over 8,100, a growth of over 5,000 in eighteen months. Mr. Martin referred to the occasion when Mr. Tesla gave a demonstration of his earlier inventions at the time of the St. Louis Convention in 1893.

Mr. Tesla said that some time ago he experienced the necessity of testing an invention he had perfected under conditions existing in a modern plant and he approached the officers of the New York Edison Company for facilities and received most cordial co-operation, for which he was greatly indebted. He introduced the subject by saying that the gift of invention and discovery is a great one, and that there is no enjoyment that he could picture in his mind so exquisite as the triumph which follows an original invention or discovery. But the world is not always ready to accept the dictum of the inventor, and doubters are plentiful, so that discoverers have often to swallow bitter pills, and he had received an ample share of bitterness as well as pleasure.

He then referred to the fact that in 1887 or 1888 he had brought out the rotating magnetic field. It was at a time when the world was not yet prepared to receive the idea and he had to stand many attacks, and when his patents were fought he had a great deal of trouble. Some went so far as to assert that he had never invented anything.

Mr. Tesla alluded to the discoveries of Hertz which startled the world. He had tried to repeat the Hertz experiments, worked on them for two or three years and had to give them up. He called on Hertz and told him of his doubts. Since that time he has satisfied himself that Hertz had seen true.

He mentioned the discovery by Roentgen in 1895. He had investigated the wonderful phenomenon which Roentgen investigated, and after long search finally ascertained the true nature of the rays and published the results in a series of papers in the ELECTRICAL REVIEW, declaring we had to deal with a new matter which was never before studied, showing that the particles projected were smaller than atoms, that they were of various sizes, that they carried electrical charges and moved with great velocities.

Photographs that originally appeared in this article can be found on pages:
48 and 146

Mr. Tesla further said that in dealing with electrical matters, there is one branch to which he had devoted a large portion of his life, and it is proper he should speak on that subject. He referred to the wireless transmission of energy. The problem presented itself to him as follows: If we can transmit energy through a closed circuit, we should also be able to transmit it through a single wire, and return being effected through the medium.

He exhibited diagrams illustrating the electrical scheme, as well as a mechanical analog, and showed in slides experiments made in 1899 in which incandescent lamps were lighted in this manner. He then exhibited other diagrams of his wireless system and produced a slide showing a lamp lighted by wireless energy. The lamp he declared could have been lighted if it had been placed at the antipodes. Dwelling on his wireless system in detail he said that it comprised five distinct inventions. The first of these was his transformer. To convey an idea of the wonderful effects which can be produced with that instrument, a slide was produced illustrating an experiment performed very frequently in the years of 1892-96. Behind a screen was placed the primary of such a transformer and before the screen a bulb of about fourteen inches in diameter and containing a drop of mercury. The experimenter holds the bulb in the air and the induction from the primary is so strong that it evaporates the mercury and produces an extremely powerful light.

He next described his "magnifying transmitter" and showed several striking experiments with the same on the screen. One slide showed the transmitter used by him in Colorado on an immensely large scale. Streamers were visible extending from the center of the coil and measuring fully forty feet, the width of the same being sixty-five feet. The discharge is so powerful that it goes through the open roof, being carried up by the heat produced.

He next showed another effect of such a magnifying transmitter with a large ball, thirty-nine inches in diameter, which was placed just a little above the building, the roof of which was removable. Several of these streamers could be followed a hundred feet into the air; from a distance it looked as if the building was on fire and the roar could be heard for ten miles. He remarked that this was one of the most difficult experiments because of the great force it takes to reach the required density.

Mr. Tesla then referred to his third invention called the "art of individualization in which the nervous system of the human body was imitated in a crude way" (indicating diagram).

"I will not bother you with theories and details," he said, "but can assure you that as long as the world exists, if all men were Faradays, they could never invent a scheme which would permit as accurate a transmission of messages or quantities of energy to a distance through a wire as has been found practicable without wire by this method; for in a wire transmission the secrecy is only the result of isolation in space, while in the wireless we get the benefit of combinations which are not practicable in a transmission through artificial channels. All the statements you read in the newspapers that wireless messages are interfered with, are because the workers in that field are laboring under delusions—they are transmitting messages by Hertz waves, and in this way no secrecy is possible."

He then showed a picture of a machine exhibited in 1898, to which he first applied this art of individualization.

After stating that his fourth invention pertaining to the system was a peculiar receiver condensing the energy, he dwelt on his discovery of the stationary waves which was the last and most important. Before he could transmit energy without wire economically he found it absolutely necessary to learn how this great body, the planet, behaved, how the current would pass through the same and what are its constants, capacity, self-induction and resistance. As he could not find opportunity in the city for investigating, he went to Colorado Springs and erected a laboratory for the purpose. Several views of the same were projected on the screen. One showed in the center of the building a coil fifty-one feet in diameter and many smaller ones within, which had been attuned to respond to higher harmonics.

Another effect of the magnifying transmitter was next illustrated, showing a display with powerful streamers shooting out in all directions from a coil, as well as a ball of thirty-nine inches in diameter placed on the top.

Mr. Tesla then said: "I had not been in Colorado Springs but a few months when I made the most marvelous discovery I ever expect to make in my life. Before explaining it to you, let me say that I was not stirred at all by its practical value, though it was immense, but by its philosophical significance. You know that through ages past, man has always attempted to project in some way or other energy into space, but in all his attempts, no matter what agent he employed, he was hampered by the inexorable law of nature which says that every effect diminishes with the distance, generally as the square of the distance, and sometimes more rapidly. Now, the discovery I have made upset all that has gone before, for there was a means of projecting energy into space, absolutely without loss from any point of the globe to another, to the antipodes if desired. In fact, a force impressed at one point could be made to increase with the distance. I saw at once that distance was annihilated in all the three aspects; in the transmission of intelligence, in the transport of our bodies and materials, and in the transmission of the energies necessary for our existence. You can imagine how profoundly I was affected by this revelation. Technically, it meant that the earth, as a whole, had a certain period of vibration, and that by impressing electrical vibrations of the same period upon it, it could be thrown into oscillation of such nature that innumerable benefits could be derived from it. Let me tell you of but one application of the principle. Vessels could be equipped with simple devices enabling them to sail across the Pacific along the shortest routes and the captain of each vessel could tell the distance, from a point of reference, within a few feet. We do not today know the exact diameter of the globe. Astronomers have been unable to determine it within a thousand feet. By this discovery without any kind of surveying instrument or even without going out of the room, an electrician can determine the diameter of the globe within four feet. Thousands of such problems, which are of immense practical importance, can be solved and I have often thought that annihilation of distance is the only means of bringing about a quick understanding and universal peace between nations. It will remain for the future to decide whether I have seen truly or not.

"On my return from Colorado I completed plans to demonstrate these principles on a larger and commercial scale, my laboratory in Colorado being only constructed for purposes of scientific demonstration. Here are some views of my plant on Long Island, erected in 1901. This plant is nothing but what I have called a magnified transmitter which, when completed, will enable you to pick up any telephone and, without the slightest change in the stations, talk as clearly as though sitting on the other side of the table to any subscriber in the world. It will make no difference where he is located, and if desired the voice may be made to come out of the ground with such force that it could be heard for miles. The plant was put up originally for the purpose of serving as such a telephone exchange, but was to serve also for other important uses. To give you an idea of the magnitude of the effects, when you speak into the telephone there will be electrical energy at the rate of one billion horsepower sending your voice across the globe, and not only this, but the plant will be so organized that hundreds of people can talk at the same time to any part of the world without the slightest interference. Of course, you will have to take my word for it now, but I hope that I shall live to realize what I have begun. I will carry out my plans exactly as they were first made.

"My project was evidently far in advance of the times. Its progress was retarded and I was compelled to devote myself for a time to other inventions which appealed more to practical men. After years of careful thinking, I found that what the world needed most, and would most readily accept, was an efficient prime mover, a converter of heat into mechanical energy. This all the more as a new world is about to be explored, the world of waste. When you consider that in the manufacture of steel and iron in this country, some thirty million horsepower could be harnessed and a proportionate income derived from that power, all of which is wasted today, you can see what value a good convertor of thermal energy into mechanical energy would have.

"But to conceive that a prime mover is valuable and to get up one, are two different things. After some thought I finally came to the following argument: suppose a number of plates are moved through a fluid medium, the medium will, of course, be dragged along with the plates, and a certain frictional loss will be incurred. Inside the casing are arrange on a shaft a number of disks with openings and spokes and there are orifices of entrance on the sides to produce a perfect balance, and the usual arrangement of outlets. This system of disks being rotated, the water or air is sucked into the channel, is taken hold of and moves in a logarithmic spiral with very nearly the velocity of the system. It was perfectly well known that a fluid would be dragged by rotating surfaces, but somehow nobody realized the conditions for economic working, nor has any one properly grasped the principles which could be applied to propulsion. So it happens again that it is my good fortune to come to the rescue, and I have produced a highly economical way of compressing or pumping fluids." Mr. Tesla then gave a practical demonstration of the working of the principle in a model pump.

"This is one of the early forms of blower which I constructed" (referring to diagram). "That was constructed three years ago. It is a two-stage blower. Far more important than the pump blower or compressor is the turbine. Here is a simple structure, a casing with two entrances, disks arranged on the shaft and outlets in the center for the escape. In this instance the power is applied to one of the openings and the fluid moves with decreasing velocity toward the center until its energy is exhausted and transferred to the shaft. If the theory is correct, I am able to take out the entire energy of steam in one single stage. In the present turbine, sixty-five per cent is the limit of efficiency; theoretically I should be able to get ninety-nine per cent of the total energy of the steam on the shaft in these turbines. These turbines are simple, they have a great torque, far better than other turbines, and a machine will develop ten horsepower for every pound of weight. This principle can also be applied to the gas turbine."

Several slides showing two turbines coupled together were then projected on the screen and a new method of power measurement described. Mr. Tesla then dwelt on the advantages of these machines and showed a number which were constructed and in operation. They have no ducts, nozzles or such complications which cause so much trouble, and besides the machines are perfectly reversible, working with the same efficiency back or forth, making a valuable machine for driving boats, locomotives, automobiles, etc. The accompanying illustrations show two of these turbines.

"In this new invention we have a beautiful solution of many mechanical problems. We have a prime mover which is reversible, ideally simple, of enormous torque, incomparably greater than the turbine possesses, so I am looking for a revolution in mechanics from the application of this principle."

Owing to the lateness of the hour, the other papers which were to have been presented at the meeting were laid over until the next meeting. The members of the Section and their guests were then entertained by an interesting vaudeville performance.

page 499   **ELECTRICAL REVIEW & WESTERN ELECTRICIAN**   Sept. 9, 1911

FLUID PROPULSION

On other pages of this issue we present Dr. Nikola Tesla's description of a new principle of fluid propulsion, which is the culmination of his labors of a number of years. As all generation of mechanical power involves the use of a fluid as the vehicle of energy, the underlying idea is a broad one and bears on all the branches of mechanics.

Dr. Tesla avails himself of the two fundamental properties of a fluid, adhesion and viscosity, in an effort to produce a highly efficient mechanism. The fluid, whether receiving or imparting energy, is made to pass along the surfaces of a system of rotating disks in free natural spirals—that is, along paths of least resistance. The efficacy of the machines he has constructed on this principle is evidenced by their remarkable performance, small turbines or rotary engines being run at a peripheral speed scarcely more than half of that of reaction turbines, and giving several times the output of the latter. For example, a small steam turbine exhibited at the Edison station in New York, having a rotor of only nine and three-quarters inches in diameter and two inches wide, was capable of developing 110 horsepower with free exhaust. This machine had no blades, vanes, valves or sliding contacts of any kind.

On account of the great simplicity of this apparatus, reversibility and extraordinary output, it will undoubtedly find an immense variety of uses, and the commercial world can not fail to be deeply interested in this new development. The electrical industry, in particular, should be greatly benefitted by this latest effort of Dr. Tesla.

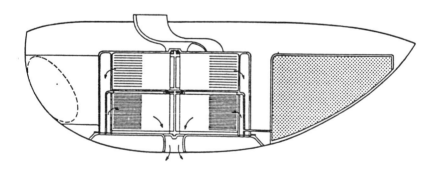

Tesla Hover Craft Design
Bladeless Compressor Pump and Bladeless Turbine Engine

page 515   **ELECTRICAL REVIEW & WESTERN ELECTRICIAN**   Sept. 9, 1911

TESLA'S NEW METHOD
OF AND
APPARATUS FOR FLUID PROPULSION

INVENTION OF A TURBINE AND PUMP.

In an address before the New York section of the National Electric Light Association on May 15 of this year, Nikola Tesla devoted a few remarks to a new mechanical principle he has developed, and exhibited diagrams and working drawings in explanation of the same. He also alluded to the fact that several of his machines were to be seen in operation at the Waterside Station of the New York Edison Company, which had courteously extended to Dr. Tesla its facilities. The ELECTRICAL REVIEW AND WESTERN ELECTRICIAN of May 20 published an exclusive and full report of Dr.Tesla's address.

We present herewith the first authoritative description in the inventor's own words, which, on account of the great importance of the subject, cannot fail to excite interest in engineering circles the world over.

"In the practical application of mechanical power based on the use of a fluid as vehicle of energy it has been demonstrated that, in order to attain the highest economy, the changes in velocity and direction of movement of the fluid should be as gradual as possible. In the present forms of such apparatus more or less sudden changes, shocks and vibrations are unavoidable. Besides, the employment of the usual devices for imparting to, or deriving energy from a fluid, as pistons, paddles, vanes and blades, necessarily introduces numerous defects and limitations and adds to the complication, cost of production and maintenance of the machine.

"The purpose of the invention is to overcome these deficiencies and to effect the transmission and transformation of mechanical energy through the agency of fluids in a more perfect manner, and by means simpler and more economical than those heretofore employed.

"This is accomplished by causing the propelled or propelling fluid to move in natural paths or stream lines of least resistance, free from constraint and disturbances such as occasioned by vanes or kindred devices, and to change its velocity and direction of movement by imperceptible degrees, thus avoiding the losses due to sudden variations while the fluid is receiving or imparting energy.

The illustrations originally appearing in this article can be found on pages: 162 (Fig. 1 and 2); p.168 (Fig 3 and 4) Tesla's Fluid Propulsion and Turbine patents.

"It is well known that a fluid possesses, among others, two salient properties; adhesion and viscosity. Owing to these a body propelled through such a medium encounters a peculiar impediment known as 'lateral,' or 'skin resistance,' which is two-fold: one arising from the shock of the fluid against the asperities of the solid substance, the other from internal forces opposing molecular separation. As an inevitable consequence a certain amount of the fluid is dragged along by the moving body. Conversely, if the body be placed in a fluid in motion, for the same reasons, it is impelled in the direction of movement. The accompanying drawings illustrate operative and efficient embodiments of the idea.

"Fig. 1 is a partial end view, and Fig. 2 a vertical cross-section of a pump or compressor, while Figs. 3 and 4 represent, respectively, in corresponding views, a rotary engine or turbine, both machines being constructed and adapted to be operated in accordance with the invention.

"Figs. 1 and 2 show a runner composed of a plurality of flat rigid disks, 1, of a suitable diameter, keyed to a shaft, 2 and held in position by a threaded nut, 3, a shoulder, 4 and washers, 5, of the requisite thickness. Each disk has a number of central openings, 6, the solid portions between which form spokes, 7, preferably curved, as shown, for the purpose of reducing the loss of energy due to the impact of the fluid.

"This runner is mounted in a two-part volute casing, 8, having stuffing boxes, 9, and inlets, 10, leading to its central portion. In addition a gradually widening and rounding outlet, 11, is provided formed with a flange for connection to a pipe as usual. The casing, 8, rests upon a base, 12, shown only in part and supporting the bearings for the shaft, 2, which, being of ordinary construction, are omitted from the drawings.

"An understanding of the principle embodied in this apparatus will be gained from the following description of its mode of operation.

"Power being applied to the shaft and the runner set in rotation in the direction of the solid arrow, the fluid, by reason of its properties of adherence and viscosity, upon entering through the inlets, 10, and coming in contact with the disks, 1, is taken hold of by the same and subjected to two forces, one acting tangentially in the direction of rotation, and the other radially outward. The combined effect of these tangential and centrifugal forces is to propel the fluid with continuously increasing velocity in a spiral path until it reaches the outlet, 11, from which it is ejected. This spiral movement, free and undisturbed and essentially dependent on these properties of the fluid, permitting it to adjust itself to natural paths or stream lines and to change its velocity and direction by insensible degrees, is characteristic of this method of propulsion and advantageous in its application.

"While traversing the chamber inclosing the runner, the particles of the fluid may complete one or more turns, or but a part of one turn. In any given case their path can be closely calculated and graphically represented, but fairly accurate estimates of turns can be obtained simply by determining the number of revolutions required to renew the fluid passing through the chamber and multiplying it by the ratio between the mean speed of the fluid and that of the disks.

"It has been found that the quantity of fluid propelled in this manner is, other conditions being equal, approximately proportionate to the active surface of the runner and to its effective speed. For this reason, the performance of such machines augments at an exceedingly high rate with the increase of their size and speed of revolution.

"The dimensions of the apparatus as a whole, and the spacing of the disks in any given machine, will be determined by the conditions and requirements of special cases. It may be stated that the intervening distance should be the greater, the larger the diameter of the disks, the longer the spiral path of the fluid and the greater its viscosity. In general, the spacing should be such that the entire mass of the fluid, before leaving the runner, is accelerated to a nearly uniform velocity, not much below that of the periphery of the disks under normal working conditions and almost equal to it when the outlet is closed and the particles move in concentric circles. It may also be pointed out that such a pump can be made without openings and spokes in the runner, as by using one or more solid disks, each in its own casing, in which form the machine will be eminently adapted for sewage, dredging and the like, when the water is charged with foreign bodies and spokes or vanes are especially objectionable.

"Another application of this principle, thoroughly practicable and efficient, is the utilization of machines such as described for the compression or rarefaction of air, or gases in general. In such cases most of the general considerations obtaining in the case of liquids, properly interpreted, hold true.

"When, irrespective of the character of the fluid, considerable pressures are desired, staging or compounding may be resorted to in the usual way, the individual runners being, preferably, mounted on the same shaft. It should be added that the same end may be attained with one single runner by suitable deflection of the fluid through rotative or stationary passages.

"The principles underlying the invention are capable of embodiment also in that field of mechanical engineering which is concerned in the use of fluids as motive agents, for while in some respects the actions in the latter case are directly opposite to those met with in the propulsion of fluids, the fundamental laws applicable in the two cases are the same. In other words, the operation above described is reversible, for if water or air under pressure be admitted to the opening, 11, the runner is set in rotation in the direction of the dotted arrow by reason of the peculiar properties of the fluid which, traveling in a spiral path and with continuously diminishing velocity, reaches the orifices 6 and 10 through which it is discharged. If the runner be allowed to turn freely, in nearly frictionless bearings, its rim will attain a speed closely approximating the maximum of that of the fluid in the volute channel and the spiral path of the particles will be comparatively long, consisting of many almost circular turns. If the load is put on and the runner slowed down, the motion of the fluid is retarded, the turns are reduced, and the path is shortened.

"Owing to a number of causes affecting the performance, it is difficult to frame a precise rule which would be generally applicable, but it may be stated that within certain limits, and other conditions being the same, the torque is indirectly proportional to the square of the velocity of the fluid relatively to the runner and to the effective area of the disks and, inversely, to the distance separating them. The machine will, generally, perform its maximum work when the effective speed of the runner is one-half of that of the fluid. But to attain the highest economy the relative speed or slip, for any given performance, should be as small as possible. This condition may be to any desired degree approximated by increasing the active area and reducing the space between the disks.

"When apparatus of the kind described is employed for the transmission of power, certain departures from similarity between transmitter and receiver may be necessary for securing the best result. It is evident that, when transmitting power from one shaft to another by such machines, any desired ratio between the speeds of rotation may be obtained by proper selection of the diameters of the disks, or by suitably staging the transmitter, the receiver, or both. But it may be pointed out that in one respect, at least, the two machines are essentially different. In the pump, the radial or static pressure, due to centrifugal force, is added to the tangential or dynamic, thus increasing the effective head and assisting in the expulsion of the fluid. In the motor, on the contrary, the first named pressure, being opposed to that of supply, reduces the effective head and the velocity of radial flow towards the center. Again, in the propelled machine a great torque is always desirable, this calling for an increased number of disks and smaller distance of separation, while in the propelling machine, for numerous economic reasons, the rotary effort should be the smallest and the speed the greatest practicable. Many other considerations, which will naturally suggest themselves, may affect the design and construction, but the preceding is thought to contain all necessary information in this regard.

"The greatest value of this invention will be found in its use for the thermodynamic conversion of energy. Reference is now made to Figs. 3 and 4, illustrative of the manner in which it is, or may be, so applied.

"As in the previous figures, a runner is provided made up of disks, 13, with openings, 14, and spokes, 15, which, in this case, may be straight. The disks are keyed to and held in position on a shaft, 16, mounted to turn freely in suitable bearings, not shown, and are separated by washers, 17, conforming in shape with the spokes and firmly united thereto by rivets, 18. For the sake of clearness but a few disks, with comparatively wide intervening spaces, are indicated.

"The runner is mounted in a casing comprising two end-castings, 19, with outlets, 20, and stuffing boxes, 21, and a central ring, 22, which is bored out to a circle of a diameter slightly larger than that of the disks, and has flanged extensions, 23, and inlets, 24, into which finished ports, or nozzles, 25, are inserted. Circular grooves, 26, and labyrinth packings, 27, are provided on the sides of the runner. Supply pipes, 28, with valves, 29, are connected to the flanged extensions of the central ring, one of the valves being normally closed.

"With the exception of certain particulars, which will be elucidated, the mode of operation will be understood from the preceding description. Steam or gas under pressure being allowed to pass through the valve at the side of the solid arrow, the runner is set in rotation in clockwise direction.

"In order to bring out a distinctive feature assume, in the first place, that the motive medium is admitted to the disk chamber through a port, that is, a channel which it traverses with nearly uniform velocity. In this case, the machine will operate as a rotary engine, the fluid continuously expanding on its tortuous path to the central outlet. The expansion takes place chiefly along the spiral path, for the spread inward is opposed by the centrifugal force due to the velocity of whirl and by the great resistance to radial exhaust. It is to be observed that the resistance to the passage of the fluid between the plates is approximately proportional to the square of the relative speed, which is maximum in the direction towards the center and equal to the full tangential velocity of the fluid. The path of least resistance, necessarily taken in obedience to a universal law of motion, is virtually, also that of least relative velocity.

"Next, assume that the fluid is admitted to the disk chamber not through a port, but a diverging nozzle, a device converting, wholly or in part, the expansive energy into velocity-energy. The machine will then work rather like a turbine, absorbing the energy of kinetic momentum of the particles as they whirl, with continuously decreasing speed, to the exhaust.

"The above description of operation is suggested by experience and observation and is advanced merely for the purpose of explanation. The undeniable fact is that the machine does operate, both expansively and impulsively. When the expansion in the nozzle is complete, or nearly so, the fluid pressure in the peripheral clearance space is small; as the nozzle is made less divergent and its section enlarged, the pressure rises, finally approximating that of the supply. But the transition from purely impulsive to expansive action may not be continuous throughout, on account of critical states and conditions, and comparatively great variations of pressure may be caused by small changes of nozzle velocity.

"In the preceding it has been assumed that the pressure of supply is constant or continuous, but it will be understood that the operation will be essentially, the same if the pressure be fluctuating or intermittent, as that due to explosions occurring in more or less rapid succession.

"A very desirable feature, characteristic of machines constructed and operated in accordance with this invention, is their capability of reversal of rotation. Fig. 3, while illustrative of a special case, may be regarded as typical in this respect. If the right hand valve be shut off and the fluid supplied through the second pipe, the runner is rotated in the direction of the dotted arrow, the operation, and also the performance, remaining the same as before, the central ring being bored to a circle with this purpose in view. The same result may be obtained in many other ways by specially designed valves, ports or nozzles for reversing the flow, the description of which is omitted here in the interest of simplicity and clearness.

"For the same reason but one operative port or nozzle is illustrated, which might be adapted to a volute but does not fit best a circular bore. It is evident that a number of suitable inlets may be provided around the periphery of the runner to improve the action and that the construction of the machine may be modified in many ways.

"Still another valuable and probably unique quality of such motors or prime movers may be described. By proper construction and observance of working conditions the centrifugal pressure, opposing the passage of the fluid, may, as already indicated, be made nearly equal to the pressure of supply when the machine is running idle. If the inlet section be large, small changes in the speed of revolution will produce great differences of flow which are further enhanced by the concomitant variations in the length of the spiral path. A self- regulating machine is thus obtained bearing a striking resemblance to a direct-current electric motor in this respect, that, with great differences of impressed pressure in a wide open channel, the flow of the fluid through the same is prevented by virtue of rotation. Since the centrifugal head increases as the square of the revolutions, or even more rapidly, and with modern high-grade steel great peripheral velocities are practicable, it is possible to attain that condition in a single-stage machine, more readily if the runner be of large diameter. Obviously this problem is facilitated by compounding. Now irrespective of its bearing on economy, this tendency which is, to a degree, common to motors of the above description, is of special advantage in the operation of large units, as it affords a safeguard against running away and destruction.

"Besides these, such a prime mover possesses other advantages, both constructive and operative. It is simple, light and compact, subject to but little wear, cheap and exceptionally easy to manufacture, as small clearances and accurate milling work are not essential to good performance. In operation it is reliable, there being no valves, sliding contacts or troublesome vanes. It is almost free of windage, largely independent of nozzle efficiency and suitable for high as well as for low fluid velocities and speeds of revolution. The principles of construction and operation are capable of embodiment in machines of the most widely different forms, and adapted for the greatest variety of purposes."

NEW YORK SUN   Sept. 15, 1911

TESLA PROMISES BIG THINGS

PLANELESS, SCREWLESS AIR-SHIP SAFE IN ANY STORM

*Says His Engine Could Convert Factory Gases Now Wasted Into
Prodigious Power for Use on Land or Sea or in the Air -
Believes He Proved It.*

Dr. Nikola Tesla leaned back in his chair at the Waldorff last night and talked calmly of airships without planes, propellers or any of the other gear of the now familiar aeroplanes hurtling through space at tremendous speed or driving more slowly carrying great loads, and in either case always as safely as the most prosaic of wheeled vehicles.

He spoke of harnessing the energy of the gases given off by the great steel plants and producing therefrom 25,000,000 or 50,000,000 horse-power with a value of say $450,000,000 a year. He spoke of these things already accomplished.

"They have called me a dreamer," he said, "but this is not a dream. It is not an experiment."

Then he went on to tell something about the new mechanical principle of which he has been at work for several years and concerning which, he said, he felt free to talk since the publication yesterday of the Electrical Review in which Dr. Tesla's invention is described. He said:

"Virtually in all generation, transmission and transformation of mechanical power we must avail ourselves of a fluid, a liquid or gas, either to impart or receive energy. In a steam engine, for instance, the fluid is a gas under pressure which transmits its potential energy to a mechanical system. In a pump just the reverse process takes place, the fluid be it a liquid or gas, having energy imparted to it by a moving material system. This invention of mine is a novel means of imparting to or deriving energy from a liquid, and therefore bears on all the branches of mechanics.

"It is rather difficult," he continued to reply to a question, "to give the average reader a correct idea of such a technical advance. But I assume that every one will understand that any fluid is possessed of two properties, one of which is to adhere to the surface of a solid and the other to hold on, as it were, to its own particles. It is a surprising fact that gases and vapors are possessed of this second property to a greater degree than are liquids such as water. Owing to these properties if a solid body is moved through a fluid more or less of the same is dragged along; conversely if a body is immersed in a fluid in motion it is impelled in the direction of movement. The new principle is based on these fundamental facts."

In reply to a question as to how the principle was applied to practical use in the new invention Dr. Tesla said:

"Let us suppose it is desired to derive energy from steam under pressure. In this case a number of disks are mounted on a shaft and the whole is placed in a casting with an inlet for the steam tangential to the disks. The steam entering into this orifice by reason of the properties mentioned exercises a pull on the disks and sets them in rotation, circulating under the influence of the centrifugal and tangential forces in a spiral with gradually diminishing velocity, giving up its energy on the rotating system and finally escaping at the center virtually devoid of dynamic energy.

"In this manner," continued Dr. Tesla, "an ideal rotary engine without any buckets, vanes or sliding contacts is obtained, and one which in performance surpasses by far any other mechanism yet invented. I have developed 110 horse-power with disks only $9^3/_4$ inches in diameter and making a thickness of about two inches. Under proper conditions the performance might have been as much as 1,000 horse-power. In fact there is almost no limit to the mechanical performance of such a machine."

Dr. Tesla said that his machine would work with gas, as in the usual type of explosion engine used in automobiles and aeroplanes, even better than it did with steam. "Tests which I have conducted have shown that the rotary effort with gas is greater than with steam," is the way he put it.

It is the utilization through his invention of energy now allowed to go to waste that seemed most to interest the inventor.

"The field of fuel waste," he said, "is the greatest of all, offering almost unlimited opportunities for exploration. In the manufacture of steel and iron, according to data which I have carefully collected in this country alone from 25,000,000 to 30,000,000 horse-power are wasted through the hot gases escaping into the atmosphere. These gases have a high heating value and by means of the new principle the energy could be readily and cheaply harnessed. If you place the value of one horse-power per annum at $15 this would mean an annual revenue from this source of $450,000,000 per annum.

The ability of his new engine to act in either direction—its "reversibility" the inventor calls it—and the wonderful energy that may be developed by a machine of little weight, Dr. Tesla says makes the engine particularly well suited to propelling ships.

"Applied to a vessel," he said, "these engines will make the carrying of reverse turbines unnecessary and will greatly reduce the expense, weight and bulk of the others."

"How about aerial navigation?" Dr. Tesla was asked . He considered for a moment or two and then replied with great deliberation:

"The application of this principle will give the world a flying machine unlike anything that has ever been suggested before. It will have no planes, no screw propellers or devices of any kind hitherto used. It will be small and compact, excessively swift, and, above all, perfectly safe in the greatest storm. It can be built of any size and can carry any weight that may be desired."

Dr. Tesla in conclusion emphasized again his assertion that the engine that is to do all this is a fact, with its performances matters of record.

"I have built a great many machines, steam and gas turbines, pumps, compressors and other apparatus," he said, and a number have been in practical use for some time past. Yes, it is a big thing, but it is for the big things only that I care to work."

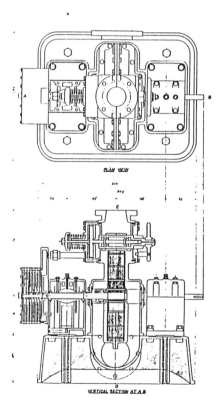

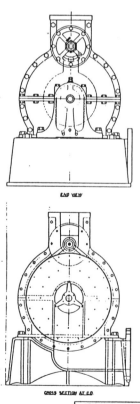

page 895   **Motor World**   Sept. 11, 1911

Possibilities of the Gas Turbine

Believing that the turbine method of converting the kinetic energy of gas into rotary motion is the most efficient and promising yet evolved, engineers continue to watch its development with keenest interest. Up to this time, however, the gas turbine, meaning that driven by products of combustion which still retain very high temperatures, has not made much head-way. Many serious obstacles remain to be overcome though there seems no logical reason why they should not be surmounted in due process of time. What is required is the application of just such mutual effort as in their days have brought forth the no less marvelous developments in submarine and aerial navigation and wireless telegraphy.

Difficulties already encountered include those resulting from high temperatures and pressures from high natural velocities and from the inadequacy of the usual devices for securing the required high degree of compression. There is reason to expect that the solution of the latter problem ultimately will be found in the turbine principle itself, while the gradual accumulation of authentic data is destined to yield in the future such information as may lead to the solving of the other incidental problems. At present there is a lack of concentration of the subject, not as regards the individual, but collectively as regards the engineering world.

The reason is that at present commercial inducement is lacking. The introduction of the steam turbine was made to await the time when the reciprocating engine had attained what seemed its maximum of efficiency in large installations. The internal combustion engine, recognized years ago as a better machine than the external combustion engine, failed to attain general use until the development of the automobile made it imperative to seek a better substitute for the small steam power plant. The large internal combustion installation, more efficient than the large steam plant today, still remains to be adopted to anything like the extent that it merits.

Efficiency alone does not govern. Elements of first cost, reliability, upkeep, flexibility and general adaptability also enter into the business problem which really governs all questions of development and production. However certain the future of a process or product may be, its marketing must be made to wait on a peculiar combination of circumstances which cannot always be foreseen.

Whether the invention of Dr. Nikola Tesla will materially assist in advancing the day and date of the successful gas turbine it is impossible at present to determine. All that is certain is that he has conceived a wonderful new theory and that on it he has based a steam engine for which almost incredible claims have been made. At the same time there is every reason to suppose that the principle is as readily applicable to the products of combustion as to steam, and that once a suitable method of supplying such products has been accomplished the rest will be relatively easy and equally marvelous. It would appear that this invention has brought the gas turbine one step nearer a successful realization, and that it should be hailed with all the enthusiasm which it seems to deserve. At the same time, as one commentator has been unkind enough to indicate, "Mr. Tesla has acquired a reputation for revolutionary inventions that never quite arrived at the point of practical utility;" though it may be contended that the observation has no material bearing in this case.

page 905   **Motor World**   Sept. 11, 1911

Tesla Points Way to Turbines

Famous Scientist Invents Radical Steam Engine With Gasoline Possibilities—New Principle in Fluid Propulsion.

Safe to say, no form of engine could be more attractive either to motorist or automobile manufacturer than that which Dr. Nikola Tesla has evolved in applying his new method of fluid propulsion. A simple form of casing, hardly more complicated than the housing over an emery wheel, a rotating shaft, a number of plain circular disks equally spaced apart and fastened to the shaft and suitable arrangements for the admission of the working fluid and release of the waste products—these few elements constitute the sole requisites of a complete and efficient engine, if the Serbian-American scientist is correct in his reasoning.

That there is nothing in the underlying principle to qualify the new form of engine more particularly for steam than for gas and that early tests have shown enormous power to be derivable from very small units lends strength to predictions that the Tesla system ultimately may exert a revolutionizing influence on the automobile industry.

So new is the invention that it is impossible to determine what are the limitations of the system nor in exactly what manner it will prove applicable. Tesla himself is authority for the statement that the action will be essentially the same whether the pressure of the working fluid be constant, fluctuating or intermittent; the latter condition being such as might obtain were the system applied to the internal combustion engine. One of the experimental steam engines, having disks, or blades, $9^3/_4$ inches in diameter and occupying a lateral space of two inches has developed 110 horsepower, as told by the Motor World last week. On the hypothesis that a practical form of gas engine ultimately may be developed it is apparent that space economy as well as high efficiency and low cost will be among its leading features.

In explaining the underlying method Tesla prefers to deal first with its application to pumping. The first authoritative description of the system, in which the Electrical Review quotes the inventor's own language, in part is as follows: *Ed. see page 83*

Illustrations that originally appeared in this article can be found on pages: 162 and 168; Tesla's Fluid Propulsion and Turbine patents.

New York Times   Sept. 13, 1911

TESLA'S NEW ENGINE

Mr. Charles Wilson Price, editor of the Electrical Review, does not say that Nikola Tesla's latest invention of a rotary engine operated by steam or gases will save most of the 30,000,000 horse-power wasted annually by manufacturing plants in this country, power that is worth upward of half a billion dollars.

He has not said, as Mr. Tesla is reported as saying, that the new engine will give the world a flying machine that without planes or screw propellers, "excessively swift, and, above all, perfectly safe in the greatest storm," will be small and compact compared with present machines, but capable of being built to carry shiploads of passengers.

What Mr. Price does say about the engine, however, arrests attention. A small turbine with a rotor two inches thick and hardly ten inches in diameter, without vanes, blades, valves, or sliding contacts, has been exhibited at the Edison station here, and has been found "capable of developing 110 horse-power." In fact, several of Tesla's engines have been tested. The ELECTRICAL REVIEW publishes his description of them, declaring that his invention "cannot fail to excite interest in engineering circles the world over."

Sir William Ramsay said in his recent address before the British Association that "a good steam engine converts about one-eighth of the potential energy of the fuel into useful work; seven-eighths are lost as unused heat and useless friction." In a good gas engine two-thirds of the fuel energy is wasted. It is quite conceivable that inventions will be made to conserve the enormous energies now wasted.

Tesla's turbine operating without the shocks or vibrations of engines that work with pistons, paddles, vanes or blades, directs the propelling fluid along rotating disks in free spirals and by its adhesive and viscous properties the fluid communicates its energy to the disks. By a reverse process the disks may be made to impart motion to fluids, thus acting as a pump which, if what is said about it is true, will effect great changes in mining operations.

As a motor its inventor says the machine will presently be seen in automobiles, working by gas or steam, in locomotives and ocean liners and in factories all over the world.

Mr. Tesla has acquired a reputation for revolutionary inventions that never quite arrived at the practical utility. But some of his invention have proved to be practical and eminently useful. The new engine may be one of them.

page 23   **Motor World**   Sept. 18, 1911

DR. TESLA TALKS OF GAS TURBINES

So Confident, He Offers to Build Them for Motor Cars
Considers New Power His Greatest Invention

Gas turbines of practical and efficient construction, light, flexible and in every way suitable for automobile propulsion, are not a dream of the future only but a probability of only a very few years hence. At least such is the conviction of Dr. Nikola Tesla, whose newly developed method of fluid propulsion, as he calls it, and which was illustrated and described in last week's Motor World, is attracting so much attention in scientific circles. Dr. Tesla himself considers it the greatest of all his inventions. By his own statement the scientist already has built, run and carefully tested internal combustion engines operating on the new turbine principle and so confident is he of the thorough practicability of the idea that on Friday of last week he informed a Motor World man that he would even be willing today to sign a contract to build and instal turbines for automobiles. He readily admits, however, that he would like to have more time, considerable more time probably, in which to develop a method of combustion entirely suited to the turbine.

Automobile motors, as a matter of fact, play a distinct part in the inventor's plans for the future. So do airship motors, pumps of various sorts, steam engines in every conceivable size, shape and capacity, and apparatus of other and varied uses. If in steam engines and pumps wonderful results already have been obtained, it is his expectation later to accomplish equally wonderful results with internal combustion engines.

Bearing in mind that a 110 horsepower steam engine already has been built so diminutive that its rotor or active part would drop into an ordinary water bucket, it would seem that the part of the program which might be supposed to concern the automobile industry would be well worth investigating. It was the tempting prospect of a pocket-size motor, therefore, which led a representative of the Motor World to seek the famous scientist in his offices high up in the Metropolitan Tower in New York.

Contrary to popular impression, not all great and famous men are inaccessible, and Tesla proved not only thoroughly approachable but extremely ready to discuss the new turbine principle in many of its bearings. His easy predictions of the future developments of the system and his confident bearing when he declared it to be the greatest of his accomplishments, might have been merely the vaporings of an over enthusiastic inventor; but the broad bearing of the man, his record and the depth of perception revealed in some of his conclusions would have laid at rest such doubts. The new principle unquestionably is a great contribution to science and engineering, great in its simplicity and breadth of application. Just when its fullest realization will be given to the markets of the world is another question; one that Tesla himself cannot answer, though he explained that he is "under great pressure from all sides" to complete the development of certain kinds of apparatus, steam engines and pumps having received a great deal of attention up to the present, and that he expects to have some of them ready for production "before very long."

Tall, erect, almost angular, with the broad brow of the philosopher and the sharply chiseled features of the habitual student, Dr. Tesla bears few of the earmarks of the traditional genius. He wears his iron-gray hair a little low in the back, to be sure, but not for an inventor, and when he walks there is just a bare suggestion of histrionic attainments utterly at variance with the hurried preoccupation of the conventional type of man whose brains are stored in the archives of the Patent Office.

"We understand that you are doing remarkable things with steam, but how far has your confidence been extended to the gas turbine?" the scientist was asked.

He laughed.

"Why, I am working with them all the time," he answered.

"You mean to say that you already have built and operated internal combustion turbines employing your principle of fluid propulsion?"

"Yes. But I am not satisfied—not yet. You see there are many things to be considered. The turbine, that is one thing; it is complete in itself and there is no question of its applicability. But when you come to the combustion of the gas you have a new difficulty. I am not satisfied with the present methods of gasification. I have tried one of my turbines discharging the gas into a chamber and then spraying water into it. You see in that way you get an intermittent flow through the nozzle, but you also have better thermal action because you get your adiabatic expansion, [meaning that in which theoretically there is no loss of heat]. And then, I have tried with gasoline using a constant jet, in which you get less efficient thermal action but better action for the turbine. But I am not yet satisfied. I think that some day we shall get better processes of combustion that will enable me to work more advantage with my turbine.

"You see, that is one great trouble," continued Dr. Tesla. "The human mind thinks but to complicate. As soon as one problem is solved, that solution introduces new complications, other problems that perhaps did not exist before. That was one of my great troubles when I was younger, I invented many things that were very fine, but always I was getting into complications. I have had to work very hard to overcome that. But here you see what I have done. Do you see how very simple it is? You take, for instance, the ordinary turbine, a bucket turbine. Here you have around the outside of the wheel a row of little jets, and within, on the periphery of a wheel, a row of buckets—many of them and very small, even on a large wheel. But don't you see that in that entire wheel you have only a narrow strip, a ring perhaps three or four inches wide, that is really useful—that is really active?

"In my invention practically the whole surface is active. In the bucket turbine the action does not even extend all the way around; you must have a series of jets. But in my turbine you have the gas traveling all the way around in free spirals—always seeking the path of least resistance—and expending its full energy."

Here he laid aside the pencil with which he had been illustrating the point, and reverted to the beginning of what he evidently considers his "big idea."

"I have been working at this a long time. Many years ago I invented a pump for pumping mercury. Just a plain disk, like this, and it would work very well. 'All right,' I said, 'that is friction.' But one day I thought it out, and I thought, 'No, that is not friction, it is something else. The particles are not always sliding by the disk, but some of them at least are carried along with it. Therefore it cannot be friction. It must be adhesion.' And that, you see, was the real beginning.

"For if you can imagine a wheel rotating in a medium, whether the fluid is receiving or imparting energy, and moving at nearly the same velocity as the fluid, then you have a minimum of friction, you get little or no 'slip.' Then you are getting something very different from friction; you are making use of adhesion alone. It's all so simple, so very simple.

"This is the greatest of my inventions," Tesla went on with great enthusiasm. "Now take my 'rotating field'— do you know my rotating field—are you familiar at all with electricity? There are millions invested in it already. Well, that is a very useful thing, but the field is limited to dynamos and motors. But here you have a new power for pumps, steam engines, gasoline motors, for automobiles, for airships, for many other uses, and all so simple."

"But is it really true that you have produced 110 horsepower from a wheel only $9\,^3/_4$ inches in diameter and two inches wide, as has been reported?" asked the interviewer incredulously.

"Oh, yes!" was the reply. "And more. We could get more power. We had 125 pounds steam pressure and no vacuum. We ran it that way for hours."

"Was it sustained power?"

"Yes, sustained power. And we could only use part of the drop in pressure; we would have twisted off the shaft, it was so light, if we had been able to use all the energy of the steam. I had to put in a smaller nozzle on that account."

"And they are very light, these steam engines?"

"I can build a steam engine that will develop one horsepower for every one tenth of a pound of weight," was the instant and amazing response. "I am now building a double turbine, one with two wheels which must revolve in opposite directions. It is for a special purpose, and I cannot talk much about that, but each wheel develops 200 horsepower, that is 400 horsepower, and it weighs 88 pounds."

A no less amazing claim made at another time was that the steam turbine could be made to return in power at the shaft no less than 97 percent of the energy of the steam. There seems to be no limit to what the inventor thinks the new system will accomplish, though, of course, a waiting world may be pardoned for withholding a full verdict of confidence until it has had opportunity to witness some of the promised marvels.

As far as demonstration of the basic principle is concerned, however, the success of the idea is unquestionable. A small pump, originally put together for purposes of exhibition before a body of scientists, to whom Dr. Tesla first disclosed his invention, was operated for the benefit of the Motor World man; the inventor himself obligingly switching on and off the current from the little electric motor which drove it, and operating the valve by means of which the discharge could be regulated to increase the flow and decrease the pressure, or vice versa.

The rotor, mounted in a casing of volute form hardly more than six inches in diameter, contained five disks of three inches diameter. From a small tank, which was part of the model, water was drawn into the casing and forced through a pipe with a lift of 18 inches or so to a long strainer in a horizontal pipe, whence, after passing a baffle plate, to break up the flow and prevent splashing, it fell back into the tank over a miniature weir in a beautiful clear sheet. The hand of a pressure gauge indicated four pounds when the valve was closed, but fell to a little under two pounds when the full discharge was permitted.

With the valve closed, the action of the disks was shown to good advantage. Rapidly snapping on and off the switch, the inventor gleefully pointed out how the hand of the gauge jumped up and fell back again so closely in response to the speed of the motor, as judged by the hum of its commutator, that eye and ear failed to detect the difference.

"And so you really believe that a practical form of gas turbine can be developed on this principle and in such shape that it could be profitably adapted to automobile use?" asked the Motor World man.

"I am so sure that I would make a contract today to build gas turbines and equip automobiles with them."

page 673   **ELECTRICAL REVIEW & WESTERN ELECTRICIAN**   Sept. 30, 1911

The Tesla Turbine

The accompanying illustrations which were taken at the request of the editor of this journal, give a very good idea of one of the small Tesla turbines which have been built and operated with slight changes of the rotors and accessories as steam, gas, air and water turbines or rotary engines, and also as pumps and compressors. The characteristics and the mechanical principles involved in the construction and operation of the Tesla turbine were discussed comprehensively in the ELECTRICAL REVIEW AND WESTERN ELECTRICIAN of September 9. Through the courtesy of the New York Edison Company the machine illustrated was installed at its Waterside station where long-continued tests were carried on under greatly varying conditions.

Mr. Tesla, when seen on Tuesday of this week by a representative of the ELECTRICAL REVIEW AND WESTERN ELECTRICIAN, gave the following statements respecting the operation and economy of his turbine: "The turbine has readily developed 110 horsepower with free exhaust, but this does not convey even an approximate idea of the possibilities offered in power production by the new principle of propulsion. It would not have been difficult to develop twice as much power were it not for the torsional stress to which the shaft was subjected. However, even with the result attained, bearing in mind that the rotor weighs only twenty pounds, and that the casing itself could have been pressed steel sheet, the weight of which together with the bearings would not exceed thirty pounds, a performance of more than two horsepower per pound of material was realized.

"As to steam economy, it is highly satisfactory, comparing well with the best turbines, the consumption being thirty-six pounds per horsepower-hour with free exhaust and back pressure of a few pounds, which would mean less than seventeen pounds for a two-stage machine of that size. This economy could still be greatly increased for the turbine was operated under conditions of maximum output and not maximum economy."

Mr. Tesla stated that there was no limit to the capacity for which this turbine could be built and said that the peculiar characteristics of this form of construction would make it possible to attain economy of operation with super-heated steam not heretofore realized. When operated as a water turbine it greatly simplified the present methods of regulation and opened up a field of application which was stupendous.

The Photographs originally appearing in this article can be found on page: 31

page 290   **Scientific American**   Sept. 30, 1911

From the Complex to the Simple

A MARKED step was taken in the simplification of prime movers when Watt's cumbersome steam engine, with its ingenious but elaborate parallel motion, gave way to the present standard reciprocating type, with only piston rod, cross head and connecting rod interposed between piston and crank. An even greater advance toward ideal simplicity occurred when, after years of effort by inventors to produce a practical rotary engine, Parsons brought out his compact, though costly, turbine, in which the energy of the steam is developed on a zig zag pattern through multitudinous rows of fixed and moving blades.

And now comes Mr. Tesla with a motor which bids fair to carry the steam engine another long step toward the ideally simple prime mover - a motor in which the fixed and revolving blades of the turbine give place to a set of steel disks of simple and cheap construction. If the flow of steam in spiral curves between the adjoining faces of flat disks is an efficient method of developing the energy of the steam, the prime mover would certainly appear to have been at last reduced to its simplest terms.

The further development of the unique turbine which we describe elsewhere will be followed with close attention by the technical world. The results attained with this small high-pressure unit are certainly flattering, and give reason to believe that the addition of a low pressure turbine and a condenser would make this type of turbine as highly efficient as it is simple and cheap in construction and maintenance.

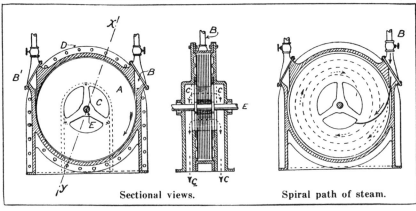

Sectional views.   Spiral path of steam.

Details of turbine.

page 296   **Scientific American**   Sept. 30, 1911

The Tesla Steam Turbine

The Rotary Heat Motor Reduced to its Simplest Terms

It will interest the readers of the SCIENTIFIC AMERICAN to know that Nikola Tesla, whose reputation must, naturally, stand upon the contribution he made to electrical engineering when the art was yet in its comparative infancy, is by training and choice a mechanical engineer, with a strong leaning to that branch of it which is covered by the term "steam engineering." For several years past he has devoted much of his attention to improvements in thermo-dynamic conversion, and the result of his theories and practical experiments is to be found in an entirely new form of prime movers shown in operation at the Waterside station of the New York Edison Company, who kindly placed the facilities of their great plant at his disposal for carrying on experimental work.

By the courtesy of the inventor, we are enabled to publish the accompanying views, representing the testing plant at the Waterside station, which are the first photographs of this interesting motor that have yet been made public.

The basic principle which determined Tesla's investigations was the well-known fact that when a fluid (steam, gas or water) is used as a vehicle of energy, the highest possible economy can be obtained only when the changes in velocity and direction of the movement of the fluid are made as gradual and easy as possible. In the present forms of turbines in which the energy is transmitted by pressure, reaction or impact, as in the De Laval, Parsons, and Curtiss types, more or less sudden changes both of speed and direction are involved, with consequent shocks, vibration and destructive eddies. Furthermore, the introduction of pistons, blades, buckets, and intercepting devices of this general class, into the path of the fluid involves much delicate and difficult mechanical construction which adds greatly to the cost both of production and maintenance.

The desiderata in an ideal turbine group themselves under the heads of the theoretical and the mechanical. The theoretically perfect turbine would be one in which the fluid was so controlled from the inlet to the exhaust that its energy was delivered to the driving shaft with the least possible losses due to the mechanical means employed. The mechanically perfect turbine would be one which combined simplicity and cheapness of construction, durability, ease and rapidity of repairs, and a small ratio of weight and space

Illustrations and Photographs which originally appeared in this article can be found on pages: 30, 34, 37, 94 and 102

occupied to the power delivered on the shaft. Mr. Tesla maintains that in the turbine which forms the subject of this article, he has carried the steam and gas motor a long step forward toward the maximum attainable efficiency, both theoretical and mechanical. That these claims are well founded is shown by the fact that in the plant at the Edison station, he is securing an output of 200 horse-power from a single-stage steam turbine with atmospheric exhaust, weighing less than 2 pounds per horse-power, which is contained within a space measuring 2 feet by 3 feet, by 2 feet in height, and which accomplishes these results with a thermal fall of only 130 B.T.U., that is, about one-third of the total drop available. Furthermore, considered from the mechanical standpoint, the turbine is astonishingly simple and economical in construction, and by the very nature of its construction, should prove to possess such a durability and freedom from wear and breakdown as to place it, in these respects, far in advance of any type of steam or gas motor of the present day.

Briefly stated, Tesla's steam motor consists of a set of flat steel disks mounted on a shaft and rotating within a casing, the steam entering with high velocity at the periphery of the disks, flowing between them in free spiral paths, and finally escaping through exhaust ports at their center. Instead of developing the energy of the steam by pressure, reaction, or impact, on a series of blades or vanes, Tesla depends upon the fluid properties of adhesion and viscosity—the attraction of the steam to the faces of the disks and the resistance of its particles to molecular separation combining in transmitting the velocity energy of the motive fluid to the plates and the shaft.

By reference to the accompanying photographs and line drawings, it will be seen that the turbine has a rotor A which in the present case consists of 25 flat steel disks, one thirty-second of an inch in thickness, of hardened and carefully tempered steel. The rotor as assembled is $3 \frac{1}{2}$ inches wide on the face, by 18 inches in diameter, and when the turbine is running at its maximum working velocity, the material is never under a tensile stress exceeding 50,000 pounds per square inch. The rotor is mounted in a casing D, which is provided with two inlet nozzles, B for use in running direct and B' for reversing. Openings C are cut out at the central portion of the disks and these communicate directly with exhaust ports formed in the side of the casing.

In operation, the steam, or gas, as the case may be, is directed on the periphery of the disks through the nozzle B (which may be diverging, straight or converging), where more or less of its expansive energy is converted into velocity energy. When the machine is at rest, the radial and tangential forces due to the pressure and velocity of the steam cause it to travel in a rather short curved path toward the central exhaust opening, as indicated by the full black line in the accompanying diagram; but as the disks commence to rotate and their speed increases, the steam travels in spiral paths the length of which increases until, as in the case of the present turbine, the particles of the fluid complete a number of turns around the shaft before reaching the exhaust, covering in the meantime a lineal path some 12 to 16 feet in length. During its progress from inlet to exhaust, the velocity and pressure of the steam are reduced until it leaves the exhaust at 1 or 2 pounds gage pressure.

The resistance to the passage of the steam or gas between adjoining plates is approximately proportionate to the square of the relative speed, which is at a maximum toward the center of the disks and is equal to the tangential velocity of the steam. Hence the resistance to radial escape is very great, being furthermore enhanced by the centrifugal force acting outwardly. One of the most desirable elements in a perfected turbine is that of reversibility, and we are all familiar with the many and frequently cumbersome means which have been employed to secure this end. It will be seen that this turbine is admirably adapted for reversing, since this effect can be secured by merely closing the right-hand valve and opening that on the left.

It is evident that the principles of this turbine are equally applicable, by slight modifications of design, for its use as a pump, and we present a photograph of a demonstration model which is in operation in Mr. Tesla's office. This little pump, driven by an electric motor of $^1/_{12}$ horse-power, delivers 40 gallons per minute against a head of 9 feet. The discharge pipe leads up to a horizontal tube provided with a wire mesh for screening the water and checking the eddies. The water falls through a slot in the bottom of this tube and after passing below a baffle plate flows in a steady stream about $^3/_4$ inch thick by 18 inches in width, to a trough from which it returns to the pump. Pumps of this character show an efficiency favorably comparing with that of centrifugal pumps and they have the advantage that great heads are obtainable economically in a single stage. The runner is mounted in a two-part volute casing and except for the fact that the place of the buckets, vanes, etc., of the ordinary centrifugal pump is taken by a set of disks, the construction is generally similar to that of pumps of the standard kind.

In conclusion, it should be noted that although the experimental plant at the Waterside station develops 200 horse-power with 125 pounds at the supply pipe and free exhaust, it could show an output of 300 horse-power with the full pressure of the Edison supply circuit. Furthermore, Mr. Tesla states that if it were compounded and the exhaust were led to a low pressure unit, carrying about three times the number of disks contained in the high pressure element, with connection to a condenser affording $28^1/_2$ to 29 inches of vacuum, the results obtained in the present high-pressure machine indicate that the compound unit would give an output of 600 horse-power, without great increase of dimensions. This estimate is conservative.

The testing plant consists of two identical turbines connected by a carefully calibrated torsion spring, the machine to the left being the driving element, the other the brake. In the brake element, the steam is delivered to the blades in a direction opposite to that of the rotation of the disks. Fastened to the shaft of the brake turbine is a hollow pulley provided with two diametrically opposite narrow slots, and an incandescent lamp placed in side close to the rim. As the pulley rotates, two flashes of light pass out of the same, and by means of reflecting mirrors and lenses, they are carried around the plant and fall upon two rotating glass mirrors placed back to back on the shaft of the driving turbine so that the center line of the silver coatings coincides with the axis of the shaft. The mirrors are so set that when there is no torsion on the spring, the light beams produce a luminous spot stationary at the zero of the scale. But as soon as load is put on, the beam is deflected through an angle which indicates directly the torsion. The scale and spring are so proportioned and adjusted that the horse-power can be read directly from the deflections noted. The indications of this device are very accurate and have shown that when the turbine is running at 9,000 revolutions under an inlet pressure of 125 pounds to the square inch, and with free exhaust, 200 brake horse-power are developed. The consumption under these conditions of maximum output is 38 pounds of saturated steam per horse-power per hour — a very high efficiency when we consider that the heat-drop, measured by thermometers, is only 130 B.T.U., and that the energy transformation is effected in one stage. Since about three times this number of heat units are available in a modern plant with super-heat and high vacuum, the above means a consumption of less than 12 pounds per horse-power hour in such turbines adapted to take up the full drop. Under certain conditions, however, very high thermal efficiencies have been obtained which demonstrate that in large machines based on this principle, in which a very small slip can be secured, the steam consumption will be much lower and should, Mr. Tesla states, approximate the theoretical minimum, thus resulting in nearly frictionless turbine transmitting almost the entire expansive energy of the steam to the shaft.

page 448   **Engineering News Record**   October 12, 1911

The Tesla Steam Turbine

A novel design of steam turbine was mentioned before a local meeting of the National Electric Light Association in New York City, on May 15, 1911, by Mr. Nikola Tesla, whose name has become famous in connection with the rotating magnetic field and other alternating-current developments. Several different types of power apparatus, both driving and driven, embodying the underlying principle of this turbine design have now been built and tested in the Tesla laboratories, including a turbine which has been running at the Waterside Station of the New York Edison Company for several months. The general results of this early work have recently been made public by Mr. Tesla.

The following outline of the designs and the underlying principle running through them all has been made after a conversation with Mr. Tesla and a study of the apparatus. The fundamental principle underlying these several designs appears to be broadly applicable to apparatus wherein a fluid moves some device or the device causes the fluid to move. This includes hydraulic, steam and internal combustion motors, hydraulic and air pumps, etc.

The study of this most interesting line of designs may be approached through the case of either prime movers or driven devices. For the purposes of this article it is perhaps simpler to consider first a pump for a fluid like air, gas, vapor, or liquid. Fig. 1 shows, more or less diagrammatically, a rotary pump in which a series of smooth, flat disks revolves in a casing, with a volute delivery passage. The disks are fastened to a driving shaft but have central openings which serve as inlets for the fluid. On rotating the shaft and disks, the fluid film in contact with the disks is set in motion, even with perfectly smooth disks, on account of the molecular adhesion between disks and fluid. The fluid between disks is also dragged along by the molecular attraction between particles of the fluid (viscosity). The motion of each point of the disk being circular, it is evident that the particles of fluid receive impelling forces which are always tangential to the circular paths. The successive points on the disk that impel given particles of fluid are at increasing distances from the center. The fluid being mechanically unconstrained by walls or vanes except in an axial direction is free to travel in spiral paths from the axis to the periphery.

Illustrations and photographs that originally appeared in this article can be found on pages: 31 (fig. 5), 34 (fig. 4), 42 (fig. 2), 58 (fig. 1), and 94 (fig. 3)

The fluid, in traversing the space from inlet to periphery, may follow a long spiral of several turns or a short one of part of a turn, depending on the quantity of fluid that is allowed to escape from the outlet. With unrestricted flow from the casing, there is little resistance to flow in a radial direction (that is from the backing up and development of pressure), and the tangential slip between disk and fluid is large. The pressure in the casing depends on the velocity with which the particles of fluid leave the periphery of the disk; the maximum pressure with the exit throttled is then proportional to the speed of the disks, the velocity head being converted to pressure head in the volute passage of the casing. The power absorbed is proportional to the square of the slip.

To one seeing such a piece of apparatus in action for the first time, the capacity of a small machine is surprising, especially in the absence of all vanes and projections of every sort which have heretofore been deemed necessary to force the fluid along. A moment's consideration, however, shows that the whole surface of each disk is effective in impelling the fluid along (solely by molecular drag), and the useful surfaces may be made very great in a machine of modest dimensions, in direct contrast with other analogous apparatus where only the relatively small area of buckets, blades, or other projections is effective.

Consideration also shows that any buckets or projecting parts that a disk might carry would constrain the fluid to travel in paths less natural or free, with the consequent development of impact and eddy friction which may be expected to decrease the efficiency over that of simple disks depending for their hold on the fluid only on natural molecular forces. In the case of the Tesla disks, the particles of fluid may be mentally pictured as rolling along on their spiral paths in orderly procession, held to the disks by some gravitation or force; whereas in the case of a disk with projections, the fluid would be pushed and crowded along by impact, with consequent disturbances.

It has been found, as theory would indicate, that the quantity of fluid discharged off the disks is proportional to the area of the disks; that is, the capacity of such machines increases nearly directly with their length along the shaft and about as the square of their diameter, the discrepancies arising naturally from the casing not having impelling surface but adding to the diameter and length of the machine.

The spacing of the disks in such a machine would depend on the conditions under which it had to operate—increasing with the viscosity and diameter and decreasing with the allowable slip. The aim of the designer would be to deliver the fluid from the disks at not much below peripheral speed under normal load conditions. When limitations of practical design would prevent the securing of desired pressures with one simple set of disks, the multiplication of stages is easily accomplished. The fluid then would pass from the exit passages of one stage to the inlet of a second, and so on.

The operations of a pump, as above described, are in general reversible for the production of power from a fluid moving with considerable velocity or under pressure. If a fluid under pressure, but of low velocity, enters the casing of the device shown in Fig.1 in order to flow along the volute of decreasing cross-section and through the inter-disk spaces to what is now the outlet, it must constantly accelerate, converting its pressure head to velocity head. This moving fluid will exert a pull on the disks on account of molecular adhesion and viscosity. If the shaft were blocked so that it could not rotate, the particles of fluid would take short spiral paths from the volute to the outlet.

If the disks are allowed to rotate, however, the particles of fluid in contact with the disks would be subjected to a force preventing travel along the shortest spirals to the outlet. The resultant of the centrifugal force exerted by the disk and that coming from the velocity of the steam constrains the fluid then to follow a longer spiral path. This reminds one of the counter E.M.F. developed in the armature windings of an electric motor opposing the impressed voltage.

It is evident that the torque developed by the disk increases with the difference in peripheral velocity of the disk and of the fluid in contact. As in the analogous case of the pump, the torque rises as the square of the slip. When the shaft runs free, without load, the speed rises and the centrifugal counter force on the fluid, traveling in very long spirals (almost concentric circles), would cause the casing pressure to rise nearly to the supply pressure, the difference being only that required to do the work of supplying energy losses.

Such a prime mover would give its maximum output at about 50% average slip, but the maximum efficiency would come with a comparatively small slip, the actual figure depending upon the fluid employed, on the working conditions, and on the mechanical limitations of design.

The greatest interest in the Tesla steam design, as outlined above, probably centers in its application to a heat motor, such as the Tesla steam turbine. While a device like Fig.1 would operate with steam, it probably would be advisable for obvious reasons to modify the mechanical features—for instance, to suppress the volute passage in the casing, coming down to the simple construction indicated in Fig 2.

If the steam is expanded in a diverging nozzle, it may be expanded over any of the usual ranges of pressure drop, the heat energy then being converted into kinetic energy. The high velocity steam escaping from the nozzle is caused to impinge tangentially on the edges of the disks. In order to escape, it has to take a spiral path from the periphery of the disks to the center openings. The velocity energy of the steam is utilized through the molecular drag on the surface of the disks. With such a nozzle it is seen that the machine is essentially of the so-called "impulse" type of turbine. The arrangement shown in Fig. 2 has a very simple and convenient means of reversing, it merely being necessary to provide a duplicate nozzle discharging against the opposite diameter of the disk and in the opposite direction. When the machine is at rest or running slowly, as in starting, the steam takes a short path from the nozzle to the exhaust and develops a comparatively large torque, since this would be proportional to the square of the difference in velocity of steam and disk. As the machine speeds up, the difference in velocity between steam and disks decreases and the centrifugal forces tend to lengthen the spiral path, so that a given quantity of steam may make several revolutions before finally passing out the exhaust.

It is not necessary, however, to expand the steam before it reaches the disks, and in place of the nozzles shown there may be simple ports. The machine then apparently will operate as a reaction type of turbine, the steam expanding as it flows in its path from port to exhaust. The expanding steam might develop a slight reactive thrust against the disk, but it would depend probably more for its influence on the peculiar action of increasing the velocity of the steam in small increments as it flows along; and absorbing the kinetic energy as fast as developed, in driving the disk.

In Figs. 3 and 4, a steam turbine tested at the Waterside Station of the New York Edison Company is shown. The rotor consists of 25 disks, 18 inches in diameter. The assembled unit, Fig. 3, occupies a floor space some 20 x 35 ins. and it stands some 5 ft. high. The numerous gages seen in Fig. 3 were attached for test purposes. With steam at 125 lbs. gage and exhausting to atmosphere, 200 HP. was developed with a speed of 9,000 r.p.m. The steam consumption under these conditions was about 38 lbs. per HP.-hr. Mr. Tesla states that with moderate superheat and the degree of vacuum ordinarily obtainable in a turbine plant, the consumption can be reduced to 10 or 12 lbs. per HP.-hr. The weight of the unit as shown was about 400 lbs., giving a unit weight of 2 lbs. per HP.

Through refinements in design in addition to the increase of capacity secured with superheat and vacuum, Mr. Tesla expects that the weight may be reduced to as little as $\frac{1}{4}$-lb. per HP. capacity and still allow for designs which will have rotational speeds low enough for direct connecting to the majority of services.

One of the interesting possibilities of the design of turbine shown is that of self-regulation. It has already been shown how the counter pressure due to the rotation of the disks amounted nearly to that of the impressed fluid when running idle. Since the centrifugal head increases as the square of the number of revolutions, and as with available materials great peripheral velocities of the disks are possible, a turbine may be designed which will not run away, the peripheral speed being limited to that value which corresponds to the maximum velocity of the fluid which can be developed.

The main principle of design may be use for an internal-combustion motor. The small machine shown in Fig. 5 has been operated with gaseous fuel burned in an auxiliary chamber and the products of combustion cooled by injecting steam or water spray. This gives a mixture of superheated steam and gases which leave the combustion chamber under high pressure, but reduced in temperature so that they may be led directly to the disks, serving in the place of steam from a boiler. The machine shown developed 110 HP., and it is stated that only the small sized shaft prevented pushing the load higher. The products of combustion instead of being cooled by the formation of superheated steam may be expanded in an insulated nozzle, the temperature falling with the reduction in pressure and the increase in velocity. At the exit of the nozzle, the temperature could be sufficiently reduced so that the gases could be caused to impinge on the disks without injuring them.

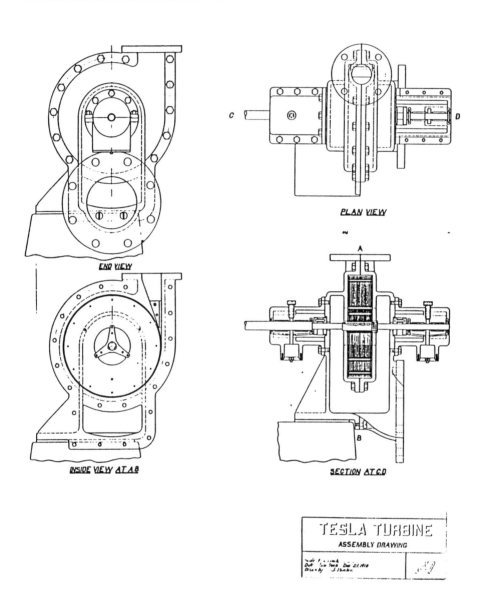

END VIEW

PLAN VIEW

INSIDE VIEW AT A B

SECTION AT C.D

TESLA TURBINE
ASSEMBLY DRAWING

Assembly Drawing for the
110 Horse Power Tesla Engine

page 657   **THE HORSELESS AGE**   Nov. 1, 1911

The Tesla Turbine

The accompanying illustrations show the new turbine invented by Nikola Tesla, the noted electrical and mechanical engineer. With slight changes of the rotors and accessories this turbine may be operated as a steam, water, air or gas engine. The rotor part of the turbine illustrated herewith is only about one foot in diameter. The inventor, in speaking of the design and operation of the machine to a representative of the HORSELESS AGE, said in part:

"The turbine consists of a set of flat steel discs mounted on a shaft and rotating within a casing, the power medium of fluid used entering with high velocity at the periphery of the discs, flowing between them in free spiral paths and escaping through the exhaust port at the centre. Instead of developing the energy of the steam or gas by pressure or impact upon vanes or buckets, the operation of this motor depends upon the adhesive and viscous properties of fluids. The attraction of the fluid to the faces of the discs and the resistance of the particles to molecular separation combine in transmitting the velocity energy of the motive fluid to the plates of the rotor."

"In order to bring out a distinctive feature assume, in the first place, that the motive medium is admitted to the disc chamber through a port; that is, a channel which it traverses with nearly uniform velocity. In this case the machine will operate as a rotary engine, the fluid continuously expanding on its tortuous path to the central outlet. The expansion takes place chiefly along the spiral path, for the spread inward is opposed by the centrifugal force due to the velocity of whirl and by the great resistance to radial exhaust. It is to be observed that the resistance to the passage of the fluid between the plates is approximately proportional to the square of the relative speed, which is maximum in the direction toward the centre and equal to the full tangential velocity of the fluid. The path of least resistance is virtually also that of least relative velocity."

"Next, assume that the fluid is admitted to the disc chamber not through a port, but a diverging nozzle, a device converting the expansive energy into velocity—energy. The machine will then work like a turbine, absorbing the energy of kinetic momentum of the particles as they whirl with continuously decreasing speed toward the exhaust."

Illustrations and photographs that originally appeared in this article can be found on pages: 114 (fig. 1) and 162 (fig. 2=1 and fig. 3=2)

Reference to the drawing in Figs. 2 and 3, of one form of the turbine now in use, shows the rotor composed of a number of flat discs A(1), keyed to a shaft B(2) and held in position against the shoulder C(4) by the nut D(3), with washers between each plate. Each disc has openings E(6) in the centre, with the solid portions F(7) forming the spokes. These spokes are curved in form so as to reduce the loss of energy due to impact of the fluid. This rotor is mounted in a volute form of casing G(8) with packing boxes H(9) in the bearings. The inlets I(10) lead to the centre, while the outlet J(11) has a gradually increasing diameter and is provided with a flange for a pipe connection.

The turbine shown in Fig.1 (below) has a rotor of only 20 pounds in weight, and is said to develop 110 horse power with a free exhaust. This weight, together with the casing and bearings, would give a performance of more than 2 horsepower per pound of motor weight.

The inventor stated that he is at present engaged in the construction of an automobile using the 110 horse power motor with gasoline as the medium of power transmission. He says the car is to be entirely gearless, but as yet is not ready to publish the details of its construction.

We publish the above because certain of our readers expressed an interest in the motor. Personally we do not believe in turbines for automobiles.

Ed. It is no wonder that the Horseless Age did not believe in this engine for autos. It would eliminated almost all of the engine components and service equipment that were the majority of this magazine's advertizing content.

page 50   **THE AUTOMOBILE**   Nov. 30, 1911

Tesla's New Mechanical Principle

Wide Field for Efficiency Increase in Motor Practice

AN engine which uses gasoline as a fuel and is capable of delivering 60 per cent. of the inherent energy of this fuel at the crankshaft instead of the customary 18 to 22 per cent. has been invented and constructed by Nikola Tesla.

"It is well known," states the inventor, "that a fluid possesses, among others, two salient properties: adhesion and viscosity. Owing to these a body propelled through such a medium encounters a peculiar impediment known as lateral or skin resistance, which is two-fold, one arising from the shock of the fluid against the aspirates of the solid substance, the other from internal forces opposing molecular separation. As an inevitable consequence a certain amount of the fluid is dragged along by the moving body; conversely, if the body be placed in a fluid in motion, for the same reasons, it is impelled in the direction of movement."

Based on these observations, Nikola Tesla, the discoverer of the polyphase alternating current, has developed a new mechanical principle broadly applicable for the generation, transformation and transmission of mechanical energy. The machines constructed by Mr. Tesla are illustrated herewith, partly by photographic reproductions and partly by sectional drawings which accompanied Mr. Tesla's original treatise in the *Electrical Review and Western Electrician,* September 9.

In the development of his machines it has been the aim of the inventor to let the energated fluid *flow along its natural paths;* that is, those of least resistance, with as small a friction loss as possible. It is important to keep in mind the fact that in his, like all other mechanical devices, *friction is inevitably equivalent to a loss in efficiency.* With these points in view Mr. Tesla uses in his construction but a few simple and economic elements creating as little resistance as possible for the fluids moving his machine or moved by them.

The machine, Fig. 1, is of simple construction and may be used as a motor or as a pump. In a steel housing, very much like to that of a centrifugal pump, is contained a runner consisting of a number of steel or bronze plates arranged in series upon a shaft, Fig. 2. Each plate or disc has three central openings A extending from the shaft to about one-third of the radius and separated by spokes. These openings arc cut or stamped out of the discs and the surfaces of the latter are kept as smooth as possible.

Illustrations and photographs that originally appeared in this article can be found on pages: 31 (fig. 1 and 2), 162 (fig. 3), and 168 (fig. 4)

If the device, Fig. 2, is mounted on bearings and rotated at considerable speed the following phenomenon takes place. The air, in direct touch with the metal discs, is held to them by molecular adhesion, clinging to the metal surfaces as water does to that of a solid it is brought in contact with, and therefore the air particles next to the discs are imparted motion in the direction of the rotation of the discs. Thus, some air is dragged along and its particles begin revolving about the shaft of the device. Since the movement of the air is rotary, centrifugal force causes it to move away from the central portions of the discs, the resultant between the rotary and centrifugal force being along a spiral line. This flow of air toward the periphery of the discs causes a fall of atmospheric pressure at the central regions, and these being occupied by the openings, air rushes in through the openings, and thus a continuous flow of air is maintained.

If the discs are enclosed in the casing seen in Fig. 1, and the shaft is rotated, the unit will work as a pump. In order to explain the office of the inlet and outlet pipes seen in the illustration, Fig. 3, is offered to illustrate the Tesla pump in partial end view and vertical cross-section. The air adjacent to the discs is dragged along in the direction of the arrows, approaching at the same time the periphery of the discs. In addition to this the particles not in direct touch with the discs, but with the moving air, are dragged along and imparted motion through viscosity, that is, the attraction of the particles of a fluid. The viscosity of air is about 100 times that of water. Thus, the entire body of air between the two discs—unless they are spaced too far—is transported to the peripheral portions of the interdiscular space and, after having reached the periphery, streams along the wall of the casing, which widens from the point 1 to 2, 3 and 4, until the air reaches the outlet where it is discharged. The quantity of the fluid propelled through this pump, according to tests made by its inventor, is approximately proportionate to the active surface of the runner—the total active surfaces of all the discs on the shaft—and to the effective speed of the machines; therefore, the performance of the pump is bettered with increasing size and number of revolutions per minute.

The machine, Figs. 1 to 3, has twenty-five plates $9\,{}^3/_4$ inches in diameter, the entire runner being 2 inches thick and the full weight including the casing of the machine being 20 pounds.

If a fluid under pressure is permitted to enter the casing through what is marked outlet, Fig. 3, it will flow along the wall of the casing, passing the points 4, 3, 2 and 1 in the order named until, when it reaches the narrowing near the outlet, which now is the inlet, it is forced to enter the interdiscular space. In doing this the adhesion of the discs to the fluid causes the former to have motion imparted to them, so that they begin to rotate, while the fluid, which is continually giving off energy, loses in velocity. Since bodies having rotary speed imparted to them are subject to a centrifugal effect, and bodies expending energy in creating rotary motion, to a centripetal one, the fluid with decreasing speed approaches the center of rotation, and is discharged dead, without pressure, through the central openings of the discs. It is exhausted by gravity through the opening marked inlet, Fig. 3.

The engine so described, when driven by a mixture of steam and the products of a gaseous fuel burned in an auxiliary chamber showed 110 horsepower on the brake, and more load could have been sustained by it except for the small dimensioned shaft. While this instance shows that the same machine may be used as a prime mover and as a pump, it is obvious that a machine of this type specially constructed for the purpose of driving machinery may be improved upon by adapting some details to the specific needs of the situation. Thus Fig. 4 shows a Tesla rotary engine, applicable for steam or hot-air drive, having a nozzle through which the pressure of the driving steam is increased. A reversing nozzle is also provided.

As in the other engine the runner is composed of discs D(13), having central openings O(14) and spokes S(15). The discs are held in position, being keyed to shaft S1(16) which is mounted on suitable bearings. Washers W(17), conforming in shape to the spokes and riveted thereto, separate the discs. For simplicity's sake, only a small number of discs is shown, with proportionally larger intervening spaces than are used in practice. The runner is mounted in a casing having two end castings S(19) with outlets E(20), stuffing boxes B(21) and a central ring R1(22) bored out to a circle of diameter slightly in increase of that of the discs. The ring has flanged extensions with inlets into which nozzles N(25) are inserted. Circular grooves G(26) and labyrinth packings P(27) are provided on the sides of the runner.

A steam engine of this type has been installed and tested at the Waterside station of the New York Edison Company. The runner consists of twenty-five discs, diameter 18 inches, the engine base being 20 by 25 inches, and the height 5 feet. This engine developed, with steam admitted at 125 pounds pressure and exhausted at 14.7 pounds, 200 horsepower at 9,000 revolutions. About 38 pounds of saturated steam were need per horsepower-hour, but Mr. Tesla stated that by the use of moderately superheated steam and the ordinary vacuum the consumption may be reduced to about one-third of the quantity stated.

If the motor runs without load, the fluid which enters at the periphery completes a number of circles before it has expended all its energy and it leaves through the central openings. As soon as the load is put on, the paths of the fluid are cut short, being changed to a spiral with fewer turns. Despite the difficulty attending the work of determining the operating conditions in this machine, the following seems to be an established fact. The torque produced by the engine is directly proportional to the square of the velocity of the fluid relatively to the runner and to the effective area of the discs, and amount of work is done when the effective speed of the runner is one-half that of the entering fluid.

There is no unsurmountable difficulty in the construction of a light and practical motor of this type for the use of liquid hydrocarbon fuels. Of course, an auxiliary combustion chamber and carburetor have to be used in connection with the rotary engine described, and a very small pump to supply the air to the gasoline, if such be used. Mr. Tesla states that he has carried out numerous experiments along this line, and by the use of his motor transforms 60 per cent. of the energy of the gasoline into mechanical work available at the shaft. This may seem very high, but since with a rotary engine (compare steam engines and turbines) it is not necessary to encounter such vast cooling losses as in common gas engine practice, the high efficiency claimed by him might perhaps be obtained even in an average gasoline engine of his construction. It has been shown in THE AUTOMOBILE, July 27, 1911, pages 147-149, that the cooling losses in an automobile engine amount to 35.9 per cent., and the heat losses in the exhaust to 35.2 per cent. These heat losses together with other small expenditures of energies leave only 21.8 per cent. available at the motor shaft, that is, one-third of what is said to be recovered by an engine of the Tesla type.

The possibility of the enormous power output of Tesla engines in proportion to their weight may be understood when the great amount of active surface of these engines is considered. This fact also accounts to some extent for the large thermal efficiency.

The 110-horsepower motor weighs 20 pounds, or 5.25 pounds per horsepower; the 200-horsepower engine at the Edison company's station weighs 400 pounds, or 2 pounds per horsepower, and by refinements of construction, the application of superheated steam and the use of vacuum exhaust Mr. Tesla expects to succeed in the building of an engine weighing $^1/_4$ pound per horsepower.

A comparison between a Tesla pump and an ordinary pump may be of interest and not out of place here. In the laboratory of the inventor a small pump of the construction here illustrated is working. It is operated by a small electric motor, consuming $^1/_{12}$ horsepower, and delivers 40 gallons per minute against a 9 foot head. The consumption of a good centrifugal pump rendering this work is about $^1/_3$ horsepower, and in no case less than $^1/_4$. This means one-third the power consumption for a given amount of work to be performed. As to the application of Mr. Tesla's principle to prime movers, it is stated by him that in large machines, by the use of superheated steam, high vacuum and the minimum of friction obtaining at these dimensions, about 95 per cent. of the fluid energy of the steam are delivered at the shaft.

page 925   **POPULAR MECHANICS**   Dec. 1911

THE TESLA TURBINE

By E. F. STEARNS

ENGINEERS and men of science throughout the world are awaiting with unusual interest the completion of tests of a new steam turbine designed by Nikola Tesla, which preliminary experiments indicate will give enormous power from a comparatively small and extremely light-weight engine. Ten horsepower to a pound of weight has already been developed with the engines that have been tested and enthusiasts who have witnessed the work of the turbine declare the perfect rotor has at last been found. To what extent this is true, time and the construction of larger units than have yet been used must prove. At present, while the practical experimental stage has not yet been passed, the entire engineering world is profoundly interested in the work that has been done, and awaits future development with much concern.

Operation of the Tesla Engine depends upon two well-known properties of fluids: adhesion—the tendency, for example, of a certain amount of water to cling to a smooth metal surface, even when the bulk of the water has been shaken off; and viscosity, the resistance of fluids to molecular separation, the tendency of one drop, in a mass of fluid, to drag adjoining drops with it, if set in motion.

In its simplest form, the new idea takes the shape of the inventor's little "air-diffuser." This consists of half a dozen very thin steel disks, some 9 or 10 in. in diameter, set horizontally, about $\frac{1}{8}$ in. apart, on the upright shaft of a small, horizontal electric motor, the center of each disk being cut away in a 3-in. circle. With current switched into the motor, the disks revolve, and instantly strong suction can be felt by the hand held several inches above the axis, while a powerful current of air is blown from the spaces between the disks. The air, in short, is being sucked into the central opening and hurled out at the periphery. Consider now that disks and shaft have been inclosed in an air-tight case, with an inlet at the axis and an outlet at one point of the periphery; we have an air pump, a Tesla Blower, one of which, now in operation, is delivering 10,000 cu. ft. of air per minute. Suppose again that water, instead of air, be the fluid admitted. Entering the cut-away space at the centers of the disks, the adhesion of the metal drags it, in a widening spiral, toward the spinning circumferences, there to hurl it away in a tangential direction; and since the water must now leave the case by its one outlet, we have the Tesla Pump, on rather new lines.

Illustrations and photographs that originally appeared in this article can be found on pages: 24, 30, 31 and 34

Assume that the pumping process is to be reversed, that the disks, instead of being turned by an outside force, are to produce power themselves, that steam under pressure has been substituted for the water. The steam, admitted to the case, strikes the edges of the disks and takes the path of least resistance between them, a narrowing spiral toward the outlet through their centers. The disks themselves are dragged around, the shaft is turned and power is being generated in an entirely new fashion.

Working under the best conditions—in the experimental laboratory—a single disk of $9\,^3/_4$ in. diameter, with a center outlet of $3\,^5/_8$ in., will develop 5 hp. Without nearly approaching the limit of strain of the materials, the pressure could be increased so that the velocity of rotation would be doubled and the power quadrupled; so that with a single steel plate, $1\,^1/_{32}$ in. in thickness, weighing about $^3/_8$ lb., and delivering 20 hp., we have a possible 53 hp. to 1 lb. of actually working material. Or a more concrete example can be found in a double Tesla turbine, built for practical service and nearly completed. In this there are two sets of disks, arranged to revolve in opposite directions and each set developing 200 hp.

Comparison between the old and the newest is best given in the inventor's own words:

"In most engines, a very small proportion of the total amount of material is actively employed in the production of power. For example, in reciprocating engines of the older type, the power-giving portion—cylinder, piston, etc.—was no more than a fraction of 1 per cent of the total weight of material used in construction. The present form of turbine, with an efficiency of about 62 per cent was a great advance, but even in this form of machine scarcely more than 1 percent or 2 percent is used in actually generating power at a given moment. The new turbine offers a striking contrast, using as it does practically the entire material of the rotor (the whole surfaces of the disks) as an active source of power, and with an efficiency of 80 percent or even 90 percent. Owing to this, it is possible to get an enormous amount of power from a small space. Assuming sufficient boiler capacity on a vessel such as the "Mauretania," it would be perfectly easy to develop, instead of some 70,000 hp., 4,000,000 hp. in the same space - and this is a conservative statement."

The following caption appeared under the photograph on page 30
A little model pump in which five disks, 3 in. in diameter, contained in the lower front, circular case, throw 40 gal. a minute when the little electric motor is started up. The water flows out of a slit at the bottom of the upper pipe and flows back to the lower tank as seen in the foreground. This model illustrates one point astonishingly: the power can be shut off when the pump is in full operation and everything stops instantly without the slightest jar. With the power switched on suddenly, the full flow is resumed so quickly that the interval between the click of the switch and the full stream of water is too small to be determined with an ordinary watch.

Page 658   **TECHNICAL WORLD MAGAZINE**   Feb., 1912

POWERFUL TURBINE A MERE TOY

By HENRY JEVONS

ALMOST any evening last fall a tall, spare man, whose discouraged looking mustache remains a glossy black without any aid from the barber in spite of the fact that its wearer is well past his fiftieth year, might have been seen wending his dignified way down East Thirty-eighth Street toward First Avenue, New York City. He was a man who would attract attention anywhere, but especially on East Thirty-eighth Street, which is not a thoroughfare one would choose for an evening stroll, unless one chanced to be hard up for strolls. If the tall man had been shadowed he would have been seen invariably to disappear within a massive brick building which covers the entire block between Thirty-eighth and Thirty-ninth streets, First Avenue and that part of Long Island Sound miscalled "East River."

Had the phenomenon been further investigated, this building would have been found to be a place of extraordinary interest, for various reasons. Together with its twin covering, the next block north, it constitutes the Waterside Station of the New York Edison Company, the largest steam power plant in the world. Of still greater interest than its size is the fact that ever since it was built there could be found within its thick walls the living history of the evolution of the steam engine epitomized and in action. Unlike all other histories of the steam engine, the opening chapter did not begin with the exploits of Hero, of Alexandria, 120 years before Christ, but started in several pages ahead of October, 1901, on which date the plant sent out its first electrical impulse.

When the New York Edison Company decided to build Waterside Station it took the bridles off the engineers and allowed them to go as far as they liked in designing a plant that would be the last word in steam engineering, for the plant was intended to be big enough to meet all demands for years to come. Power was furnished by vertical, three cylinder compound engines of 5,000 horse power, which were considered something marvelous both in size and economy, eleven years ago. But before steam had been turned on for the first time the Curtis turbine had thrown down the gauntlet to reciprocating engines of whatever size or kind, offering to give them cards and spades and beat them out in the matter of economy. So a turbine of 2,000 horse power was installed almost at the beginning to show what it could do. It did so well that a turbine of 10,000 horse power soon took its place beside the pioneer. All the various examples of different periods in the evolution of the steam engine worked together in harmony, sending their currents out over the same wires in one united stream to light the Great White Way and more useful, if less popular, places.

Illustration and Photographs which originally appeared in this article can be found on pages: 22, 31, 34 and 94

Before the plant could be started up the company realized that forty thousand horse power, instead of being enough to meet all demands for years, wasn't even enough to begin business with; so the architect was routed out of bed and told to get busy on an extension. Since then neither architect nor engineer have had time to go out to lunch, for the plant has been steadily increasing in capacity until now it aggregates approximately three hundred thousand horse power, and it is still growing night and day. At the present time the company is replacing its vertical compound engines of 5,000 horse power with Curtis steam turbines of 27,000 horse power, by far the largest steam engines the world has ever seen. A single one of these monsters would supply electric current enough to meet the requirements of a city of 250,000 inhabitants; yet one of them takes up no more space than that occupied by the vertical compound engines of one-fifth their power.

This may seem to be going some, yet the evolution of the steam engine is proceeding at such a terrific pace that even so persevering a corporation as the Edison Company might be pardoned for feeling discouraged. In a gloomy corner of this titanic power plant a new idea has sprouted which may oblige the Edison Company to send the first of its 27,000 horse power Curtis turbines to the scrap heap before the last one can be installed. And this brings us back to the tall man.

He is none other than Nikola Tesla, whom the American Institute of Electrical Engineers, by vote of its members, placed seventh in the list of the greatest twenty-five names in electrical science. Tesla has invented a steam turbine. Of course this in itself is nothing worth mentioning, for everybody who is anybody has invented a steam turbine. And as there are steam turbines aggregating 5,166,000 horse power hard at work in the United States today, nearly all installed within the last six years, there is nothing sensational in the mere existence of such a prime mover.

But Tesla's turbine is different. Everything that Tesla does is different. Instead of studying for the priesthood as his father wished, Tesla went out to the stable at his home in far-off Hungary one day when he was very much younger than he is now and tried to fly from the roof with no other aid than that afforded by an old umbrella. The next six weeks he spent in bed. Since then he has been careful to keep his corporeal substance on solid ground; but his fancy essays some marvelous flights. It was Tesla, for instance, who proposed to signal from Long Island to the people on Mars by means of Hertzian waves of exceptional force. It was Tesla, too, who conceived the idea of wireless transmission of power, not to mention other enterprises daringly original. All this goes to show that while Tesla has a long list of practical achievements to his credit he is, in many things, decades, if not centuries, ahead of his times.

When such a man turns his attention to the things of every day life he may confidently be counted upon to produce something original. As every one who is informed upon the subject knows, the fundamental feature of the steam turbine is a wheel bearing upon its periphery a series of vanes or buckets. A jet of steam blowing upon the buckets pushes the wheel around and thus generates power. Many variations have been embroidered upon this elementary feature to produce the long list of turbines upon the market; but in none of them is the bucket dispensed with. It took Tesla to do that, though E. C. Thrupp, of England, tried to do it eleven years ago, and others have also tinkered vainly at the idea.

Tesla's turbine is the apotheosis of simplicity. Its working parts consist of nothing in the world but some smooth disks of steel only one thirty-second of an inch in thickness mounted about seven sixty-fourths of an inch apart upon a shaft. This assemblage of disks upon a shaft, called a "rotor," being placed within a steam-tight steel casing in which is an opening on the periphery to admit steam and another at the center of one side to allow it to escape, completes the turbine. Lacking the essential element of a turbine, the bucket, it really isn't a turbine; but as the inventor has not yet had time to think up a suitable name for it the familiar designation must answer present purposes.

To go into more minute particulars, the opening for the admission of steam is placed so that the jet strikes the periphery of the disks tangentially. As for the disks themselves, a part of their center is cut away as near as possible to the shaft so that there are three passages from side to side parallel with the shaft at equal distances apart. At one side of the casing opposite these openings is the exhaust port.

At first glance it might appear that when steam was admitted it would simply blow through between the disks and out at the exhaust port without causing the rotor to turn over. And really it almost does this, but not quite. Striking the periphery of the disks at a tangent the steam does follow a short curve to the center at first, but still the curve is long enough to allow the steam to begin to push the disks around. As the disks begin to revolve the steam follows them part way, thus increasing the distance it has to travel to reach the outlet and at the same time giving it a greater hold upon the surface of the disks. This process continues until the rotor has attained full speed, when the steam is pursuing a spiral course from inlet to outlet which takes it several times around the disks in a course six or seven feet long before it finally escapes.

Tesla's turbine is so violently opposed to all precedent that it seems unbelievable, even when you see it at work. In the reciprocating engine the steam has the immovable cylinder head to brace itself against while it expands and pushes the movable piston ahead of it. In the reaction turbine it follows exactly the same principle, expanding between fixed buckets on the sides of a chamber and buckets on the rotor. Even in the impulse turbine there are buckets to give the steam a purchase. In the Tesla turbine there is not so much as a scratch for the steam to grip—nothing but smooth steel.

But the advantages of the earlier forms of the steam turbine and the seeming disadvantages of the Tesla motor are more apparent than real. Steam is a fluid; and when any fluid is used as the medium through which power is developed the most economical results are obtained when the changes in velocity and direction of the current are made as gradual and easy as possible. A diagram of the path followed by a jet of steam in a reaction turbine would look like the thread from an old chain stitch sewing machine ravelled out and thrown down loose. With such a zigzag course destructive eddies, vibration and shocks are inevitable. This is not saying that steam turbines are not highly efficient, for they are; but still they are a long way short of perfection. Another point that counts against the impossibility of attaining the ideal with the older forms of turbines is their delicate and difficult construction. The large ones contain many thousand blades or buckets each one of which has to be machined and fitted separately. While turbines are much more economical than reciprocating engines in their own particular field they are, nevertheless, costly to build and maintain.

Tesla gets the cost of construction and maintenance down to an irreducible minimum by the extreme simplicity of his turbine. He can do this because he approaches the problem from an entirely new angle. Instead of developing power by pressure, reaction or impact on buckets or vanes he depends upon the properties of adhesion and viscosity which are common to all fluids, including steam.

The characteristic of viscosity is best exemplified by cold molasses. Any one who has had to go out to the smoke house in winter to draw a pitcher of molasses for the matutinal buckwheats does not need to look in the dictionary to ascertain what viscosity is. Nor is an unduly vivid imagination required to figure out what would happen if a stream of cold molasses were directed against the rotor of a Tesla turbine. There would be such an excess of viscosity that nothing whatever would happen except the machine would be all mussed up. But by heating the molasses its viscosity would be so much reduced that the fluid might trickle down slowly between the disks.

Water has much slighter powers of adhesion than hot molasses, but it does pretty well, even at that. Test the matter by twirling a big button by twisting strings passed through the eyes as children do to make a familiar plaything, holding the rim of the button in a basin of water. The way the water will fly will show very strikingly how so thin a liquid will adhere to a smooth disk.

Steam is less adhesive than water, but the difference is in degree only, not in kind. When steam is admitted to the Tesla turbine a thin film of it adheres to the faces of the disks with tenacity enough to exert a pull in the direction in which the jet is moving. At the same time the steam in the thin space between the disks is also held back by the molecular attraction between its particles and those adhering to the disks, which is another way of expressing viscosity, so that all the steam between the disks is helping to drag the rotor around. Of course the disks do not move as fast as the steam, for the velocity of steam is very great.

If the disks were placed too far apart the greater bulk of the steam would flow swiftly through, like the current in a river which flows more swiftly in the center than near its banks, without doing any useful work; but the space is carefully calculated so as to make each molecule of steam exert a long pull, a strong pull and a pull all together with its neighbors, and thus do all the work it is capable of doing under the circumstances.

After Tesla had worked out the theory of his turbine he had one built, then obtained of the Edison Company permission to conduct his experiments at Waterside Station where there is an abundance of superheated steam, vacuum and all other essentials, including surroundings which might be supposed to be inspiring in such an undertaking, for the very air in the great buildings seems to vibrate with irresistible power.

On a base which raises it a few inches above the steel floor is an object shaped like a cheese, actually no bigger than a derby hat of average size. Within the black casing is a rotor made up of steel disks $9\,{}^3/_4$ inches in diameter and measuring but two inches across the face. Yet this insignificant black cheese makes a fifty kilowatt generator hump itself. Actually it is capable of developing 110 horse power. It has to be geared down, for it is too swift for any generator that ever was built.

When Tesla escorted the first installment of guests around to inspect the new turbine he remarked casually that it ran at 16,000 revolutions per minute. To ask any engineer to believe such a tall statement was putting altogether too great a strain upon credulity. The guests smiled indulgently and winked at each other behind Tesla's back. But when the inventor applied a revolution counter, that bit of brass mechanism went into spasms, then calmed down enough to indicate 16,000 revolutions per minute, whereat the eyes of the visitors protruded until they were unable to wink again for a fortnight.

Beside this first Tesla turbine stand two larger ones, coupled together by a flexible shaft so that one may be used as a brake to test the power developed by the other. Taking steam at 125 pounds pressure and exhausting into the open air, making 9,000 revolutions per minute this larger turbine develops 200 horse power. At 185 pounds pressure as used by its big neighbors, it is capable of developing 300 horse power. Yet this new turbine stands on a base only 20 by 35 inches and measures but 5 feet from the floor to the top of the throttle valve. The weight is only 400 pounds, or two pounds per horse power. The rotor is composed of 25 disks 18 inches in diameter, spaced so that they measure 3 $\frac{1}{2}$ inches across the face. So compact is this newest of steam engines that one developing 27,000 horse power would only occupy about one-tenth of the space required for the wonderful Curtis turbines on the farther side of the room. The pair of larger turbines are thickly studded with gauges of various sorts used by the inventor in his tests and experiments.

The method of testing the capacity of the turbine is interesting. The two turbines, exact counterparts of each other, are connected by a torsion spring which has been carefully calibrated so that its strength is accurately known. Steam is admitted to the turbine used as a brake in the direction opposite to that in which the disks revolve. On the shaft of the brake turbine is a hollow pulley in which are two slots diametrically opposite each other with an electric light inside close to the rim. As the pulley revolves two flashes of light are seen which with the aid of mirrors and lenses are carried around so that they fall upon two revolving mirrors placed back to back on the shaft of the driving turbine. The mirrors are set so that when there is no torsion on the spring the light is a stationary spot at zero on a scale. As soon as a load is thrown on the spring the beam of light moves up the scale which is so proportioned to the spring that the horse power can be accurately read from it.

In various tests this turbine has consumed 38 pounds of saturated steam per horse power per hour, which is a high efficiency, considering that the steam only gave up 130 British thermal units, and that power is developed in a single stage instead of in several as in other turbines or in triple expansion reciprocating engines. This is equivalent to a consumption of less than 12 pounds per horsepower per hour of the superheated steam with the high vacuum used by the monster Curtis turbines near by. Tesla declares that with a large multiple stage turbine of his own type he will be able to develop 97 per cent. of the available energy in the steam, and this with a motor weighing but a quarter of a pound per horse power capacity. Certainly he is doing remarkable things.

A notable advantage possessed by the Tesla turbine is the ease with which it can be reversed. The great drawback to the marine turbines now in use is the difficulty of reversing. It is necessary to have two turbines on each shaft; one for going ahead and one for backing. In the Tesla turbine all that is necessary is to shut off steam on one side of the casing and admit it on the opposite side. There are no ponderous levers to throw, no reversing mechanism whatever, no moving parts but the valves in the steam pipes.

Yet more marvelous is the fact that the new motor is as well adapted to the use of gas as of steam. For years dozens of inventors have racked their brains, squandered their money and sacrificed their sleep in vain efforts to produce a practical gas turbine. But the obstacles in the way appeared insurmountable. **Tesla has solved the problem.** He has two gas turbines now approaching completion which are to be sent to Europe. The time may not be far distant when automobile manufacturers may be announcing new models with turbine motors. The gas turbine is identical with the steam turbine, the gasoline being exploded in a separate combustion chamber and its heat reduced by a spray of steam or water when the jet is introduced at great velocity into the turbine.

As if this was not versatile enough for one invention, the Tesla steam and gas turbine is also a pump and an air compressor. All that is necessary to transform the turbine into a pump is to take the rotor out of its casing and put it into another of slightly different form,—a "volute" casing, the engineers call it, and reverse the direction of the fluid. That is, the water to be pumped enters through the center of the side casing, passes through the interstices between the disks from center to circumference and flows out through the periphery of the casing.

The same molecular adhesion between the disks and the fluid and the molecular attraction between the film adhering to the disks and the fluid between them that imparts power to the steam turbine gives force to the stream of water passing through the pump or the air passing through the compressor. As the water enters at the center and as the motion of each point on the disk is circular, its particles receive an impetus always at a tangent to the circular paths; and so it moves in a spiral path from center to circumference. If the outlet is wide open there is little resistance to flow in a radial direction. Pressure in the casing of the pump depends upon the velocity of the particles leaving the periphery of the rotor. By throttling the outlet the pressure is increased in proportion to the speed of the rotor, velocity being converted into pressure.

The capacity of the new pump is amazing. A nickel plated model in Tesla's office that one could carry comfortably in his overcoat pocket pumps forty gallons a minute against a head of nine feet. With a pump having disks 18 inches in diameter the inventor declares he can deliver 3,500 gallons a minute against a head of 300 feet.

But perhaps the most interesting feature about this unique invention is the use to which its proceeds are to be put. Upon being told that steps were being taken to place the turbine on the market, I suggested to Tesla that he would soon be able to retire.

"Oh, no!" he exclaimed. "I shall be ready to begin work. I am going to use the money I get from my turbine to develop wireless transmission of power."

Tesla's Dual Engine Test Dynamometer Fully Assembled

Page 263   THE BOY'S BOOK OF NEW INVENTIONS   1912

THE TESLA TURBINE

By HARRY E. MAULE

DR. NIKOLA TESLA TELLS OF HIS
NEW STEAM TURBINE ENGINE
A MODEL OF WHICH, THE SIZE OF A DERBY HAT,
DEVELOPS MORE THAN 110 HORSEPOWER

HOW would you like to have an engine for your motor boat that you could almost cover with a man's derby hat and yet which would give 110 horsepower?" asked the scientist of his young friend one day when they had been talking about boats and engines.

"I never heard of any real engine as small as that," said the boy. "I used to play with toy engines, but they wouldn't give anywhere near one horsepower, much less 110."

"Well, I think I can show you a little engine that, for mechanical simplicity and power is about the most wonderful thing you ever have seen, if you would like to make another visit to Dr. Nikola Tesla, who told us all about his invention for the wireless transmission of power the other day. Doctor Tesla invented this little engine and he is going to do great things with it."

Of course the boy jumped at the opportunity, for what real boy would miss a chance to find out all about a new and powerful engine?

"Is it a gasoline engine?" he asked.

"No, it is a steam turbine, but if you know anything at all about turbines you will see that it is entirely different from any you ever have seen, for Doctor Tesla has used a principle as old as the hills and one which has been known to men for centuries, but which never before has been applied in mechanics."

After a little more talk the scientist promised to arrange with Tesla to take the young man over to the great Waterside power-house, New York, where the inventor is testing out his latest invention. We will follow them there and see what this wonderful little turbine looks like.

Picking his way amid the powerful machinery and the maze of switchboards, the scientist finally stopped in front of a little device that seemed like a toy amid the gigantic machines of the power-house.

"This is the small turbine," says Tesla. "It will do pretty well for its size."

Illustrations and Photographs which originally appeared in this article can be found on pages: 21, 30, 31, 34, 94 and 139

The little engine looked like a small steel drum about ten inches in diameter and a couple of inches wide, with a shaft running through the centre. Various kinds of gauges were attached at different points. Outside of the gauges and the base upon which it was mounted, the engine almost could have been covered by a derby hat. The whole thing, gauges and all, practically could have been covered by an ordinary hat box.

Yet when Tesla gave the word, and his assistant turned on the steam, the small dynamo to which the turbine shaft was geared, instantly began to run at terrific speed. Apparently the machine began to run at full speed instantly instead of gradually working up to it. There was no sound except the whir of well-fitted machinery. "Under tests," said Tesla, "this little turbine has developed 110 horse-power."

Just think of it, a little engine that you could lift with one hand, giving 110 horsepower!

"But we can do better than that," added the inventor, "for with a steam pressure of 125 pounds at the inlet, running 9,000 revolutions per minute, the engine will develop 200 brake-horsepower."

Nearby was another machine a little larger than the first, which seemed to be two identical Tesla turbines with the central shafts connected by a strong spring. Gauges of different kinds, to show how the engine stood the tests, were attached at various places. When Tesla gave the word to open the throttle on the twin machines the spring connecting the shafts, without a second's pause, began to revolve, so that it looked like a solid bar of polished steel. Outside of a low, steady hum and a slight vibration in the floor, that steadied down after the engine had been running a little while, there was no indication that enough horsepower to run machinery a hundred times the weight and size of the turbine was being generated.

"You see, for testing purposes," said Doctor Tesla, "I have these two turbines connected by this torsion spring. The steam is acting in opposite directions in the two machines. In one, the heat energy is converted into mechanical power. In the other, mechanical power is turned back into heat. One is working against the other, and by means of this gauge we can tell how much the spring is twisted and consequently how much power we are developing. Every degree marked off on this scale indicates twenty-two horsepower." The beam of light on the gauge stood at the division marked "10."

"Two hundred and twenty horsepower," said Doctor Tesla. "We can do better than that." He opened the steam valves a trifle more, giving more power to the motive end of the combination and more resistance to the "brake" end. The scale indicated 330 horsepower. "These casings are not constructed for much higher steam pressure, or I could show you something more wonderful than that. These engines could readily develop 1,000 horse-power.

"These little turbines represent what mechanical engineers have been dreaming of since steam power was invented — the perfect rotary engine," continued Doctor Tesla, as he led the way back to his office. "My turbine will give at least twenty-five times as much power to the pound of weight as the lightest weight engines made to date. You know that the lightest and most powerful gasoline engines used on aeroplanes nowadays generally develop only one horsepower to two and one half pounds of weight. With that much weight my turbine will develop twenty-five horsepower.

"That is not all, for the turbine is probably the cheapest engine to build ever invented. Its mechanical simplicity is such that any good mechanic could build it, and any good mechanic could repair such parts as get out of order. When I can show you the inside of one of the turbines, in a few moments, however, you will see that there is nothing to get out of order such as most turbines have, and that it is not subjected to the heavy strains and jerks that all reciprocating engines and other turbines must stand. Also you will see that my turbine will run forward or backward, just as we desire, will run with steam, water, gas, or air, and can be used as a pump or an air compressor, just as well as an engine."

"But most of your research as been in electricity," Tesla was reminded, for no one can forget that Tesla's inventions largely have made possible most of the world's greatest electrical power developments.

"Yes," he answered, "but I was a mechanical engineer before I was an electrical engineer, and besides, this principle was worked out in the course of my search for the ideal motor for airships, to be used in conjunction with my invention for the wireless transmission of electrical power. For twenty years I worked on the problem, but I have not given up. When my plan is perfected the present-day aeroplanes and dirigible balloons will disappear, and the dangerous sport of aviation, as we know it now with its hundreds of accidents, and its picturesque birdmen, will give way to safe, seaworthy airships, without wings or gas bags, but supported and driven by mechanical means.

"As I told you before when we were talking of the wireless transmission of power, the mechanism will be a development of the principle on which my turbine is constructed. It will be so tremendously powerful that it will make a veritable rope of air above the great machine to hold it at any altitude the navigators may choose, and also a rope of air in front or in the rear to send it forward or backward at almost any speed desired. When that day comes, airship travel will be as safe and prosaic as travel by railroad train today, and not very much different, except that there will be no dirt, and it will be much faster. One will be able to dine in New York, retire in an aero Pullman berth in a closed and perfectly furnished car, and arise to breakfast in London."

Tesla's plans for the airship are far in the future, but his turbine is a thing of the present, and it has been declared by some of the most eminent authorities in the world in mechanical engineering to be the greatest invention of a century. The reason for this is not altogether on account of the wonderful feats of Tesla's model turbines, but because in them he has shown the world an entirely unused mechanical principle which can be applied in a thousand useful ways.

James Watt discovered and put to work the expansive power of steam, by which the piston of an engine is pushed back and forth in the cylinder of an engine, but it has remained for Nikola Tesla to prove that it is not necessary for the steam to have something to push upon — that the most powerful engine yet shown to the world works through a far simpler mechanism than any yet used for turning a gas or a fluid into the driving force of machinery.

"How did you come to invent your turbine while you were busy with your wonderful electrical inventions?" Tesla was asked.

"You see," he answered, "while I was trying to solve the problem of aerial navigation by electrical means, the gasoline motor was perfected; and aviation as we know it today became a fact. I consider the aeroplane as it has been developed little more than a passing phase of air navigation. Aeroplaning makes delightful sport, no doubt, but as it is now it can never be practical in commerce. Consequently I abandoned for the time being my attempts to find the ideal airship motor in electricity, and for several years studied hard on the problem as one of mechanics. Finally I hit upon the central idea of the new turbine I have just been showing you."

"What is this principle?"

"The idea of my turbine is based simply on two properties known to science for hundreds of years, but never in all the world's history used in this way before. These properties are adhesion and viscosity. Any boy can test them. For instance, put a little water on a sheet of metal. Most of it will roll off, but a few drops will remain until they evaporate. The metal does not absorb the water so the only thing that makes the water remain on the metal is adhesion — in other words, it adheres, or sticks to the metal.

"Then, too, you will notice that the drop of water will assume a certain shape and that it will remain in that form until you make it change by some outside force — by disturbing it by touch or holding it so that the attraction of gravitation will make it change.

"The simple little experiment reveals the viscosity of water, or, in other words, reveals the property of the molecules which go to make up the water, of sticking to each other. It is these properties of adhesion and viscosity that cause the "skin friction" that impedes a ship in its progress through the water, or an aeroplane in going through the air. All fluids have these qualities —

and you must keep in mind that air is a fluid, all gases are fluid, steam is fluid. Every known means of transmitting or developing mechanical power is through a fluid medium.

"It is a surprising fact that gases and vapours are possessed of this property of viscosity to a greater degree than are liquids such as water. Owing to these properties, if a solid body is moved through a fluid, more or less of the fluid is dragged along, or if a solid is put in a fluid that is moving it is carried along with the current. Also you are familiar with the great rush of air that follows a swiftly moving train. That simply means that the train tends to carry the air along with it, as the air tries to adhere to the surface of the cars, and the particles of air try to stick together. You would be surprised if you could have a picture of the great train of moving air that follows you about merely as you walk through this room.

"Now, in all the history of mechanical engineering, these properties have not been turned to the full use of man, although, as I said before, they have been known to exist for centuries. When I hit upon the idea that a rotary engine would run through their application, I began a series of very successful experiments."

Tesla went on to explain that all turbines, and in fact all engines, are based on the idea that the steam must have something to push against. We shall see a little later how these engines were developed, but it will suffice for the moment to listen to Doctor Tesla's explanation.

"All of the successful turbines up to the time of my invention," he says, "give the steam something to push upon. For instance" — taking a pencil and a piece of paper — "we will consider this circle, the disk, or rotor of an ordinary turbine. You understand it is the wheel to which the shaft is attached, and which turns the shaft, transmitting power to the machinery. Now it is a large wheel and along the outer edge is a row of little blades, or vanes, or buckets. The steam is turned against these blades, or buckets, in jets from pipes set around the wheel at close intervals, and the force of the steam on the blades turns the wheel at very high speed and gives us the power of what we call a "prime mover" — that is, power which we can convert into electricity, or which we can use to drive all kinds of machinery. Now see what a big wheel it is and what a very small part of the wheel is used in giving us power — only the outer edge where the steam can push against the blades.

"In my new turbine the steam pushes against the whole wheel all at once, utilizing all the space wasted in other turbines. There are no blades or vanes or sockets or anything for the steam to push against, for I have proved that they hinder the efficiency of the turbine rather than increase it."

Comparing his turbine to other engines Tesla says, "In reciprocating engines of the older type the power-giving portion — the cylinder, piston, etc. — is no more than a fraction of 1 per cent. of the total weight of material used in construction. The present form of turbine, with an efficiency of about 62 per cent., was a great advance, but even in this form of machine scarcely more than 1 per cent. or 2 per cent. is used in actually generating power at a given moment. The only part of the great wheel that is used in actually making power is the outside edge where the steam pushes on the buckets.

"The new turbine offers a striking contrast using as it does practically the entire material of the power-giving portion of the engine. The result is an economy that gives an efficiency of 80 per cent. to 90 per cent. With sufficient boiler capacity on a vessel such as the *Mauretania,* it would be perfectly easy to develop, instead of some 70,000 horsepower, 4,000,000 horsepower in the same space — and this is a conservative estimate.

"You see this is obtained by the new application of this principle in physics which never has been used before, by which we can economize on space and weight so that most of the engine is given over to power producing parts in which there is little waste material."

Tesla then went on to explain the details of his new turbine. Leading the way to a small model in his office he unscrewed a few bolts and lifted off the top half of the round steel drum or casing. Inside were a number of perfectly smooth, circular disks mounted upon one central shaft — the shaft that extends through the machine, and corresponds to the crankshaft of an ordinary engine. The disks all were securely fastened to the rod so that they could not revolve without making it also turn in its carefully adjusted bearings. The disks, which were only about one sixteenth of an inch in thickness, and which he said were constructed of the finest quality of steel, were placed close together at regular intervals, so that a space of only about an eighth of an inch intervened between them. They were solid with the exception of a hole close to the centre. The set of disks is called the rotor or runner.

When the casing is clamped down tight, the steam is sent through an inlet or nozzle at the side, so that it enters at the periphery or outside edge of the set of disks, at a tangent to the circle of the rotor. Of course the steam is shot into the turbine under high pressure so that all its force is turned into speed, or what the scientists call velocity-energy. The steel casing of the rotor naturally gives the steam the circular course of the disks, and as it travels around the disks the vapour adheres to them, and the particles of steam adhere to each other. By the law that Tesla has invoked, the steam drags the disks around with it. As the speed of the disks increases the path of the steam lengthens, and at an average speed the steam actually travels a distance of twelve to fifteen feet. Starting at the outside edge of the disks it travels around and around in constantly narrowing circles as the steam pressure decreases until it finally reaches the holes in the disks at their centre, and there passes out. These holes, then, we see act as the exhaust for the used-up steam, for by the time the steam, which was shot into the turbine by the nozzle under high pressure, reaches the exhaust, it registers no more than about two pounds gauge pressure.

For reasons which will be explained later, ordinary turbines cannot be reversed, but Tesla's invention can run backward just as easily as forward. The reverse action is accomplished simply by placing another nozzle inlet on the other side of the rotor so that the steam can be turned off from the right side of the engine, for instance, and turned into the left side, immediately reversing its direction, with the change in the direction of the steam. The action is instantaneous, too, for as we saw in the experiments Tesla showed us, the turbine began to run at practically top speed as soon as the steam was turned on.

The disks in the little 110-horsepower engine which we saw, were only a little larger than a derby hat were only nine and three quarter inches in diameter, while in his larger turbines he simply increases the diameter of the disks.

Tesla further explained that the 110-horsepower turbine represented a single stage engine, or one composed simply of one rotor. Where greater power is required he explained that it would be easy to compound a number of rotors to a double, or triple or even what he calls a multi, or many stage, turbine. In engineering the single stage is called one complete power unit, and a large engine could be made up of as many units as needed, or practicable.

"Then do you mean to say," Tesla was asked, "that the only thing that makes the engine revolve at this tremendous speed is the passage of steam through the spaces between those smooth disks?"

"Yes, that is all," he answered, "but as I explained before, the steam travels all the way from the outer edge to the centre of the disks, working on them all the time; whereas in the ordinary turbines the steam only works on the outside edge, and all the rest of the wheel is useless. By the time it leaves the exhaust of my engine practically all the energy of the steam has been put into the machine."

This is only one of the many advantages that Tesla points out in his invention, for the turbine is the exemplification of a principle, and hence more than a mechanical achievement. "With a 1,000-horsepower engine weighing only 100 pounds, imagine the possibility in automobiles, locomotives, and steamships," he says.

Explaining the large engines that he is testing, one against the other, at the power plant, the inventor said:

"Inside of the casings of the two larger turbines the disks are eighteen inches in diameter and one thirty-second of an inch thick. There are twenty-three of them, spaced a little distance apart, the whole making up a total thickness of three and one half inches. The steam, entering at the periphery, follows a spiral path toward the centre, where openings are provided through which it exhausts. As the disks rotate and the speed increases the path of the steam lengthens until it completes a number of turns before reaching the outlet — and it is working all the time.

"Moreover, every engineer knows that, when a fluid is used as a vehicle of energy, the highest possible economy can be obtained only when the changes in the direction and velocity of movement of the fluid are made as gradual and easy as possible. In previous forms of turbines more or less sudden changes of speed and direction are involved.

"By that I mean to say," explained Doctor Tesla, "that in reciprocating engines with pistons, the power comes from the backward and forward jerks of the piston rod, and in other turbines the steam must travel a zigzag path from one vane or blade to another all the whole length of the turbine. This causes both changes in velocity and direction and impairs the efficiency of the machine. In my turbine, as you saw, the steam enters at the nozzle and travels a natural spiral path without any abrupt changes in direction, or anything to hinder its velocity."

But the Tesla turbine engine, claims the inventor, will work just as well by gas as by steam, for as he points out gases have the properties of adhesion and viscosity just as much as water or steam.

Further, he says that if the gas were introduced intermittently in explosions like those of the gasoline engine, the machine would work as efficiently as it does with a steady pressure of steam. Consequently Tesla declares that his turbine can be developed for general use as a gasoline engine.

The engine is only one application of the principle of Tesla's turbine, because he has used the same idea on a pump and an air compressor as successfully as on his experimental engines. In his office in the Metropolitan Tower he has a number of models. Pointing to a little machine on a table, which consisted of half a dozen small disks three inches in diameter, he said: "This is only a toy, but it shows the principle of the invention just as well as the larger models at the power plant." Tesla turned on a small electric motor which was connected with a shaft on which the disks were mounted, and it began to hum at a high number of revolutions per second.

"This is the principle of the pump," said Tesla. "Here the electric motor furnishes the power and we have these disks revolving in the air. You need no proof to tell you that the air is being agitated and propelled violently.

"If you will hold your hand down near the centre of these disks — you see the centres have been cut away — you will feel the suction as air is drawn in to be expelled from the outer edges.

"Now, suppose these revolving disks were enclosed in an air-tight case, so constructed that the air could enter only at one point and be expelled only at another — what would we have?"

"You'd have an air pump," was suggested.

"Exactly — an air pump or a blower," said Doctor Tesla. "There is one now in operation delivering ten thousand cubic feet of air a minute.

But this was not all, for Tesla showed his visitors a wonderful exhibition of the little device at work. "To make a pump out of this turbine," he explained; "we simply turn the disks by artificial means and introduce the fluid, air or water at the centre of the disks, and their rotation, with the properties of adhesion and viscosity immediately suck up the fluid and throw it off at the edges of the disks."

The inventor led the way to another room, where he showed his visitors two small tanks, one above the other. The lower one was full of water but the upper one was empty. They were connected by a pipe which terminated over the empty tank. At the side of the lower tank was a very small aluminum drum in which, Tesla told his visitors, were disks of the kind that are used in his turbine. The shaft of a little one twelfth horsepower motor adjoining was connected with the rotor through the centre of the casing. "Inside of this aluminum case are several disks mounted on a shaft and immersed in water," said Doctor Tesla. "From this lower tank the water has free access to the case enclosing the disks. This pipe leads from the periphery of the case. I turn the current on, the motor turns the disks, and as I open this valve in the pipe the water flows."

He turned the valve and the water certainly did flow. Instantly a stream that would have filled a barrel in a very few minutes began to run out of the pipe into the upper part of the tank and thence into the lower tank.

"This is only a toy," smiled the inventor. "There are only half a dozen disks — "runners," I call them — each less than three inches in diameter, inside of that case. They are just like the disks you saw on the first motor — no vanes, blades or attachments of any kind. Just perfectly smooth, flat disks revolving in their own planes and pumping water because of the viscosity and adhesion of the fluid. One such pump now in operation, with eight disks, eighteen inches in diameter, pumps 4,000 gallons a minute to a height of 360 feet.

"From all these things, you can see the possibilities of the new turbine," he continued. "It will give ten horsepower to one pound of weight, which is twenty-five times as powerful as many light weight aeroplane engines, which give one horsepower of energy for every two and one half pounds of weight.

"Moreover, the machine is one of the cheapest and simplest to build ever invented and it has the distinct advantage of having practically nothing about it to get out of order. There are no fine adjustments, as the disks do not have to be placed with more than ordinary accuracy, and there are no fine clearances, because the casing does not have to fit more than conveniently close.

"As you see, there are no blades or buckets to get broken or to get out of order. These things, combined with the easy reversibility, simplicity of the machine when used either as an engine, a pump or an air compressor, and the possibility of using it either with steam, gas, air, or water as motive power, all combine to afford limitless possibilities for its development."

Doctor Tesla calls the invention the most revolutionary of his career, and it certainly will be if it fulfills the predictions that so many eminent experts are making for it.

It is interesting to think that although this latest and most modern of all steam engines is a turbine, the first steam engine ever invented, also was a turbine.

Though most of us usually think of James Watt as the inventor of the steam engine, he was not first by any means, for the very first of which history gives us any record was a turbine, which was described by Hero of Alexandria, an ancient Egyptian scientist, who wrote about 100 B.C.

Hero's engine was a hollow sphere which was made to turn by the reaction of steam as it escaped from the ends of pipes, so placed that they would blow directly upon the ball.

Centuries later — in 1629, about the time the New England States were being colonized — a scientist named Branca made use of the oldest mechanical principle in the world — the paddle-wheel — which, turned by the never-ceasing river, goes on forever in the service of mankind. Branca's invention was simply a paddle-wheel turned by a jet of steam instead of by a water current. The engine was really a turbine, for that type is simply a very high development of this idea — the pushing power of a fluid on a paddle-wheel.

The picture of Branca's crude machine shows the head and shoulders of a great bronze man suspended over a blazing wood fire. Evidently it is intended to convey the idea that the figure's lungs are filled with boiling water, for he is pictured breathing a jet of steam on to the blades of a paddle-wheel, the revolving of which sets some crude machinery in motion.

After Branca, however, the turbine dropped from view and what few inventors did experiment with steam worked on the idea of a reciprocating engine.

The principle of the reciprocating engine, as most boys know from their own experiments with toy steam engines, and as was discovered by Watt, is simply the utilization of the power of steam for expanding with great force when let into first one side, and then the other side of the cylinder. Thus, as the steam expands, it pushes the piston back and forth at a high rate of speed, transmitting motion to shafts and flywheels.

In 1888 the world was ready for a bigger and more powerful type of steam engine; and C.A. Parsons, an Englishman, and Dr. G. de Laval of Stockholm, brought forth successful turbines at about the same time.

The machines were developed to a high state of efficiency, and are still in general use, although most turbines for driving heavy electrical machinery in the United States are the great Curtiss engines, which are a combination of the principles of both the De Laval and Parsons machines. All of them are run by the old principle of the water-wheel. Instead of the steam being turned into a cylinder to push the piston, it is turned into a steel drum or casing in which wheels or disks are mounted on the central shaft. All along the edge of these wheels are hundreds of little vanes or blades or buckets against which the steam flows from many nozzles placed all around the inside of the casing. The steam flows with great force, and naturally pushing against the blades, starts the wheels and the engine shaft to revolving. After expending its force on the blades that turn the steam passes on to a set of stationary blades which then shoot it out against the next set of moving blades.

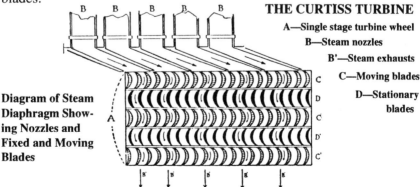

THE CURTISS TURBINE

A—Single stage turbine wheel

B—Steam nozzles

B'—Steam exhausts

C—Moving blades

D—Stationary blades

Diagram of Steam Diaphragm Showing Nozzles and Fixed and Moving Blades

In the Curtiss turbine the wheels at one end of the shaft are smaller than those at the other, and the steam enters at the small end, where it is under heavy pressure. After having expended its force on the blades of the first wheel, the steam passes through holes in a partition at the side and zigzags back so that it strikes the vanes or blades on the next larger disk. It then repeats the process, expands a little, and goes to a larger disk. Finally, by the time the steam has expanded to its full capacity, the greater part of its force has been expended against the disks of the turbine.

From this we see the main points of difference between reciprocating engines and turbines, and between most turbines and Tesla's invention.

While most turbines take advantage of the expansive power of steam, the main idea is to make use of the velocity of the vapour as it is driven from a set of nozzles around the turbine wheel, under high pressure.

Also it will be seen that Tesla's invention is a turbine in form, but that it is entirely different from either of the two earlier types, because instead of giving the steam something to push against, it is allowed to follow its own natural course around between the smooth disks, and drag them after it.

Some kind of a crank motion is necessary in all reciprocating engines, to convert the backward and forward movement of the piston to the rotary motion of the shaft, but this is done away with entirely in the turbine. What engineers call a "direct drive" is substituted in its place. In other words, the turbine wheels or disks, fastened to the shaft, turn it, and drive the machinery directly from the source of power. The speed of the machine is regulated by gears.

The great advantage of the "direct drive," particularly for big steamships and for turning big electric dynamos, will be plain to every boy when he thinks of the long narrow body of a ship in which can lie the turbine engines working directly on the propeller shafts (with the exception of certain gears, of course, for regulating the speed) instead of the big flywheels, and flying cranks of marine reciprocating engines. Also with dynamos it is just as important to have the power applied directly to save space and increase the general efficiency of the machine.

The greatest disadvantage of the usual kinds of turbines for most machinery, including steamships, is the fact that they cannot be reversed. To solve this difficulty, all the great ocean and coast liners, battleships, cruisers, and torpedo boats that are equipped with turbines have two sets of engines, one for straight ahead and one for backward.

With the Tesla turbine this disadvantage, as we have seen, is entirely done away with, and the one turbine can be reversed as easily and simply as it can be started.

And so, while we are waiting for the world-moving wireless transmission of power and for the completion of Tesla's invention for safe and stable airships, we can look for the speedy development of his turbine in practically all departments of mechanical engineering.

page 543   **THE WORLD'S WORK**   March 1920

THE TESLA TURBINE
A MACHINE AS BIG AS A DERBY HAT THAT GENERATES 110 HORSEPOWER

By FRANK PARKER STOCKBRIDGE

WE FOLLOWED Dr. Nikola Tesla through the Waterside Power Station of the New York Edison Company - along narrow passages lined with huge electric switches, the turning of any one of which would throw a whole section of Manhattan into darkness or a blaze of light. We stumbled in the shadows of whirring dynamos, skirted great Corliss engines that seemed to rise from the very bowels of the earth beneath us and detoured past thundering turbines. Before the largest turbine we paused for a moment.

"Here," said Dr. Tesla, pointing to the huge machine, "is a triumph of engineering skill. This turbo-dynamo, the largest ever made, developing 30,000 horsepower, was built from plans worked out on paper. It was never tested until it was erected here and it worked perfectly from the first turning on of steam. That is engineering. But that is not what we are here for."

We pressed on until we reached an open space where a mechanic in blue jeans was wiping the oil and grease from a machine so tiny in comparison with the gigantic turbine we had just inspected that it seemed like a toy.

"Here it is," said the tall, thin man - or rather he shouted, for the noise of a hundred thousand horsepower of moving machinery is not conducive to free vocal expression. "Better take off your coats," he continued, "for it is a cold night and it gets pretty hot in here."

We followed his advice and example and stripped down to shirt-sleeves.

"Turn on the steam," said the inventor to the mechanic. The workman gave a valve a short turn. From inside the little machine, which seemed to be composed of two identical parts connected by a spiral spring, came a humming sound; the connecting spring began to revolve so rapidly that it looked like a solid bar of steel and the floor under our feet shook with rapid vibrations which died down. I glanced at a speed-gauge attached to what seemed to be the main shaft of the device and saw that it was registering 7,000 revolutions a minute. I looked up at the main steam gauge overhead and saw a pressure of ninety pounds to the square inch indicated.

Illustrations originally appearing in this article can be found on pages:
31, 94 and 128

Page 545 featured the photo from which the drawing on page 22 was made. The caption read:
DR. TESLA WHO, IN HIS SEARCH FOR AN ENGINE SUFFICIENTLY LIGHT AND POWERFUL TO OPERATE THE IDEAL FLYING MACHINE, HAS INVENTED A WONDERFUL LITTLE TURBINE MOTOR, FOR GENERAL USE, THAT IS AN ENTIRELY NEW APPLICATION OF MECHANICAL PRINCIPLES

Dr. Nikola Tesla, inventor of the alternating-current motor, and pioneer in research into high-tension electric currents generally, was demonstrating his latest invention - a steam turbine, different in principle from any heretofore in use and one which will take less room and less coal per horsepower than the best engines now running. "It's up to its normal speed now - about nine thousand revolutions," said Dr. Tesla, and the tachometer bore out his statement. "You see, for testing purposes, I have these two turbines connected by this torsion spring. The steam is acting in opposite directions in the two machines. In one, the heat energy is converted into mechanical power. In the other, mechanical power is turned back into heat. One is working against the other, and by means of this beam of light we can tell how much the spring is twisted and consequently how much power we are developing. Every degree marked off on this scale indicates twenty-two horsepower." We looked at the division marked "10."

"Two hundred and twenty horsepower," said Dr. Tesla. "We can do better than that." He opened the steam valves a trifle more, giving more power to the motive end of the combination and more resistance to the "brake" end. The scale indicated 330 horsepower. "These casings are not constructed for much higher steam pressures, or I could show you something more wonderful than that. These engines could readily develop 1,000 horsepower," he said, as we watched the turbine running smoothly, steadily, almost noiselessly except for that single clear, musical note.

Standing nearby was another and smaller machine of the same type, connected through a gear-box with a dynamo. The engine itself would almost go into an ordinary hat-box. At a signal from Dr. Tesla the mechanic turned on the steam. Instantly, without the fraction of a second's apparent delay, the dynamo was under full speed, and from the end containing the motor rose the same clear note, indicating a well-balanced machine running freely at its normal speed.

"This little turbine has developed 110 horsepower under tests," said Dr. Tesla. It was about the size of a derby hat.

"Careful tests have shown that the single-stage turbine, running at 9,000 revolutions per minute, with a steam pressure of 125 pounds at the inlet, developing 200 brake horsepower, consumes 38 pounds of saturated steam per horsepower hour," said Dr. Tesla.

"But I can do better than that by compounding," he added. "The heat-drop under the conditions I named is only 130 British thermal units, and that is less than one third of the amount available under modern conditions of superheated steam and high vacuum. By compounding the turbines I shall get a steam consumption of not more than eight pounds per horse-power hour.

"The most efficient steam engines in America, big, slow-moving pumping engines working under ideal conditions and constant load, use about eleven pounds. I have undertaken a contract to produce one which will consume less than nine.

"The idea on which all steam engines - gas engines, too - have been built in the past was that there must be something solid and substantial for the steam to push against. The piston of a reciprocating engine and the blades and buckets of modern turbine engines are examples of what I mean. That idea has made them rather complicated devices, requiring careful fitting for efficient operation, great expense for repairs, and, especially in the case of turbines, great liability to damage. It has also made them bulky and heavy.

"What I have done is to discard entirely the idea that there must be a solid wall in front of the steam and to apply in a practical way, for the first time, two properties which every physicist knows to be common to all fluids (including steam and gas) but which have not been utilized. These are adhesion and viscosity.

"You know that water has a tendency to stick to a solid surface. That is the property of adhesion which every fluid - gas, steam, water, or whatever it be - possesses. You also know that a drop of water tends to retain its form, even against a considerable force, such as gravity. That is viscosity, the tendency to resist molecular separation, and all fluids have this property, too.

"It occurred to me that if I should take circular disks, mount them on a shaft through their centres, space them a little distance apart, and let some fluid under pressure, such as steam or gas, enter the interstices between the disks in a tangential direction, the fluid, as it moved, owing to these properties of adhesion and viscosity, would tend to drag the disks along and transmit its energy to them. It happened just as I had thought it would, and that is the principle of this turbine. It utilizes the very properties which cause all the loss of power in other turbines.

"Inside of the casings of those engines you saw - instead of buckets or blades or vanes on the edge of a wheel, there are simple disks of steel mounted on the shaft. In the two larger turbines these disks are eighteen inches in diameter and one thirty-second of an inch thick. There are twenty-three of them, spaced a little distance apart, the whole making up a total thickness of three and one half inches. The steam, entering at the periphery, follows a spiral path toward the centre, where openings are provided through which it exhausts. As the disks rotate and the speed increases, the path of the steam lengthens until it completes a number of turns before reaching the outlet - and it is working all the time. In the ordinary turbine the steam passes only around the periphery and the central portion of the wheel is useless. Moreover, every engineer knows that, when a fluid is used as a vehicle of energy, the highest possible economy can be obtained only when the changes in the direction and velocity of movement of the fluid are made as gradual and easy as possible. In previous forms of turbines more or less sudden changes of speed and direction are involved."

Later, in his laboratory in the Metropolitan Tower, discussing the commendations which eminent engineers, many of them with international reputations, have expressed concerning his turbine, Dr. Tesla summarized the points that make it a long step in advance in mechanical engineering.

"To say nothing of it being a new application of mechanical principles," he said, "it has many decided advantages. First of these is its simplicity. It is comparatively inexpensive to construct, because nothing but the bearings need be accurately fitted, and exact clearances are not essential. Then there is nothing in it to get out of order and the disks can easily be replaced by any competent mechanic. It can be reversed without complex or cumbersome apparatus - all that is needed is a two-way valve to let the steam in at one side or the other, as desired. Reversing an ordinary turbine is next to impossible.

"My machine occupies, as you saw little space - the 110 horsepower turbine has disks only $9\,^3/_4$ inches in diameter - and in consequence it weighs very little. The lightest engines now in use weigh $2\,^1/_2$ pounds to the horsepower, while these, in their crudest forms, weigh less than that, and I expect to be able to produce 10 horsepower to the pound. Using gas instead of steam it gives most gratifying results, doing away with the complicated valves and springs of the prevailing types of gas engines. Another interesting application of it is as a pump, either for water or for air. The same disk arrangement is used, but the casing is so arranged, when built as a pump, that the fluid enters at the centre and is ejected at the periphery." He led the way into an adjoining room where a tiny turbine pump, with disks only three inches in diameter, operated by a one twelfth horsepower electric motor, was pumping 40 gallons of water a minute against a 9-foot head.

"How did you happen to turn your attention to mechanics instead of electricity?" I asked.

"I was a mechanical engineer before I ever took up electricity," replied Dr. Tesla. "I went into electricity," replied Dr. Tesla. "I went into electric science years ago because I thought, in that direction, I was going to solve the problem I have been working on all my life - the production of an engine sufficiently light and powerful to operate the ideal flying machine. All my work in the wireless transmission of power, which has attracted more public attention than anything else I have ever done, was toward that end. I do not expect to build that ideal machine tomorrow, any more than I expect every steam engine in the world to be thrown into the scrap-heap because of this new application of mechanical principles, but such a flying machine will come some day, and meantime I have succeeded in developing something new in prime movers. I am young yet and have plenty of time ahead of me."

I remembered that it was twenty-seven years ago that he had come over from Lika with the principle of the rotating field for alternating current motors already worked out, and began some mental calculations, which Dr. Tesla noticed.

"My age? What do you think it is?" he asked.

"If I didn't know better, I'd say around forty," I ventured. "Fifty, for a guess."

"Fifty-four," was the answer.

"And you still expect to perfect your flying machine?"

"Why not? I have half a century yet to live, if no accident happens. One of my grandfathers lived to be 118, the other past 100. One of my mother's grandfathers won a footrace at the age of 73. I hope it will not take me fifty years to perfect the flying machine, but if it does, I expect to be young enough at 104 to make a flight in it. The Tesla turbine will be on the market long before that, however."

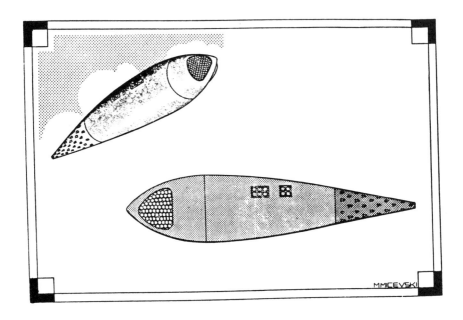

Tesla's Vision of a Turbine Powered Flying Machine

Tesla's Dual Engine Test Dynamometer Fully Assembled
The engines are set up in a slightly different configuration than that
pictured on page 128. Note the separate steam feeds to each engine
instead of the common supply appearing earlier.

PRODIGAL GENIUS

The Life of Nikola Tesla - Inventor Extraordinary

By JOHN J. O'NEILL (1943)

When his World Wireless System project crashed, Tesla turned again to a project to which he had given considerable thought at the time he was developing his polyphase alternating-current system: that of developing a rotary engine which would be as far in advance of existing steam engines as his alternating-current system was ahead of the direct-current system, and which could be used for driving his dynamos.

All of the steam engines in use in powerhouses at that time were of the reciprocating type; essentially the same as those developed by Newcomer and Watt, but larger in size, better in construction and more efficient in operation.

Tesla's engine was of a different type—a turbine in which jets of steam injected between a series of disks produced rotary motion at high velocity in the cylinder on which these disks were mounted. The steam entered at the outer edge of the disks, pursued a spiral path of a dozen or more convolutions, and left the engine near the central shaft.

When Tesla informed a friend in 1902 that he was working on an engine project, he declared he would produce an engine so small, simple and powerful that it would be a "powerhouse in a hat." The first model, which he made about 1906, fulfilled this promise. It was small enough to fit into the dome of a derby hat, measured a little more than six inches in its largest dimension, and developed thirty horsepower. The power producing performance of this little engine vastly exceeded that of every known kind of prime mover in use at that time. The engine weighed a little less than ten pounds. Its output was therefore three horsepower per pound. The rotor weighed only a pound and a half, and its light weight and high power yield gave Tesla a slogan which he used on his letterheads and envelopes— "Twenty horsepower per pound."

There was nothing new, of course, in the basic idea of obtaining circular motion directly from a stream of moving fluid. Wind-mills and water wheels, devices as old as history, performed this feat. Hero, the Alexandrian writer, about 200 B.C., described, if he did not invent, the first turbine. It consisted of a hollow sphere of metal mounted on an axle, with two tubes sticking out of the sphere at a tangent to its surface. When water was placed in the sphere and the device was suspended in a fire, the reaction of the steam coming out of the tubes caused the device to rotate.

Tesla's ingenious and original development of the turbine idea probably had its origin in that amusing and unsuccessful experiment he made when, as a boy, he tried to build a vacuum motor and observed its wooden cylinder turn slightly by the drag of the air leaking into the vacuum chamber. Later, too, when as a youth he fled to the mountains to escape military service and played with the idea of transporting mail across the ocean through an underwater tube, through which a hollow sphere was to be carried by a rapidly moving stream of water, he had discovered that the friction of the water on the walls of the tube made the idea impracticable. The friction would slow down the velocity of the stream of water so that excessive amounts of power would be required to move the water at a desired speed and pressure. Conversely, if the water moved at this speed, the friction caused it to try to drag the enclosing tube along with it.

It was this friction which Tesla now utilized in his turbine. A jet of steam rushing at high velocity between disks with a very small distance separating them was slowed down by the friction—but the disks, being capable of rotation, moved with increasing velocity until it was almost equal to that of the steam. In addition to the friction factor, there exists a peculiar attraction between gases and metal surfaces; and this made it possible for the moving steam to grip the metal of the disks more effectively and drag them around at high velocities. The first model which Tesla made in 1906 had twelve disks five inches in diameter. It was operated by compressed air, instead of steam, and attained a speed of 20,000 revolutions per minute. It was Tesla's intention eventually to use oil as fuel, burning it in a nozzle and taking advantage of the tremendous increase in volume, in the change from a liquid to burned highly expanded gases, to turn the rotor. This would eliminate the use of boilers for generating steam and give the direct process proportional increased efficiency.

Had Tesla proceeded with the development of his turbine in 1889 when he returned from the Westinghouse plant, his turbine might perhaps have been the one eventually developed to replace the slow, big, lumbering reciprocating engines then in use. The fifteen years, however, which he devoted to the development of currents of high potential and high frequency, had entailed a delay which gave opportunity for developers of other turbine ideas to advance their work to a stage which now was effective in putting Tesla in the status of a very late starter. In the mean-time, turbines had been developed which were virtually wind-mills in a box. They consisted of rotors with small buckets or vanes around the circumference which were struck by the incoming steam jet. They lacked the simplicity of the Tesla turbine; but by the time Tesla introduced his type, the others were well entrenched in the development stage.

Tesla's first tiny motor was built in 1906 by Julius C. Czito, who operated at Astoria, Long Island, a machine shop for making inventor's models. He also built the subsequent 1911 and 1925 models of the turbine, and many other devices on which Tesla worked up to 1929. Mr. Czito's father had been a member of Tesla's staff in the Houston Street laboratories, from 1892 to 1899, and at Colorado Springs.

Mr. Czito's description of the first model is as follows:

The rotor consisted of stack of very thin disks six inches in diameter, made of German silver. The disks were one thirty-second of an inch thick and were separated by spacers of the same metal and same thickness but of much smaller diameter which were cut in the form of a cross with a circular center section. The extended arms served as ribs to brace the disks.

There were eight disks and the edgewise face of the stack was only one-half inch across. They were mounted on the center of a shaft about six inches long. The shaft was nearly an inch in diameter in the mid section and was tapered in steps to less than half an inch at the ends. The rotor was set in a casing made in four parts bolted together.

The circular chamber where the rotor turned was accurately machined to allow a clearance of one sixty-fourth of an inch between the casing and the face of the rotor. Mr. Tesla desired an almost touching fit between the rotor face and the casing when the former was turning. The large clearance was necessary because the rotor attained tremendously high speeds, averaging 35,000 revolutions per minute. At this speed the centrifugal force generated by the turning movement was so great it appreciably stretched the metal in the rotating disks. Their diameter when turning at top speed was one thirty-second of an inch greater than when they were standing still.

A larger model was built by Tesla in 1910. It had disks twelve inches in diameter, and with a speed of 10,000 revolutions per minute it developed 100 horsepower, indicating a greatly improved efficiency over the first model. It developed more than three times as much power at half the speed.

During the following year, 1911, still further improvements were made. The disks were reduced to a diameter of 9.75 inches and the speed of operation was cut down by ten per cent, to 9,000 revolutions per minute—and the power output increase by ten per cent, to 110 horsepower!

Following this test, Tesla issued a statement in which he declared:
I have developed 110 horsepower with disks nine and three quarter inches in diameter and making a thickness of about two inches. Under proper conditions the performance might have been as much as 1,000 horsepower. **In fact there is almost no limit to the mechanical performance of such a machine.** *This engine will work with gas, as in the usual type of explosion engine used in automobiles and airplanes, even better than it did with steam. Tests which I have conducted have shown that the rotary effort with gas is greater than with steam.*

Enthusiastic over the success of his smaller models of the turbine, operated on compressed air, and to a more limited extent by direct combustion of gasoline, Tesla designed and built a larger, double unit, which he planned to test with steam in the Waterside Station, the main powerhouse of the New York Edison Company.

This was a station which had originally been designed to operate on the direct-current system developed by Edison—but it was now operating throughout on Tesla's polyphase alternating-current system.

Now Tesla, invading the Edison sanctum to test a new type of turbine which he hoped would replace the types in use, was definitely in enemy territory. The fact that he had Morgan backing, and that the Edison Company was a "Morgan company," had no nullifying effect on the Edison-Tesla feud.

This situation was not softened in any way by Tesla's method of carrying on his tests. Tesla was a confirmed "sun dodger;" he preferred to work at night rather than in the daytime. Power-houses, not from choice but from necessity, have their heaviest demands for current after sunset. The day load would be relatively light; but as darkness approached, the dynamos started to groan under the increasing night load. The services of the workers at the Waterside Station were made available to Tesla for the setting up and tests of his turbine with the expectation that the work would be done during the day when the tasks of the workers were easiest.

Tesla, however, would rarely show up until five o'clock in the afternoon, or later, and would turn a deaf ear to the pleas of workers that he arrive earlier. He insisted that certain of the workers whom he favored remain after their five-o'clock quitting time on the day shift to work with him on an overtime basis. Nor did he maintain a conciliatory attitude toward the engineering staff or the officials of the company. The attitudes, naturally, were mutual.

The turbine Tesla built for this test had a rotor 18 inches in diameter which turned at a speed of 9,000 revolutions per minute. It developed 200 horse-power. The overall dimensions of the engine were—three feet long, two feet wide and two feet high. It weighed 400 pounds.

Two such turbines were built and installed in a line on a single base. The shafts of both were connected to a torque rod. Steam was fed to both engines so that, if they were free to rotate, they would turn in opposite directions. The power developed was measured by the torque rod connected to the two opposing shafts.

At a formal test, to which Tesla invited a great many guests, he issued a statement in which he said, as reported, in part:

It should be noted that although the experimental plant develops 200 horse-power with 125 pounds at the supply pipe and free exhaust it could show an output of 300 horsepower with full pressure of the supply circuit. If the turbine were compounded and the exhaust were led to a low pressure unit carrying about three times the number of disks contained in the high pressure element, with connection to a condenser affording 28.5 to 29.0 inches of vacuum the results obtained in the present high pressure machine indicate that the compounded unit would give an output of 600 horsepower without great increase of dimensions. This estimate is very conservative.

Tests have shown that when the turbine is running at 9,000 revolutions per minute under an inlet pressure of 125 pounds to the square inch and with free exhaust 200 brake horsepower are developed. The consumption under these conditions of maximum output is 38 pounds of saturated steam per horse-power per hour, a very high efficiency when we consider that the heat drop, measured by thermometers, is only 130 B.T.U. and that the energy transfor-mation is effected in one stage. Since three times the number of heat units are available in a modern plant with superheat and high vacuum the utilization of these facilities would mean a consumption of less than 12 pounds per horsepower hour in such turbines adapted to take the full drop.

Under certain conditions very high thermal efficiencies have been obtained which demonstrate that in large machines based on this principle steam consumption will be much lower and should approximate the theoretical minimum thus resulting in the nearly frictionless turbine transmitting almost the entire expansive energy of the steam to the shaft.

It should be kept in mind that all the turbines which Tesla built and tested were single-stage engines, using about one-third of the energy of the steam. In practical use, they were intended to be installed with a second stage which would employ the remaining energy and increase the power output about two or three fold. (The two types of turbines in common use each have a dozen and more stages within a single shell.)

Some of the Edison electric camp, observing the torque-rod tests and appar-ently not understanding that in such a test the two rotors remain stationary—their opposed pressures staging a tug of war measured as torque—circulated the story that the turbine was a complete failure; that this turbine would not be practical if its efficiency had been increased a thousand fold. It was stories such as these that contributed to the imputation that Tesla was an impractical visionary. The Tesla turbine, however, used as a single-stage engine, functioning as a pygmy power producer, in the form in which it was actually tested, anticipated by more than twenty-five years a type of turbine which has been installed in recent years in the Waterside Station. This is a very small engine, with blades on its rotor, known as a "topping turbine," which is inserted in the steam line between the boilers and the ordinary turbines. Steam of increased pressure is supplied, and the topping turbine skims this "cream" from the steam and exhausts steam that runs the other turbines in their normal way.

The General Electric Company was developing the Curtis turbine at that time, and the Westinghouse Electric and Manufacturing Company was developing the Parsons turbine; and neither company showed the slightest interest in Tesla's demonstration.

Further development of his turbine on a larger scale would have required a large amount of money—and Tesla did not possess even a small amount.

FINALLY he succeeded in interesting the Allis Chalmers Manufacturing Company of Milwaukee, builders of reciprocating engines and turbines, and other heavy machinery. In typical Tesla fashion, though, he manifested in his negotiations such a lack of diplomacy and insight into human nature that he would have been better off if he had completely failed to make any arrangements for exploiting the turbine.

Tesla, an engineer, ignored the engineers on the Allis Chalmers staff and went directly to the president. While an engineering report was being prepared on his proposal, he went to the Board of Directors and "sold" that body on his project before the engineers had a chance to be heard. Three turbines were built. Two of them had twenty disks eighteen inches in diameter and were tested with steam at eighty pounds pressure. They developed at speeds of 12,000 and 10,000 revolutions per minute, respectively, 200 horsepower. This was exactly the same power output as had been achieved by Tesla's 1911 model, which had disks of half this diameter and was operated at 9,000 revolutions under 125 pounds pressure. A much larger engine was tackled next. It had fifteen disks sixty inches in diameter, was designed to operate at 3,600 revolutions per minute, and was rated at 500 kilowatts capacity, or about 675 horsepower.

Hans Dahlstrand, Consulting Engineer of the Steam Turbine Department, reports, in part:

We also built a 500 kw steam turbine to operate at 3,600 revolutions. The turbine rotor consisted of fifteen disks 60 inches in diameter and one eighth inch thick. The disks were placed approximately one eighth inch apart. The unit was tested by connecting to a generator. The maximum mechanical efficiency obtained on this unit was approximately 38 per cent when operating at steam pressure of approximately 80 pounds absolute and a back pressure of approximately 3 pounds absolute and 100 degrees F superheat at the inlet.

When the steam pressure was increased above that given the mechanical efficiency dropped, consequently the design of these turbines was of such a nature that in order to obtain maximum efficiency at high pressure, it would have been necessary to have more than one turbine in series.

The efficiency of the small turbine units compares with the efficiency obtainable on small impulse turbines running at speeds where they can be directly connected to pumps and other machinery. It is obvious, therefore, that the small unit in order to obtain the same efficiency had to operate at from 10,000 to 12,000 revolutions and it would have been necessary to provide reduction gears between the steam turbine and the driven unit.

Furthermore, the design of the Tesla turbine could not compete as far as manufacturing costs with the smaller type of impulse units. It is also questionable whether the rotor disks, because of light construction and high stress, would have lasted any length of time if operating continuously.

The above remarks apply equally to the large turbine running at 3,600 revolutions. It was found when this unit was dismantled that the disks had distorted to a great extent and the opinion was that these disks would ultimately have failed if the unit had been operated for any length of time.

The gas turbine was never constructed for the reason that the company was unable to obtain sufficient engineering information from Mr. Tesla indicating even an approximate design that he had in mind.

Tesla appears to have walked out on the tests at this stage.

In Milwaukee, however, there was no George Westinghouse to save the situation. Later, during the twenties, the author asked Tesla why he had terminated his work with the Allis Chalmers Company. He replied:

"They would not build the turbines as I wished"
and he would not amplify the statement further.

The Allis Chalmers Company later became the pioneer manufacturers of another type of gas turbine that has been in successful operation for years.

While the Dahlstrand report may appear to be severely critical of the Tesla turbine and to reveal fundamental weaknesses in it not found in other turbines, such is not the case. The report is, in general, a fair presentation of the results; and the description of apparent weakness merely offers from another viewpoint the facts which Tesla himself stated about the turbine in his earlier test—that when employed as a single-stage engine it uses only about a third of the energy of the steam, and that to utilize the remainder, it would have to be compounded with a second turbine.

The reference to a centrifugal force of 70,000 pounds resulting from the high speed of rotation of the rotor, causing damage to the disks, refers to a common experience with all types of turbines. This is made clear in a booklet on "The Story of the Turbine," issued during the past year by the General Electric Company, in which it is stated:

It [the turbine] had to wait until engineers and scientists could develop materials to withstand these pressures and speeds. For example, a single bucket in a modern turbine travelling at 600 miles per hour has a centrifugal force of 90,000 pounds trying to pull it from its attachment on the bucket wheel and shaft....

In this raging inferno the high pressure buckets at one end of the turbine run red hot while a few feet away the large buckets in the last stages run at 600 miles per hour through a storm of tepid rain—so fast that the drops of condensed steam cut like a sand blast.

Dahlstrand reported that difficulties were encountered in the Tesla turbine from vibration, making it necessary to re-enforce the disks. That this difficulty is common to all turbines is further indicated by the General Electric booklet, which states:

Vibration cracked buckets and wheels and wrecked turbines, sometimes within a few hours and sometimes after years of operation. This vibration was caused by taking such terrific amounts of power from relatively light machinery—in some cases as much as 400 horsepower out of a bucket weighing but a pound or two....

The major problems of the turbine are four—high temperatures, high pressures, high speeds and internal vibration. And their solution lies in engineering, research and manufacturing skill.

These problems are still awaiting their final solution, even with the manufacturers who have been building turbines for forty years; and the fact that they were encountered in the Tesla turbine, and so reported, is not a final criticism of Tesla's invention in the earliest stages of its development.

There have been whisperings in engineering circles during the past year or two to indicate a revival of interest in the Tesla turbine and the possibility that the makers of the Curtis and Parsons types may extend their lines to include the Tesla type for joint operation with the others. The development of new alloys, which can now almost be made to order with desired qualities of mechanical stability under conditions of high temperature and great stresses, is largely responsible for this turn of events.

It is a possibility that if the Tesla turbine were constructed with the benefit of two or more stages, thus giving it the full operating range of either the Curtis or the Parsons turbine, and were built with the same benefits of engineering skill and modern metallurgical developments as have been lavished on these two turbines, the vastly greater simplicity of the Tesla turbine would enable it to manifest greater efficiencies of operation and economies of construction.

REPORT OF FRITZ LOWENSTEIN
July 1911

ON CERTAIN APPARATUS INVENTED AND DESIGNED BY NIKOLA TESLA FOR THE PROPULSION OF FLUIDS AND CONVERSION OF ENERGY BY FLUID PROPULSION.

I, the undersigned, Fritz Lowenstein, am a mechanical and electrical engineer, thirty seven years of age, residing at 231 West 141st St., New York, N.Y. My office address is 115 Nassau St., where I conduct a consulting engineering business, in which I have been engaged since 1903.

I am a graduate of the mechanical electrical faculty of the Polytechnic School of Vienna, Austria, 1897, and have had varied experience in mechanical and electrical work in Austria, Germany, France and the United States. More particularly, I held the position of Chief Draughtsman with Ritchell & Company, Vienna, and was thereafter engaged by the German Thomson-Houston Company, (Union El. Ges.) in Munich, and then, in 1898 by Nikola Tesla, in New York and Colorado.

Subsequently I served as engineer for the Parville Freres, Paris, France, and afterwards was engaged by the German Westinghouse Electric & Manufacturing Co., with an establishment in Frankfurt a/Main. In 1902 I re-entered the employ of Mr. Tesla and assisted him in his work in high frequency oscillations and on steam engines, in New York and Long Island. Since 1903 I have followed the profession of a consulting engineer.

I have devoted a great deal of time, both as a student and practitioner, to thermo-dynamic questions, and believe that I am fully capable of independent and valuable judgment on questions relating to steam and fluid propulsion generally.

I have made tests on a great number of steam engines for the purpose of determining their power and efficiency, and regard myself as well equipped with theoretical and practical knowledge necessary for making such tests intelligently and correctly.

I have had occasion to witness the operation and to participate in a number of tests of Tesla turbines, and I have been requested to submit a sworn statement of the results of such tests and my opinion as to the novelty, efficiency and commercial value of such apparatus.

The first test with a Tesla turbine witnessed by me was made in Bridgeport, Conn., at the works of the American & British Manufacturing Company in the summer of 1910. I was present during tests, at these works, on three other occasions when two different turbines were used, which I may designate, respectively, as the 100 H.P. Tesla turbine and the 600 H.P. Tesla turbine.

The 100 H.P. turbine was loaded by a Prony Brake and gages were provided for reading the steam pressure at various points in the turbine, viz; at the feed pipe, at the nozzle, beyond the nozzle and at the exhaust. A tachometer was employed for indicating the revolutions of the shaft. On two of the occasions above mentioned the readings were taken and recorded by myself, while in another instance the record was kept by Mr. Tesla. The turbine developed in the various tests made on these three occasions from 50 to 105 H.P., according to the setting of the brake. The steam pressure was approximately 90 lbs. per square inch gage pressure, the exhaust varying from one inch to ten inches vacuum, according to the load and other conditions. For so small a prime mover of 100 H.P. the efficiency was remarkably high.

The rotor was nine and three quarter inches in diameter and two and one half inches long, and was composed of smooth disks mounted upon a shaft with openings near the centers for exhaust. The steam consumption was measured by means of a surface condenser, and an accurate scale was employed to weigh the condensed water for a given period of time.

The accompanying photograph which I have marked "Exhibit A" represents a drawing of the 100 H.P. Tesla turbine above described. [Ed. see page 52] The steam was made to enter a nozzle chamber located at the top of the turbine, the nozzle being carried by a rotative member provided with a hand wheel, by means of which the steam was made to impinge on the rotor in opposite tangential directions at will. I witnessed the reversing of the turbine on several occasions. The sectional view in photograph Exhibit A illustrates the construction of the rotor, which was composed of spaced, plane smooth disks with openings near the centers to permit exit of the steam which entered the rotor tangentially and traveled in a free spiral path toward the center, leaving through the holes above mentioned. The readings of the pressure gages taken during the tests indicated clearly a conversion of heat into mechanical power, taking place partly in the nozzle and partly in the free spiral path of the steam through the rotor. I recognize the accompanying drawing marked "Tesla Reversible Turbine, Nov. 30, 1908", as a drawing of the 100 H.P. Tesla turbine described, with the exception, however, that the exhaust was located on the side as shown in photograph hereto annexed and marked "B", and not at the bottom as shown in photograph A.

Photograph B and that also attached hereto and marked "C" show the same turbine disconnected from the same pipes. In both of these photographs the reversing nozzle, which is mounted at the top, as well as the exhaust, may be plainly seen. I have read the applications for patent filed by Mr. Tesla for this invention, namely, Serial No. 523,832, filed Oct. 21, 1909, and Serial No. 603,049, filed January 17, 1911, and I find that the turbine above referred to was constructed exactly on the principle described in said applications and illustrated more particularly in Figures 2 thereof, and I am of the opinion that the turbine operates precisely on the principle set forth in said applications.

The following data, selected from a number of readings taken, refer to measurements of this turbine at which I assisted Mr. Tesla, the record being kept by Professor C.D. Richards, Professor Emeritus of the Engineering Faculty of Yale University:

R.P.M.	Steam Gage at nozzle	Vacuum Gage at exhaust
18,000	100 lbs.	15"

Water consumed per hour	Brake H.P.	Steam consumption per Brake H.P. per hour
5481 lbs	102.8	53.4

No allowance was made in these tests for loss of power in gear.

Many similar tests with the Tesla turbine have unmistakably shown that conversion of heat into mechanical power takes place during the passage of the steam through the rotor. It is therefore, entirely unlike other smooth disk turbines as that proposed and illustrated, for example, in the United States patent to Thrupp, No. 699,636, dated May 6, 1902 or the corresponding British patent No. 6422 of 1901, inasmuch as in the latter the conversion of heat into mechanical power takes place in the nozzle only, while the Tesla turbine works as an expansion engine, the rotor deriving mechanical power from the expansion of the steam therein.

So far as I have knowledge of the subject the Tesla turbine is the first engine utilizing the expansion of steam without the use of pistons, blades or vanes.

The 600 H.P. Tesla turbine, illustrated in photograph D hereto annexed, was of the same design as that above described, the steam entering at the circumference of the rotor, which consisted of plane disks, and leaving the same at the center through the openings provided. This turbine was coupled directly to a Tesla pump, the construction of which is substantially the same as that of the turbine, and the output was measured by the hydraulic performance of the pump. [Ed: see page 33]

This 600 H.P. Tesla turbine had a rotor 6 feet in diameter, and in the test which I witnessed was run from 1400 to 1600 R.P.M. The set equipped with steam and hydraulic gages which were used for taking measurements in which I assisted Mr. Tesla on two different occasions. I recognize in photograph D. this 600 H.P. turbo-pump.

I have assisted in a number of tests with another 100 H.P. Tesla turbine, which was installed in the spring of 1911 in the large power house, called the Waterside Plant of the New York Edison Company, located at 38th St., and First Avenue, New York City, and I have also witnessed the installation and preliminary tests of two other Tesla turbines of 200 H.P. each.

The 100 H.P. turbine at the Edison plant, as shown in photographs E and F hereto annexed was used to drive an alternating current generator through reducing gears, and was equipped with all devices for measuring steam consumption and the pressures of the different points in the path of the steam, and the electrical work done by the generator was accurately indicated by a wattmeter. [Ed. see page 48]

In many of these instances I have recorded myself the pressures and temperatures of the steam, the speed of the turbine and the electrical performance of the generator, and I have found the turbine to be more economical in steam consumption than any other as given by the guarantee of steam consumption of well known manufacturers. The tests have shown that thermo-dynamic work is being performed by the steam on its free spiral path through the rotor, a unique feature of these turbines constructed by Mr. Tesla.

The 100 H.P. Tesla turbine at the Edison plant, above referred to, is shown in the accompanying photograph E of drawing No. 147, and photograph F. The rotor, as shown in the longitudinal section of the said drawing is composed of plane disks riveted together with interstices between them. The sectional view in drawing No. 147 shows the central openings of the disks by which the steam leaves the rotor after having traversed it in its free spiral path. As seen in section at C, D the steam, entering tangentially from above, leaves the rotor at both sides, passing into the exhaust chamber. [Ed. see pages 31 and 112]

The following table gives the results of tests made by Mr. Tesla and myself to show the performance of this turbine.

R.P.M.	Gauge pressure at nozzle	Vacuum at Exhaust
18,000	**176 lbs.**	**21"**

Effective Load	Water Consumption per hour	Steam Consumed per H.P. hour
77 H.P.	**2700 lbs.**	**35 lbs.**

The application of vacuum to that turbine at the same load and speed did not change the steam consumption on account of the small exhaust ports and pipe; from which I draw the conclusion that with an exhaust pressure above atmospheric pressure the steam consumption would have been still better.

This efficiency of conversion of heat into mechanical power is indeed superior to the best guarantee of any turbine, of corresponding size that I have any knowledge of. The rotor of this machine was only nine and three quarter inches in diameter and not more than two inches wide. I recognize photograph E of drawing No. 147 as correctly representing the construction of the said turbine, and photograph F as correctly showing the said turbine in working condition at the Edison power house, and I furthermore know that this turbine was operated in accordance with the instructions and descriptions in Mr. Tesla's applications for patent above referred to. On the left side of photograph F is shown the turbine proper driving through the reduction gear (shown in the center of the photograph), the generator on the right side of the photograph. [Ed. see page 48]

The two 200 H.P. turbines mentioned above are shown in photograph G of drawing No. 135, and photograph H, both of which are hereto annexed, with the singe exception that the regulating attachment on the left hand side of the longitudinal section was replaced in the tests which I witnessed by an auxiliary device for measuring torque. Both of these machines were provided with reversing nozzles as shown in the photographs. Their rotors were composed of plane disks riveted together, as indicated, with spaces between them. The steam entered tangentially and, after describing its free spiral path, issued from the center through the three openings at both sides into the exhaust chamber. [Ed. see pages 37, 128 and 146]

I recognize photographs G and H as showing the two 200 H.P. turbines installed at the Edison Waterside Plant, New York City, and I know these machines were constructed and operated in accordance with the descriptions and illustrations in the above mentioned Tesla applications for patent. They were coupled together by a torsion spring shown in photograph H so that horsepower measurements could be taken without recourse to reduction gears, one turbine being used as a driver and the other as a brake.

The Tesla turbine is particularly valuable on account of its reversibility, its efficiency being the same for both directions of rotation. Other advantageous features are its extreme simplicity and adaptability to varying speeds without the marked drop in efficiency which is unavoidable in bucket turbines. The great torque at low speed which it possesses makes it especially adaptable for traction work, and by its compactness and small weight per horse power yield it is superior to existing machines.

It is also a prominent characteristic of the Tesla turbine, and this is a matter of the greatest practical importance, that there is a very much smaller slip or relative velocity of steam and metal surface than in my other practical forms of turbines. This contributes very greatly to its efficiency. I may also note that I believe it is the only turbine which utilizes the viscosity of the steam to transmit the kinetic energy of the intermediate layers between the disks to the outer layers in contact with the surfaces of the disks, which in turn impart power to the rotor.

Fritz Lowenstein

State of New York,   )
) SS:
County of New York.)

Personally appeared before me Fritz Lowenstein, to me now and known to me to be the person who subscribed to the above document entitled "Report of Fritz Lowenstein on certain apparatus invented and designed by Nikola Tesla for the Propulsion of Fluid and the conversion of Energy by Fluid propulsion," and he being duly sworn deposes and says that he has read the said report and knows the contents thereof, and that the same is true except as to matters of opinion, and as to these he verily believes to be true. Subscribed and sworn to before me this day of July, 1911.

TESLA PUMPS GENERATING SALES IN THE MULTI-MILLIONS

Opportunists Charge Premium Prices for Tesla's Pumping Technology; Claim Patent Protection

Tesla's pumps have recently been introduced commercially at premium prices generating sales in the multi-millions. Individuals were issued bladeless pumping patents in the 1980's despite the fact that Tesla was refused these patents in 1913. This has resulted in an ongoing battle over who is the rightful owner of the lucrative Tesla pumping technology.

These individuals have claimed in the past that *they*, each individually, are the rightful and true "*inventor*" of modern bladeless pumping technology, stating that Tesla was not a pump engineer, claiming Tesla's field was electrical not mechanical.

Nothing, however, could be further from the truth. Tesla was by training and **first love** a mechanical engineer. Without Tesla's marvelous mechanical insight his electrical devices could not have functioned. They are, after all, **mechanical** devices operating electrically.

These individuals have been made aware of the **fact** that bladeless pumping devices were issued to Tesla under U.S. Patent No. 1,061,142 granted May 6, 1913. This patent, featured on the next page, is entitled "Fluid Propulsion" and describes how bladeless pumps can be used to "impart energy to a vessel." In other words, a replacement for the bladed propeller of a ship. During this same period Tesla applied for a pumping patent to "impart energy to a fluid," Serial No. 735,914, reference of which is made in the Fluid Propulsion patent. The U.S. Patent Office rejected this application on the grounds that it was duplicative. Bladeless pumping devices, by their judgement, were covered under Tesla's Fluid Propulsion patent.

Tesla formally objected and unsuccessfully argued that separate pumping patents be issued, there being a substantial difference in construction between the two devices including but not limited to, variations in inlet, outlet, and disk spacing. The decision of the patent office in this matter, as well as correspondence with Tesla's attorney, recorded and archived in the patent wrappers, clearly establishes that bladeless pumping applications fall under and are fully protected by Tesla's Fluid Propulsion patent.

TESLA'S PATENTS ARE NOW PUBLIC DOMAIN.

N. TESLA.
FLUID PROPULSION.
APPLICATION FILED OCT. 21, 1909.

1,061,142.

Patented May 6, 1913.

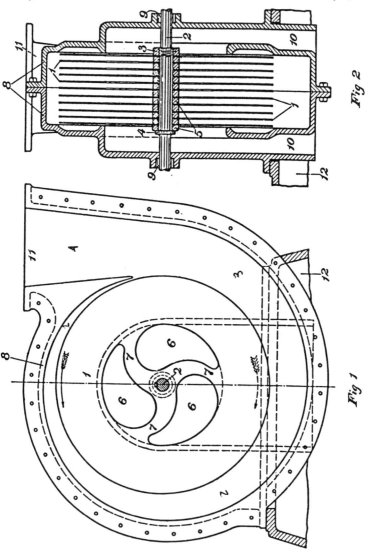

Fig 2

Fig 1

Witnesses:
R. Diez Buitago
J. J. Dunham

Nikola Tesla,
Inventor

By his Attorneys
Kerr, Page Cooper & Hayward

United States Patent   **May 6, 1913**

FLUID PROPULSION

1,061,142

Application filed October 21, 1909.   Serial No. 523,832

To all whom it may concern:

Be it known that I, Nikola Tesla, a citizen of the United States, residing at New York, in the county and State of New York, have invented certain new and useful Improvements in Fluid Propulsion, of which the following is a full, clear, and exact description.

In the practical application of mechanical power based on the use of a fluid as the vehicle of energy, it has been demonstrated that, in order to attain the highest economy, the changes in velocity and direction of movement of the fluid should be as gradual as possible. In the present forms of such apparatus more or less sudden changes, shocks and vibrations are unavoidable. Besides, then employment of the usual devices for imparting energy to a fluid, as pistons, paddles, vanes and blades, necessarily introduces numerous defects and limitations and adds to the complication, cost of production and maintenance of the machine.

The object of my present invention is to overcome these deficiencies in apparatus designed for the propulsion of fluids and to effect thereby the transmission and transformation of mechanical energy through the agency of fluids in a more perfect manner, and by means simple and more economical than those heretofore employed. I accomplish this by causing the propelled fluid to move in natural paths or stream lines of least resistance, free from constraint and disturbance such as occasioned by vanes or kindred devices, and to change its velocity and direction of movement by imperceptible degrees, thus avoiding the losses due to sudden variations while the fluid is receiving energy.

It is well known that a fluid possesses, among others, two salient properties: *adhesion* and *viscosity*. Owing to these a body propelled through such a medium encounters a peculiar impediment known as "lateral" or "skin resistance", which is two-fold; one arising from the shock of the fluid against the asperities of the solid substance, the other from internal forces opposing molecular separation. As an inevitable consequence, a certain amount of the fluid is dragged along by the moving body. Conversely, if the body be placed in a fluid in motion, for the same reasons, it is impelled in the direction of movement. These effects, in themselves, are of daily observation, but I believe that I am the first to apply them in a practical and economical manner for imparting energy to or deriving it from a fluid.

The subject of this application is an invention pertaining to the art of imparting energy to fluids, and I shall now proceed to describe its nature and the principles of construction of the apparatus which I have devised for carrying it out by reference to the accompanying drawings which illustrate an operative and efficient embodiment of the same.

Figure 1 is a partial end view, and **Fig. 2** is a vertical cross section of a pump or compressor constructed and adapted to be operated in accordance with my invention.

In these drawings the device illustrated contains a runner composed of a plurality of flat rigid disks **1** of a suitable diameter, keyed to a shaft **2**, and held in position by a threaded nut **3**, a shoulder **4** and washers **5**, of the requisite thickness. Each disk has a number of central openings **6**, the solid portions between which form spokes **7**, preferably curved, as shown, for the purpose of reducing the loss of energy due to the impact of the fluid. The runner is mounted in a two part volute casing **8**, having stuffing boxes **9**, and inlets **10** leading to its central portion. In addition a gradually widening and rounding outlet **11** is provided, formed with a flange for connection to a pipe as usual. The casing **8** rests upon a base **12**, shown only in part, and supporting the bearings for the shaft **2**, which, being of ordinary construction, are omitted from the drawings.

An understanding of the principle embodied in this device will be gained from the following description of its mode of operation. Power being applied to the shaft and the runner set in rotation in the direction of the solid arrow the fluid by reason of its properties of adherence and viscosity, upon entering through the inlets **10** and coming in contact with the disks **1** is taken hold of by the same and subjected to two forces, one acting tangentially in the direction of rotation, and the other radially outward. The combined effect of these tangential and centrifugal forces is to propel the fluid with continuously increasing velocity in a spiral path until it reaches the outlet **11** from which it is ejected. This spiral movement, free and undisturbed and essentially dependent on the properties of the fluid, permitting it to adjust itself to natural paths or stream lines and to change its velocity and direction by insensible degrees, is characteristic of this method of propulsion and advantageous in its application. While traversing the chamber inclosing the runner, the particles of the fluid may complete one or more turns, or but a part of one turn. In any given case their path can be closely calculated and graphically represented, but fairly accurate estimate of turns can be obtained simply by determining the number of revolutions required to renew the fluid passing through the chamber and multiplying it by the ratio between the mean speed of the fluid and that of the disks. I have found that the quantity of fluid propelled in this manner is, other conditions being equal, approximately proportionate to the active surface of the runner and to its effective speed. For this reason, the performance of such machines augments at an exceedingly high rate with the increase of their size and speed of revolution.

The dimensions of the device as a whole, and the spacing of the disks in any given machine will be determined by the conditions and requirements of special cases. It may be stated that the intervening distance should be the greater, the larger the diameter of the disks, the longer the spiral path of the fluid and the greater its viscosity. In general, the spacing should be such that the entire mass of the fluid, before leaving the runner, is accelerated to a nearly uniform velocity, not much below that of the periphery of the disks under normal working conditions and almost equal to it when the outlet is closed and the particles move in concentric circles. It may also be pointed out that such a pump can be made without openings and spokes in the runner, as by using one or more solid disks, each in its own casing, in which form the machine will be eminently adapted for sewage, dredging and the like, when the water is charged with foreign bodies and spokes or vanes especially objectionable.

Another application of this principle which I have discovered to be not only feasible, but thoroughly practicable and efficient, is the utilization of machines such as above described for the compression or rarefaction of air, or gases in general. In such cases it will be found that most of the general considerations obtaining in the case of liquids, properly interpreted, hold true.   When, irrespective of the character of the fluid, considerable pressures are desired, staging or compounding may be resorted to in the usual way the individual runners being, preferably, mounted on the same shaft. It should be added that the same end may be attained with one single runner by suitable deflection of the fluid through rotative or stationary passages.

The principles underlying the invention are capable of embodiment also in that field of mechanical engineering which is concerned in the use of fluids as motive agents, for while in some respects the actions in the latter case are directly opposite to those met with in the propulsion of fluids, the fundamental laws applicable in the two cases are the same. In other words, the operation above described is reversible, for if water or air under pressure be admitted to the opening **11** the runner is set in rotation in the direction of the dotted arrow by reason of the peculiar properties of the fluid which traveling in a spiral path and with continuously diminishing velocity, reaches the orifices **6** and **10** through which it is discharged.

When apparatus of the general character above described is employed for the transmission of power, however, certain departures from structural similarity between transmitter and receiver may be necessary for securing the best result. I have, therefore, included that part of my invention which is directly applicable to the use of fluids as motive agents in a separate application filed January 17, 1911, Serial No. 603,049. It may be here pointed out, however, as is evident from the above considerations, that when transmitting power from one shaft to another by such machines, any desired ratio between the speeds of rotation may be obtained by proper selection of the diameters of the disks, or by suitably staging the transmitter, the receiver, or both.

But it may be stated that in one respect, at least, the two machines are essentially different. In the pump, the radial or static pressure, due to centrifugal force, is added to the tangential or dynamic, thus increasing the effective head and assisting in the expulsion of the fluid. In the motor, on the contrary, the first named pressure, being opposed to that of supply, reduces the effective head and velocity of radial flow toward the center. Again, in the propelled machine a great torque is always desirable, this calling for an increased number of disks and smaller distance of separation, while in the propelling machine, for numerous economic reasons, the rotary effort should be the smallest and the speed the greatest practicable. Many other considerations, which will naturally suggest themselves, may affect the design and construction, but the preceding is thought to contain all necessary information in this regard.

It will be understood that the principles of construction and operation above set forth, are capable of embodiment in machines of the most widely different forms, and adapted for the greatest variety of purposes. In the above, I have sought to describe and explain only the general and typical applications of the principle which I believe I am the first to realize and turn to useful account.

I do not claim in this application the method herein described of imparting energy to a fluid, having made that discovery the subject of a copending application Serial No. 735,914.

What I claim is:

1. A machine for propelling or imparting energy to fluids comprising in combination a plurality of spaced disks rotatably mounted and having plane surfaces, an inclosing casing, ports of inlet at the central portion of said casing and through which the fluid is adapted to be introduced to the axial portions of the disks, and ports of outlet at the peripheral portion of the casing through which the fluid, when the machine is driven by power, is adapted to be expelled, as set forth.

2. A machine for propelling or imparting energy to fluids, comprising in combination a volute casing provided with ports of inlet and outlet at its central and peripheral portions, respectively, and a runner mounted within the casing and composed of spaced disks with plane surfaces having openings adjacent to the axis of rotation.

3. A rotary pump, comprising in combination a plurality of spaced disks with plane surfaces mounted on a rotatable shaft and provided with openings adjacent thereto, a volute casing inclosing the said disks, means for admitting a fluid into that portion of the casing which contains the shaft and an outlet extending tangentially from the peripheral portion of said casing.

In testimony whereof I affix my signature in the presence of two subscribing witnesses.

NIKOLA TESLA.

Witnesses

    M. Lawson Dyer,

    Drury W. Cooper.

N. TESLA.

TURBINE.

APPLICATION FILED JAN. 17, 1911.

1,061,206.

Patented May 6, 1913.

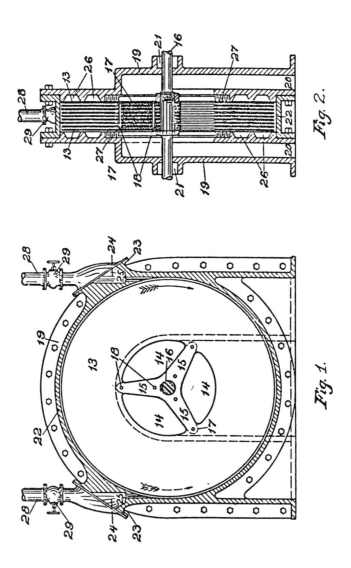

Fig. 2.

Fig. 1.

Witnesses:
R. Diaz Armitage
Wm. Cohleber

Nikola Tesla, Inventor

By his Attorneys

Kerr Page Cooper & Hayward

United States Patent   **May 6, 1913**

TURBINE
1,061,206

Application filed October 21, 1909.   Serial No. 523,832.

To all whom it may concern:

Be it known that I, Nikola Tesla, a citizen of the United States, residing at New York, in the county and State of New York, have invented certain new and useful Improvements in Rotary Engines and Turbines, of which the following is a full, clear, and exact description.

In the practical application of mechanical power, based on the use of fluid as the vehicle of energy, it has been demonstrated that, in order to attain the highest economy, the changes in the velocity and direction of movement of the fluid should be as gradual as possible. In the forms of apparatus heretofore devised or proposed, more or less sudden changes, shocks and vibrations are unavoidable. Besides, the employment of the usual devices for imparting to, or deriving energy from a fluid, such as pistons, paddles, vanes and blades, necessarily introduces numerous defects and limitations and adds to the complication, cost of production and maintenance of the machines.

The object of my invention is to over-come these deficiencies and to effect the transmission and transformation of mechanical energy through the agency of fluids in a more perfect manner and by means simpler and more economical than those heretofore employed. I accomplish this by causing the propelling fluid to move in natural paths or stream lines of least resistance, free from constraint and disturbance such as occasioned by vanes or kindred devices, and to change its velocity and direction of movement by imperceptible degrees, thus avoiding the losses due to sudden variations while the fluid is imparting energy.

It is well known that a fluid possesses, among others, two salient properties, adhesion and viscosity. Owing to these a solid body propelled through such a medium encounters a peculiar impediment known as "lateral" or "skin resistance," which is two fold, one arising from the shock of the fluid against the asperities of the solid substance, the other from internal forces opposing molecular separation. As an inevitable consequence a certain amount of the fluid is dragged along by the moving body. Conversely, if the body be placed in a fluid in motion, for the same reasons, it is impelled in the direction of movement. These effects, in themselves, are of daily observation, but I believe that I am the first to apply them in a practical and economical manner in the propulsion of fluids or in their use as motive agents.

In an application filed by me October 21st, 1909, Serial Number 523,832 of which this case is a division, I have illustrated the principles underlying my discovery as embodied in apparatus designed for the propulsion of fluids. The same principles, however, are capable of embodiment also in that field of mechanical engineering which is concerned in the use of fluids as motive agents, for while in certain respects the operations in the latter case are directly opposite to those met with in the propulsion of fluids, and the means employed may differ in some features, the fundamental laws applicable in the two cases are the same. In other words, the operation is reversible, for if water or air under pressure be admitted to the opening constituting the outlet of a pump or blower as described, the runner is set in rotation by reason of the peculiar properties of the fluid which, in its movement through the device, imparts its energy thereto.

The present application, which is a division of that referred to, is specially intended to describe and claim my discovery above set forth, so far as it bears on the use of fluids as motive agents, as distinguished from the applications of the same to the propulsion or compression of fluids.

In the drawings, therefore, I have illustrated only the form of apparatus designed for the thermo-dynamic conversion of energy, a field in which the applications of the principle have the greatest practical value.

Figure 1 is a partial end view, and **Figure 2** a vertical cross-section of a rotary engine or turbine, constructed and adapted to be operated in accordance with the principles of my invention.

The apparatus comprises a runner composed of a plurality of flat rigid disks **13** of suitable diameter, keyed to a shaft **16**, and held in position thereon by a threaded nut **11**, a shoulder **12**, and intermediate washers **17**. The disks have openings **14** adjacent to the shaft and spokes **15**, which may be substantially straight. For the sake of clearness, but a few disks, with comparatively wide intervening spaces, are illustrated.

The runner is mounted in a casing comprising two end castings **19**, which contain the bearings for the shaft **16**, indicated but not shown in detail; stuffing boxes **21** and outlets **20**. The end castings are united by a central ring **22**, which is bored out to a circle of a slightly larger diameter than that of the disks, and has flanged extensions **23**, and inlets **24**, into which finished ports or nozzles **25** are inserted. Circular grooves **26** and labyrinth packing **27** are provided on the sides of the runner. Supply pipes **28**, with valves **29**, are connected to the flanged extensions of the central ring, one of the valves being normally closed.

For a more ready and complete understanding of the principle of operation it is of advantage to consider first the actions that take place when the device is used for the propulsion of fluids for which purpose let it be assumed that power is applied to the shaft and the runner set in rotation say in a clockwise direction. Neglecting, for the moment, those features of construction that make for or against the efficiency of the device as a pump, as distinguished from a motor, a fluid, by reason of its properties of adherence and viscosity, upon entering through the inlets **20**, and coming in contact with the disks **13**, is taken hold of by the latter and subjected to two forces, one acting tangentially in the direction of rotation, and the other radially outward. The combined effect of these tangential and centrifugal forces is to propel the fluid with continuously increasing velocity in a spiral path until it reaches a suitable peripheral outlet from which it is ejected. This spiral movement, free and undisturbed and essentially dependent on the properties of the fluid, permitting it to adjust itself to natural paths or stream lines and to change its velocity and direction by insensible degrees, is a characteristic and essential feature of this principle of operation.

While traversing the chamber inclosing the runner, the particles of the fluid may complete one or more turns, or but a part of one turn, the path followed being capable of close calculation and graphic representation, but fairly accurate estimates of turns can be obtained simply by determining the number of revolutions required to renew the fluid passing through the chamber and multiplying it by the ratio between the mean speed of the fluid and that of the disks. I have found that the quantity of fluid propelled in this manner, is, other conditions being equal, approximately proportionate to the active surface of the runner and to its effective speed. For this reason, the performance of such machines augments at an exceedingly high rate with the increase of their size and speed of revolution.

The dimensions of the device as a whole, and the spacing of the disks in any given machine will be determined by the conditions and requirements of special cases. It may be stated that the intervening distance should be the greater, the larger the diameter of the disks, the longer the spiral path of the fluid and the greater its viscosity. In general, the spacing should be such that the entire mass of the fluid, before leaving the runner, is accelerated to a nearly uniform velocity, not much below that of the periphery of the disks under normal working conditions, and almost equal to it when the outlet is closed and the particles move in concentric circles.

Considering now the converse of the above described operation and assuming that fluid under pressure be allowed to pass through the valve at the side of the solid arrow, the runner will be set in rotation in a clockwise direction, the fluid traveling in a spiral path and with continuously diminishing velocity until it reaches the orifices **14** and **20**, through which it is discharged. If the runner be allowed to turn freely, in nearly frictionless bearings, its rim will attain a speed closely approximating the maximum of that of the adjacent fluid and the spiral path of the particles will be comparatively long, consisting of many almost circular turns. If load is put on and the runner slowed down, the motion of the fluid is retarded, the turns are reduced, and the path is shortened.

Owing to a number of causes affecting the performance, it is difficult to frame a precise rule which would be generally applicable, but it may be stated that within certain limits, and other conditions being the same, the torque is directly proportionate to the square of the velocity of the fluid relatively to the runner and to the effective area of the disks and, inversely, the distance separating them. The machine will, generally, perform its maximum work when the effective speed of the runner is one-half of that of the fluid; but to attain the highest economy, the relative speed or slip, for any given performance should be as small as possible. This condition may be to any desired degree approximated by increasing the active area of and reducing the space between the disks.

When apparatus of the kind described is employed for the transmission of power certain departures from similarity between transmitter and receiver are necessary for securing the best results. It is evident that, when transmitting power from one shaft to another by such machines, any desired ratio between the speeds of rotation may be obtained by a proper selection of the diameters of the disks, or by suitably staging the transmitter, the receiver or both. But it may be pointed out that in one respect, at least, the two machines are essentially different. In the pump, the radial or static pressure, due to centrifugal force, is added to the tangential or dynamic, thus increasing the effective head and assisting in the expulsion of the fluid. In the motor, on the contrary, the first named pressure, being opposed to that of supply, reduces the effective head and the velocity of radial flow toward the center. Again, in the propelled machine a great torque is always desirable, this calling for an increased number of disks and smaller distance of separation, while in the propelling machine, for numerous economic reasons, the rotary effort should be the smallest and the speed the greatest practicable. Many other considerations, which will naturally suggest themselves, may affect the design and construction, but the preceding is thought to contain all necessary information in this regard.

In order to bring out a distinctive feature, assume, in the first place, that the motive medium is admitted to the disk chamber through a port, that is a channel which it traverses with nearly uniform velocity. In this case, the machine will operate as a rotary engine, the fluid continuously expanding on its tortuous path to the central outlet. The expansion takes place chiefly along the spiral path, for the spread inward is opposed by the centrifugal force due to the velocity of whirl and by the great resistance to radial exhaust. It is to be observed that the resistance to the passage of the fluid between the plates is, approximately, proportionate to the square of the relative speed, which is maximum in the direction toward the center and equal to the full tangential velocity of the fluid. The path of least resistance, necessarily taken in obedience to a universal law of motion is, virtually, also that of least relative velocity. Next, assume that the fluid is admitted to the disk chamber not through a port, but a diverging nozzle, a device converting wholly or in part, the expansive into velocity-energy. The machine will then work rather like a turbine, absorbing the energy of kinetic momentum of the particles as they whirl, with continuously decreasing speed, to the exhaust.

The above description of the operation, I may add, is suggested by experience and observation, and is advanced merely for the purpose of explanation. The undeniable fact is that the machine does operate, both expansively and impulsively. When the expansion in the nozzles is complete, or nearly so, the fluid pressure in the peripheral clearance space is small; as the nozzle is made less divergent and its section enlarged, the pressure rises, finally approximating that of the supply. But the transition from purely impulsive to expansive action may not be continuous throughout, on account of critical states and conditions and comparatively great variations of pressure may be caused by small changes of nozzle velocity.

In the preceding it has been assumed that the pressure of supply is constant or continuous, but it will be understood that the operation will be, essentially the same if the pressure be fluctuating or intermittent, as that due to explosions occurring in more or less rapid succession.

A very desirable feature, characteristic of machines constructed and operated in accordance with this invention, is their capability of reversal of rotation. **Fig. 1**, while illustrative of a special case, may be regarded as typical in this respect. If the right hand valve be shut off and the fluid supplied through the second pipe, the runner is rotated in the direction of the dotted arrow, the operation, and also the performance remaining the same as before, the central ring being bored to a circle with-this purpose in view. The same result may be obtained in many other ways by specially designed valves, ports or nozzles for reversing the flow, the description of which is omitted here in the interest of simplicity and clearness. For the same reasons but one operative port or nozzle is illustrated which might be adapted to a volute but does not fit best a circular bore. It will be understood that a number of suitable inlets may be provided around the periphery of the runner to improve the action and that the construction of the machine may be modified in many ways.

Still another valuable and probably unique quality of such motors or prime movers may be described. By proper construction and observance of working conditions the centrifugal pressure, opposing the passage of the fluid, may, as already indicated, be made nearly equal to the pressure of supply when the machine is running idle. If the inlet section be large, small changes in the speed of revolution will produce great differences in flow which are further enhanced by the concomitant variations in the length of the spiral path. A self-regulating machine is thus obtained bearing a striking resemblance to a direct-current electric motor in this respect that, with great differences of impressed pressure in a wide open channel the flow of the fluid through the same is prevented by virtue of rotation. Since the centrifugal head increases as the square of the revolutions, or even more rapidly, and with modern high grade steel great peripheral velocities are practicable, it is possible to attain that condition in a single stage machine, more readily if the runner be of large diameter. Obviously this problem is facilitated by compounding, as will be understood by those skilled in the art. Irrespective of its bearing on economy, this tendency which is, to a degree, common to motors of the above description, is of special advantage in the operation of large units, as it affords a safeguard against running away and destruction. Besides these, such a prime mover possesses many other advantages, both constructive and operative. It is simple, light and compact, subject to but little wear, cheap and exceptionally easy to manufacture as small clearances and accurate milling work are not essential to good performance. In operation it is reliable, there being no valves, sliding contacts or troublesome vanes. It is almost free of windage, largely independent of nozzle efficiency and suitable for high as well as for low fluid velocities and speeds of revolution.

It will be understood that the principles of construction and operation above generally set forth, are capable of embodiment in machines of the most widely different forms, and adapted for the greatest variety of purposes. In my present specification I have sought to describe and explain only the general and typical applications of the principle which I believe I am the first to realize and turn to useful account.

What I claim is:

1. A machine adapted to be propelled by a fluid consisting in the combination with a casing having inlet and outlet ports at the peripheral and central portions, respectively, of a rotor having plane spaced surfaces between which the fluid may flow in natural spirals and by adhesive and viscous action impart its energy of movement to the rotor, as described.

2. A machine adapted to be propelled by a fluid, comprising a rotor composed of a plurality of plane spaced disks mounted on a shaft and open at or near the same, an inclosing casing with a peripheral inlet or inlets, in the plane of the disks, and an outlet or outlets in its central portion, as described.

3. A rotary engine adapted to be propelled by adhesive and viscous action of a continuously expanding fluid comprising in combination a casing forming a chamber, an inlet or inlets tangential to the periphery of the same, and an outlet or outlets in its central portion, with a rotor composed of spaced disks mounted on a shaft, and open at or near the same, as described.

4. A machine adapted to be propelled by fluid, consisting in the combination of a plurality of disks mounted on a shaft and open at or near the same, and an inclosing casing with ports or passages of inlet and outlet at the peripheral and central portions, respectively, the disks being spaced to form passages through which the fluid may flow, under the combined influence of radial and tangential forces, in a natural spiral path from the periphery toward the axis of the disks, and impart its energy of movement to the same by its adhesive and viscous action thereon, as set forth.

5. A machine adapted to be propelled by a fluid comprising in combination a plurality of spaced disks rotatably mounted and having plane surfaces, an inclosing casing and ports or passages of inlet and outlet adjacent to the periphery and center of the disks, respectively, as set forth.

6. A machine adapted to be propelled by a fluid comprising in combination a runner composed of a plurality of disks having plane surfaces and mounted at intervals on a central shaft, and formed with openings near their centers, and means for admitting the propelling fluid into the spaces between the disks at the periphery and discharging it at the center of the same, as set forth.

7. A thermo-dynamic converter, comprising in combination a series of rotatably mounted spaced disks with plane surfaces, an inclosing casing, inlet ports at the peripheral portion and outlet ports leading from the central portion of the same, as set forth.

8. A thermo-dynamic converter, comprising in combination a series of rotatably mounted spaced disks with plane surfaces and having openings adjacent to their central portions, an inclosing casing, inlet ports in the peripheral portion, and outlet ports leading from the central portion of the same as set forth.

In testimony whereof I affix my signature in the presence of two subscribing witnesses.

NIKOLA TESLA.

Witnesses:

M. LAWSON DYER,

WM BOHLEBER

N. TESLA.
SPEED INDICATOR.
APPLICATION FILED MAY 29, 1914.

1,209,359.   Patented Dec. 19, 1916.

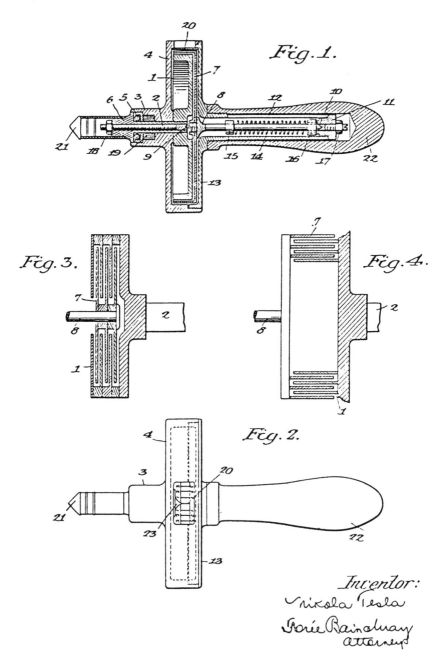

Fig. 1.

Fig. 3.

Fig. 4.

Fig. 2.

Inventor:
Nikola Tesla
Rosie Bainchnay
attorney

United States Patent   **December 19, 1916**

SPEED INDICATOR
1,329,559

Application filed May 29, 1914.   Serial No. 841,726.

NIKOLA TESLA, OF NEW YORK, N. Y., ASSIGNOR TO WALTHAM
WATCH COMPANY, OF WALTHAM, MASSACHUSETTS,
A CORPORATION OF MASSACHUSETTS.

To all whom it may concern:

Be it known that I, Nikola Tesla, a citizen of the United States, residing at New York, in the county and State of New York, have invented certain new and useful Improvements in Speed-Indicators, of which the following is a full, clear, and exact description.

In the provision of speed indicators, that give direct readings of rate of motion,—for example shaft speeds in terms of revolutions per minute or vehicle speeds in miles per hour—it is obviously important that the instrument be simple, inexpensive and durable, and that its indications be correct throughout a wide range of speed. Likewise it is very desirable that its operation shall be subject to little or no appreciable deviation from accuracy under normal or expected extraneous changes, such as those of atmospheric density, temperature, or magnetic influence, in order that the structure may be free from any complications incident to the employment of specific means compensating for such varying conditions.

My present invention supplies a speed measuring appliance amply satisfying commercial demands as above stated, in a structure wherein the adhesion and viscosity of a gaseous medium, preferably air, is utilized for torque-transmission between the driving and driven members.

More particularly, my invention provides a rotatable primary and a mechanically resistant or biased pivoted secondary element, cooperating through an intervening fluid medium to produce, inherently, without the use of compensating instrumentalities, angular displacements of the secondary element in linear proportion to the rate of rotation of the primary, so that the reading scale may be uniformly graduated. This latter advantage is secured through the application of novel principles, discovered by me, which will be presently elucidated.

In investigating the effects of fluids in motion upon rotative systems I have observed that under certain conditions to be hereafter defined, the drag or turning effort exerted by the fluid is exactly proportionate to its velocity relative to the system. This I have found to be true of gaseous and liquid media, with the distinction however, that the limits within which the law holds good are narrower for the latter, especially so when the specific gravity or the viscosity of the liquid is great.

Having determined the conditions under which the law of proportionality of torque to speed (rather than to the square of the speed or to some higher exponential function of the same) holds good, I have applied my discoveries in the production of new devices—essentially indicators of speed but having wider fields of use—which are, in many aspects, superior to other forms of speedometers.

Specifically I have devised rate-of-motion indicators which comprise driving and driven members with confronting, closely-adjacent, noncontacting, smooth, annular surfaces of large area, coacting in the transmission of torque through the viscosity and adhesion of interposed thin films of air,—mechanical structures offering numerous constructive and operative advantages. Furthermore, by properly designing and coordinating the essential elements of such instruments I have secured substantial linear proportionality between the deflections of the indicating or secondary element and the rate of rotation of the driving or primary member.

The conditions more or less indispensable for this most perfect embodiment of my invention—that is to say, embodiment in a speed indicator approximating rigorous linear proportionality of deflection to speed—are:

1. The arrangement should be such that the exchange of fluid acting on the system is effectively prevented or minimized. If new fluid were permitted to pass freely between the elements there would be, as in a pump, with the rise and fall of velocity, corresponding changes of quantity and the torque would not vary directly as the speed, but as an exponential function of the same. Broadly speaking, such provision as is commonly made in hydraulic brakes for free circulation of fluid with respect to the rotative system, with the attendant acceleration and retardation of the flow, will generally produce a torque varying as the square of the speed, subject however, in practice, to influences which may cause it to change according to still higher powers. For this reason confinement of the fluid intervening between the primary and secondary elements of the system so that such active, torque-transmitting medium may remain resident, and not be constantly renewed, is vital to complete attainment of the desired linear proportionality.

2. The spaces or channels inclosing the active medium should be as narrow as practicable, although within limits this is relative, the range of effective separation increasing with the diameter of the juxtaposed rotative surfaces.

My observations have established that when the spacing is so wide as to accommodate local spiral circulation in the resident fluid between the confronting area, marked departures from rigorous proportionality of torque to speed occur. Therefore in small instruments with primary members of but few inches diameter, it is desirable that the channels should be as narrow as is mechanically feasible with due regard to the importance of maintaining the noncontacting relation of the rotative parts.

3. The velocity of the fluid relative to the system should be as small as the circumstances of the case will permit. When a gas such as air is the active medium, it may be 100 feet per second or even more, but with liquids speeds of that order cannot be used without detriment.

4. The bodies exposed to the action of the fluid should be symmetrically shaped and with smooth surfaces, devoid or corners or projections which give rise to destructive eddies that are particularly hurtful.

5. The system should be so shaped and disposed that no part of the moving fluid except that contained in the spaces or channels can effect materially the torque. If this rule is not observed the accuracy of the instrument may be impaired to an appreciable degree, for even though torque transmission between the confronting surfaces is proportional, there may yet be a component of the rotary effort (through the fluid coacting with the external surfaces) proportional to an exponential function of the speed. Hence it is desirable that by a closely investing casing, or other means, the torque-transmitting effect of fluid outside of the channels between the rotative parts be minimized.

6. In general the flow of the medium should be calm and entirely free from all turbulent action. As soon as there is a break of continuity the law above stated is violated and the indications of the device cease to be rigorously precise.

These requirements can be readily fulfilled and the above discoveries applied to a great many valuable uses, as for indicating the speed of rotation or translation, respectively, of a shaft, or a vehicle, such as an automobile, locomotive, boat or aerial vessel; for determining the velocity of a fluid in motion; for measuring the quantity of flow in steam, air, gas, water or oil supply; for ascertaining the frequency of mechanical and electrical impulses or oscillations; for determining physical constants; and for numerous other purposes of scientific and practical importance.

The nature and object of the invention will be clearly understood from the succeeding description with reference to the accompanying drawings in which:

Figure 1 represents a vertical cross section of a speed indicator or hand tachometer embodying the above principles; **Fig. 2** is a horizontal view of the instrument disclosing part of the scale, and **Figs.** 3 and 4 are diagrammatic illustrations showing modified constructions of the main parts in a similar device.

Referring to **Fig. 1**, 1 is a pulley-shaped metal disk from three to four inches in diameter constituting the freely-rotatable primary element. It is fastened to a drive-shaft 2 which is turned to fit a hole in the central hub 3 of the casting 4. A ball bearing 5 set in a recess of the former, serves to take up the thrust against the shoulder 6 of the shaft and insures free running of the same. In close proximity to the disk 1 is the thin shell 7 in the form of a cup, this being the secondary element of the system. It is made of stiff and light material, as hard aluminum, and is fixed to a spindle 8, supported in nearly frictionless bearings or pivots 9 and 10. As before remarked the spacing between the two elements, (1 and 7), should best be as small as manufacturing conditions may make feasible. By way of example, a separation,— in an instrument of the diameter suggested,—of say .015" to .025" will be found effective for working purposes and also within a reasonable range of inexpensive mechanical attainment. Still smaller spacing is, however, theoretically desirable. One of the bearings aforesaid is screwed into the end of a slotted tubular extension 12 of a casting 13. The running bearing in the shaft, though not of perceptible influence on the indications, may be replaced by a stationary support behind and close to shell 7, as at 8. A torsional spring 14 is provided, for biasing the pivoted element 7, having its ends held in collars 15 and 16, which can be clamped, as by the set screws shown, the one to the spindle 8 and the other to the plug 11. The bearings 9 and 10 are capable of longitudinal adjustment and can be locked in any position by check nuts 17, and 18, but this refinement is generally unnecessary. The casting 4 and 13, in the construction specifically shown, when screwed together form a casing that closely invests the rotative system. This casing forms one available means for preventing communication of torque from the primary element 1 to the secondary member 7 through the medium contacting with the external surfaces of both, to any extent sufficient for materially modifying the torque due to the films between the elements, but other means to this end may be substituted. The chamber inclosed within the casting should be airtight for highest accuracy in order that the density of the contained medium may remain constant, although in the vast majority of cases where air is used as the active agent, the slight effects of ordinary changes of temperature and density of the external atmosphere can be ignored, as they are in a measure neutralized by the concomitant variations in the resilience of the torsional spring and as they do not seriously affect the proportionality of deflections observed. However, when great precision is essential, a seal 19 of suitable packing, paste or amalgam may be employed. Obviously the working parts may be contained in a separate, perfectly tight reservoir filled with fluid of any desired character, the rotating member or disk 1 being driven by a magnet outside. This expedient has been adopted in numerous instances and is quite familiar. The casting **4** has a window or opening **20**, closed by a piece of transparent substance, such as celluloid, for enabling the readings to be made on the scale which is engraved upon or glued to the rim of the indication-controlling element or shell **7**. The shaft **2** is armed with a steel or rubber tip **21**, and a handle **22** of fiber or other material is fastened to the central hub of casting **13**, completing the hand tachometer.

Fig. 2 in which like numbers designate corresponding parts is self-explanatory.

Attention may be called to the pointed index **23** placed in the opening **20** and marking, when the instrument is not in use, zero on the scale. The latter can be readily put in proper position by turning the collar **16** to the desired angle.

As described the device is adapted for use in the manner of an ordinary hand tachometer. In taking the revolutions of a shaft, the tip **21** is placed firmly into the central cavity of the former, as usual, with the result of entraining the disk **1** and bringing it to full speed by friction. The active medium, preferably air, in the narrow channels between the rotating and pivoted members, by virtue of its adhesion and viscosity, is set in circular motion by the primary element, and, giving up the momentum imparted to it on the light secondary shell **7**, causes the latter to turn until the torque exerted is balanced by the retractile force of spring **14**. Care should be taken to employ a spring the resistance of which increases linearly with displacement, so that the deflections are exactly proportionate to the torsional effect, as otherwise the indications will not be true to scale, even though the instrument be perfect in other respects. In order that the torque should vary rigorously as the speed, the fluid particles in the minute channels between the rotating and pivoted members should move in circles and not in spirals, as necessarily would be the case in a device in which pumping action could take place, and either by making both the primary and secondary elements effectively-imperforate to prevent central admission of air, or otherwise so constructed and conditioned that air may not freely pass from center to periphery between the elements of the moving system unchanging residence of a definite body of the active medium within the system is insured. Where pumping action,—that is to say, acceleration or retardation of fluid movement other than circularly with the primary element,—takes place the deflections increase more rapidly than the speed. It follows that centrifugal force, which is the essential active principle in pumping, must be negligible to avoid compression of the air at the periphery which might result in a sensibly increased torque. To appreciate this, it should be borne in mind that the resistance of a circular strip of the active area would, under such conditions, be proportionate to the fourth power of the diameter so that a slight compression and attendant increase of density of the medium in the peripheral portion would cause a noticeable departure from rigorous proportionality. Experience has demonstrated that when the space is very narrow, as is indispensable for the fullest attainment of the desired proportionality, the centrifugal effect of the active fluid, be it gaseous or liquid, is so small as to be unobservable. The inference is that the actions in the narrow space between the rotative members are capillary or molecular and wholly different in principle from those taking place in a pumping device in which the fluid masses are alternately retarded and accelerated. The scale, which, as will be apparent from the preceding, is uniform in an instrument best embodying my invention, may be so graduated that each degree corresponds to a certain number of revolutions per unit of time, and for convenience, (in shaft-speed indicators as herein shown), the constant is made a round number, as 100. The establishment of this relation through the adjustment of the torsional spring is facilitated by varying the distance between the parts **1** and **7**, thus modifying the torque and consequently the deflection, (the torque varying inversely as the distance) while always keeping within the range throughout which linear proportionality is attainable. In calibrating it is necessary to make but one observation comparative with some positive standard and to plot the balance of the scale accordingly. The conditions above set forth being realized, the reading will be accurately proportionate to the speed and the constant will be correct through the whole range contemplated in the design. Therein lies a very important advantage bearing on manufacture and introduction of devices of this character over those now in use which are based on an empirical scale, tedious to prepare, and unreliable. When desired, the instrument may be rendered dead beat through magnetic or mechanical damping, but by making the torque very great, and the inertia of the secondary element very small, such objectionable complication may be avoided. With a given separation the turning effort is proportionate to the product of the velocity of rotation, the density of the fluid and the aggregate area of the active surfaces, hence by increasing either of these factors the torsion can be augmented at will. It obviously follows that the pull exerted on a circular disk will be as the third power of the diameter and one way of attaining the object is to use a large plate. Other and better ways are illustrated in **Fig. 3** and **4** in which the rotating and pivoted elements are composed of interleaved disks or cylinders. The first arrangement permits an indefinite increase of the torque, the second commends itself through the facility of adjustment of the force by varying the active area.

For many reasons it is decidedly advantageous to employ air as the agent in an instrument intended for popular purposes, especially those involving rough use and inexpert handling, since thereby the cost of manufacture may be kept low, the need for ensealing minimized and susceptibility of the parts to easy disassembling and replacement attained. It is, therefore, desirable that the annular confronting surface of the elements,— whether of disk or cylindrical form,—be sufficiently extensive for securing ample torque to make the instrument approximately dead beat and to minimize the percentage of error due to mechanical imperfections.

The foregoing description contains, I believe, all the information necessary for enabling an expert to carry my invention into successful practice. When using the indicator in the manner of an ordinary vehicle speedometer, as in an automobile, the shaft 2 is rigidly or flexibly geared to the driving axle or other suitable part and readings are made in miles per hour, as is customary. As will be apparent many other valuable uses may be served, since the primary element may be connected in suitable electrical or mechanical manner with any rotating part, the speed of which may be translated through a linearly proportionate constant into the desired terms of time and quantity, and the reading scale may be calibrated in such terms. It will also be evident that by accurate workmanship, following the teachings of my invention, instruments at once simple, rugged, and scientifically accurate may be constructed for a very wide range of uses in either huge or tiny sizes; and, since the commercial requirements of accuracy in many fields gives a reasonable range of permissive error, manufacturing considerations may lead to deviations from strict observance of some of the conditions that I have indicated as best attaining a rigorous proportionality of reading. The provision of simple mechanical elements, cooperating primarily only through the viscosity and adhesiveness of the air films intervening therebetween and substantially free from need for ensealing and from error caused by changes of extraneous conditions, especially temperature, affords striking commercial advantages unattainable in any form of speedometer of which I am aware. Therefore while I have described in detail for the purpose of full disclosure a specific and highly advantageous embodiment of my invention, it will be understood that wide variations in the mechanical development thereof may be made without departure from its spirit within the scope of the appended claims.

What I claim is:

1. In combination, fixed supporting means, disconnected aligned driving and driven shafts rotatably mounted in said supporting means, relatively thin spaced rigid pieces of material rigidly connected to and arranged coaxially about said driven shaft with broad surfaces opposite each other, and other relatively thin spaced rigid pieces of material rigidly connected to and arranged coaxially with the driving shaft, and being alternated with the first-mentioned pieces between them and having their broad surfaces adjacent to and spaced from the broad surfaces of said other pieces, said pieces all arranged in air, through which torque is frictionally transmitted from the second-mentioned pieces to those first-mentioned.

2. In combination, in a speedometer, disconnected aligned driving and driven shafts, a fixed support, said shafts being mounted in said support, a coiled spring having one end secured to said fixed support and the other end secured to said driven shaft, relatively thin spaced rigid pieces of material rigidly connected to and arranged coaxially with the driving shaft, and being alternated between said first-mentioned pieces and spaced therefrom, and an air body filling the spaces between said pieces and constituting the torque-transmitting friction medium therebetween.

3. In combination, in a speedometer, disconnected aligned driving and driven shafts, a frame having bearings for said shafts, a coiled spring whose inner end is secured to said driven shaft and having its outer end secured to said frame, spaced rigid pieces of material rigidly connected to and arranged about said driven shaft, and other spaced rigid pieces of material rigidly connected to and arranged about said driving shaft, the former pieces being alternated between the latter pieces in spaced relation with their broad surfaces in close juxtaposition, and with the interspaces between said spaced pieces forming a convoluted air-containing channel therebetween open to the surrounding air.

4. In combination, disconnected aligned driving and driven shafts, a fixed support, bearings therefor in said support, a coiled spring having one end secured to the driven shaft and its other end secured to said fixed support, a cup-shaped body secured to one end of said driving shaft coaxially, spaced rigid relatively thin plates secured to said body in parallel relation to each other, another cup-shaped body secured coaxially to said driven shaft and inclosing said plates at their outer edges in spaced relation thereto, other spaced rigid relatively thin plates secured to the second-mentioned body and extending between the first-mentioned body and extending between the first-mentioned plates in spaced relation thereto, and an air body filling the spaces between said pieces frictionally to transmit torque from the driving structure to the driven structure.

5. The combination with means for support and driving and driven shafts rotatably supported thereby, of means to transmit torque from the driving shaft to the driven shaft comprising opposed material pieces respectively connected with the driving shaft and the driven shaft and arranged to present toward each other relatively-extensive, non-contacting, closely-adjacent surfaces, and a gaseous medium in which said pieces work, said gaseous medium serving frictionally to connect the said opposed material-pieces for transmission of torque from the driving shaft to the driven shaft.

6. In combination, driving and driven elements suitably supported and having confronted annuli always presenting to each other relatively-extensive, non-contacting, closely-adjacent surfaces, said surfaces disposed in a gaseous friction medium, whereby the driving member, by its rotation, induces rotary motion of the driven member through the drag of the gaseous medium intervening between said annuli.

7. In combination, driving and driven elements having in opposed, closely adjacent, non-contacting relation, relatively extensive friction surfaces, and an interposed gaseous body, through which the driving member frictionally drags the driven element.

8. In a speedometer, the combination with supporting means, separately-rotatable driving and driven shafts mounted therein, biasing means for the driven shaft, and means to indicate rotary displacement of the biased shaft in terms of speed, of pieces rotatively carried by said respective shafts, having relatively-extensive, non-contacting, closely-adjacent surfaces arranged to confront each other, and a gaseous medium intervening between said confronting surfaces to coact therewith frictionally to transmit torque from the driving shaft to the biased driven shaft.

9. In a speedometer, the combination of a primary element rotatable at varying speeds, having a plurality of spaced annuli, a biased secondary element, arranged for separate rotary movement and adapted and arranged to indicate speed variations by the extent of its displacement, said secondary element having a plurality of spaced, thin, light annuli, the annuli of said two elements interleaved in non-contacting, closely-adjacent relation always to present toward each other extensive friction surfaces, and an air body, through the films of which, intervening between said annuli, rotation of the primary element may induce speed-indicating displacement of the secondary element.

10. A speedometer wherein a primary, variable-speed element, and a biased, speed-indication-controlling secondary element, that are suitably supported for separate movement, have opposed extensive friction surfaces in non-contacting juxtaposition for frictional communication of power from the primary element to the secondary element through a gaseous medium that intervenes between said friction surfaces.

11. An air drag speedometer, wherein a primary, variable-speed element and a biased speed-indication-controlling secondary element, that are suitably mounted for separate rotary movement in an air-containing casing, have opposed, extensive friction-surfaces in non-contacting juxtaposition, for frictional communication of torque from the primary element to the secondary element through the medium of the casing contained air.

12. In a speedometer, the combination of an air containing casing, a primary element and a secondary element mounted in said casing for separate movement, said elements having extensive surfaces exposed toward each other in closely contiguous but non-contacting relation for frictional communication of power to one from the other through the intervening air, means resiliently to resist displacement of the secondary element, and means to indicate displacement of the secondary element in terms of speed.

13. In combination, in a speedometer, disconnected shafts respectively carrying driving and driven elements that have annuli affording continuous extensive friction surfaces in always confronting non-contacting closely - spaced relation, the driven element being light and biased by a light spring, for ready response to torque transmitted frictionally by air, and the air film-spaces between the elements constituting an open tortuous channel; and an air containing casing inclosing the driving and driven elements, its contained air body forming the sole effective means of torque transmission between the elements.

14. In a speedometer, the combination of rotatable driving and driven elements having in opposed, closely-adjacent non-contacting relation, relatively extensive friction surfaces, means to bias the driven element, means to indicate rotary displacement of said driven element in terms of speed, a casing inclosing said elements and containing air, said contained air body extending in films between the friction surfaces, and forming the sole effective means of torque transmission between the driving and driven elements.

15. In combination, driving and driven elements having in opposed non-contacting relation relatively extensive friction surfaces so closely adjacent that through an interposed gaseous body the driving member frictionally drags the driven member with a torque linearly proportionate to the speed of the former.

16. A rate indicator wherein a freely-rotatable primary and a biased, indication-controlling secondary member, suitably supported for separate movement, have opposed, non-contacting surfaces in such close proximity that through an intervening viscous fluid medium torque is transmitted to the secondary member in linear proportion to the speed of the primary.

17. A rate indicator wherein a freely rotatable primary and a biased, indication-controlling secondary element, suitably supported for separate movement are operatively linked through an intervening viscous and adhesive air body, said elements having opposed, extensive non-contacting surfaces so closely adjacent that the torque transmitted to the secondary element through said air body is substantially in linear proportion to the speed of the primary element.

18. In a speed indicator the combination of two rotatively movable driving and driven members having opposed non-contacting extensive surfaces confining between them a practically constant body of torque-transmitting fluid medium, said surfaces being so closely proximate that the torque transmitted from the driving to the driven member is substantially proportional to the rate of rotation of the former.

19. A speed indicator comprising, in combination, a rotatable body, a second angularly movable body, means to resist displacement of the latter proportionately to the torque applied thereto, and a fluid medium interposed between them, said bodies having opposed annular surfaces in such close proximity that pumping of the medium therebetween is prevented and the deflections of the second body are made proportionate to the speed of the other.

20. A speed indicator, comprising, in combination, a rotatable, variable speed primary element, and a light, pivoted, torsionally-resisted, indication-controlling secondary element, suitably mounted for separate movement and operatively linked with the former through an interposed gaseous medium, said elements having opposed, annular, non-contacting surfaces so extensive and closely proximate that the whirling medium exerts a strong and steady turning effort upon the secondary element, substantially in linear proportion to the speed of the primary.

21. The combination, in a rate indicator, of a freely rotatable primary and a torsionally-resisted indication controlling secondary member mounted for separate movement, with their opposed non-contacting symmetrical surfaces confining therebetween a resident fluid body and arranged in such close proximity that the fluid, entrained in circles by the rotating primary exerts a torque on the secondary member in substantially linear proportion to the speed of the former.

22. In combination, in a speed-indicator, a rotatable primary element, a biased secondary element, a fluid body between and around them, said elements having opposed non-contacting extensive surfaces in such close proximity that the resident fluid body therebetween transmits torque to the secondary in substantially linear proportion to the speed of the primary element, and means for minimizing the rotary effort transmitted through the fluid around the elements.

23. A rate indicator comprising a structure confining a substantially unchanging body of fluid and including an extensive annular surface of a freely rotatable member, arranged to impart circular motion to the fluid, and a confronting annular surface of an indication-controlling angularly-displaceable member, arranged to take up momentum of the fluid, said surfaces being so closely proximate that the torque transmitted through the fluid is proportional to the speed of the rotatable member.

24. A speed indicator comprising two elements mounted for separate movement in a fluid medium, one of the elements being freely rotatable at varying speeds, and the other pivoted and biased against angular displacement, said elements having opposed non-contacting extensive symmetrical surfaces in such close proximity that torque is transmitted through the intervening fluid body in substantially linear proportion to the speed of the primary element, and a member surrounding said elements and minimizing the flow of the fluid along the exterior surfaces of said secondary element.

25. In a device of the character described, the combination of a rotatable primary element, a spring-biased secondary element, a casing surrounding the same and a fluid body filling the casing, said elements having opposed non-contacting annular surfaces in such close proximity that the rotary effort exerted through the fluid body on the secondary element is proportionate to the speed of the primary element, some parts of said casing being so closely proximate to said elements as to minimize torque-transmitting flow of the fluid along the exterior surfaces of the secondary element.

26. An air drag speedometer wherein a rotatable primary variable-speed element, mounted for separate movement in an air-containing casing, have opposed extensive smooth annular surfaces in such close juxtaposition that torque is transmitted through the air intervening between said surfaces in substantially linear proportion to the speed of the rotatable primary element.

27. A speed indicator comprising a closed fluid-filled casing, primary and secondary elements mounted therein, the one for rotation and the other for torsionally resisted angular displacement, said elements having opposed non-contacting extensive annular surfaces forming therebetween a smooth intervening channel wherein confined fluid may move in circles under the influence of the primary member, and between them and the interior surfaces of the casing surrounding channels wherein fluid contiguous to the secondary element may receive circular movement from the primary element, said surfaces being so closely proximate that torque transmission through the fluid is linearly proportionate to the speed of the primary element.

28. The combination, in a speed indicator, of a closed casing, a fluid body and two rotatively-movable members therein, means for rotating one of the members, means for resisting displacement of the other, and means controlled by the last named member for reading its displacement in terms of speed, said two members having opposed, non-contacting imperforate annular surfaces in such close proximity as to confine there-between a film of fluid through which torque is transmitted to the resistant member in linear proportionality to the speed of the rotatable member.

29. The combination with a closed fluid containing casing, of a plurality of symmetrical bodies with smooth surfaces rotatably mounted therein, means for torsionally restraining some of said bodies, and means for rotating the other, said bodies being placed with their surfaces in such close proximity to each other and to the walls of the casing that the rotating bodies will cause an even and undisturbed circular motion of the fluid and transmit torque to the torsionally restrained bodies in proportion to the speed of the others.

30. In a speed measuring instrument, the combination of driving and driven members having in opposed closely adjacent non-contacting relation relatively extensive smooth friction surfaces, and an interposed gaseous body through which the driving member frictionally drags the driven member.

31. A tachometer comprising, in combination, a rotatably mounted shaft, a smooth annular body fixed thereto, a similar pivoted body, a torsion spring for the latter, indicating means movable with said pivoted body, and an air-containing casing, said bodies having their annular surfaces in such close, non-contacting proximity that the intervening air transmits torque to the pivoted body in substantially linear proportion to the speed of the rotatable body.

32. A tachometer comprising, in combination, a rotatably mounted shaft, a primary element carried thereby, a pivoted secondary element, a torsion spring therefor permitting its angular displacement substantially in proportion to the torque, indicating means operated by the pivoted element and graduated with substantial uniformity, and a fluid-containing casing closely investing part of said rotative system, the opposed surfaces of the elements being so closely proximate to each other and to part of the casing that the fluid-transmitted torque causing deflections of the pivoted body is substantially proportionate to the speed of the primary element.

In testimony whereof I affix my signature in the presence of two subscribing witnesses

NIKOLA TESLA

Witnesses:

M. Lawson Dyer,

Thomas J. Byrne.

N. TESLA.

VALVULAR CONDUIT.

APPLICATION FILED FEB. 21, 1916. RENEWED JULY 8, 1919.

1,329,559.

Patented Feb. 3, 1920.

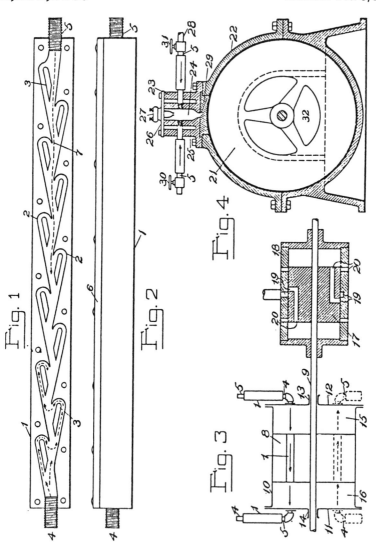

INVENTOR

Nikola Tesla

BY

Kerr, Page, Cooper & Hayward

ATTORNEY

United States Patent   **February 3, 1920**

VALVULAR CONDUIT

1,329,559

Application filed February 21, 1916.   Serial No. 79,703.

To all whom it may concern:

Be it known that I, Nikola Tesla, a citizen of the United States, residing at New York, in the county and State of New York, have invented certain new and useful Improvements in Valvular Conduits, of which the following is a full, clear, and exact description.

In most of the machinery universally employed for the development, transmission and transformation of mechanical energy, fluid impulses are made to pass, more or less freely, through suitable channels or conduits in one direction while their return is effectively checked or entirely prevented. This function is generally performed by devices designated as valves, comprising carefully fitted members the precise relative movements of which are essential to the efficient and reliable operation of the apparatus. The necessity of, and absolute dependence on these, limits the machine in many respects, detracting from its practical value and adding greatly to its cost of manufacture and maintenance. As a rule the valve is a delicate contrivance, very liable to wear and get out of order and thereby imperil ponderous, complex and costly mechanism and, moreover, it fails to meet the requirements when the impulses are extremely sudden or rapid in succession and the fluid is highly heated or corrosive.

Though these and other correlated facts were known to the very earliest pioneers in the science and art of mechanics, no remedy has yet been found or proposed to date so far as I am aware, and I believe that I am the first to discover or invent any means, which permit the performance of the above function without the use of moving parts, and which it is the object of this application to describe.

Briefly expressed, the advance I have achieved consists in the employment of a peculiar channel or conduit characterized by valvular action.

The invention can be embodied in many constructions greatly varied in detail, but for the explanation of the underlying principle it may be broadly stated that the interior of the conduit is provided with enlargements, recesses, projections, baffles or buckets which, while offering virtually no resistance to the passage of the fluid in one direction, other than surface friction, constitute an almost impassable barrier to its flow in the opposite sense by reason of the more or less sudden expansions, contractions, deflections, reversals of direction, stops and starts and attendant rapidly succeeding transformations of the pressure and velocity energies.

For the full and complete disclosure of the device and of its mode of action reference is made to the accompanying drawings in which
Figure 1 is a horizontal projection of such a valvular conduit with the top plate removed.

Fig. 2 is side view of the same in elevation.

Fig. 3 is a diagram illustrative of the application of the device to a fluid propelling machine such as, a reciprocating pump or compressor, and

Fig. 4 is a plan showing the manner in which the invention is, or may be used, to operate a fluid propelled rotary engine or turbine.

Referring to **Fig. 1**, **1** is a casing of metal or other suitable material which may be cast, milled or pressed from sheet in the desired form. From its side-walls extended alternatively projections terminating in buckets **2** which, to facilitate manufacture are congruent and spaced at equal distances, but need not be. In addition to these there are independent partitions **3** which are deemed of advantage and the purpose of which will be made clear. Nipples **4** and **5**, one at each end, are provided for pipe connection. The bottom is solid and the upper or open side is closed by a fitting plate **6** as shown in **Fig. 2**. When desired any number of such pieces may be joined in series, thus making up a valvular conduit of such length as the circumstances may require.

In elucidation of the mode of operation let it be assumed that the medium under pressure be admitted at **5**. Evidently, its approximate path will be as indicated by the dotted line **7**, which is nearly straight, that is to say, if the channel be of adequate cross-section, the fluid will encounter a very small resistance and pass through freely and undisturbed, at least to a degree. Not so if the entrance be at the opposite end **4**. In this case the flow will not be smooth and continues, but intermittent, the fluid being quickly deflected and reversed in direction, set in whirling motion, brought to rest and again accelerated, these processes following one another in rapid succession. The partitions **3** serve to direct the stream upon the buckets and to intensify the actions causing violent surges and eddies which interfere very materially with the flow through the conduit. It will be readily observed that the resistance offered to the passage of the medium will be considerable even if it be under constant pressure, but the impediments will be of full effect only when it is supplied in pulses and, more especially, when the same are extremely sudden and of high frequency. In order to bring the fluid masses to rest and to high velocity in short intervals of time energy must be furnished at a rate which is unattainable, the result being that the impulse cannot penetrate very far before it subsides and gives rise to movement in the opposite direction. The device not only acts as a hinderment to the bodily return of particles but also, in a measure, as a check to the propagation of a disturbance through the medium. Its efficacy is chiefly determined; first, by the magnitude of the ratio of the two resistances offered to disturbed and to undisturbed flow, respectively, in the directions from **4** to **5** and from **5** to **4**, in each individual element of the conduit; second, by the number of complete cycles of action taking place in a given length of the valvular channel and, third, by the character of the impulses themselves. A fair idea may be gained from simple theoretical considerations.

Examining more closely the mode of operation it will be seen that, in passing from one to the next bucket in the direction of disturbed flow, the fluid undergoes two complete reversals or deflections through 180 degrees while it suffers only two small deviations from about 10 to 20 degrees when moving in the opposite sense. In each case the loss of head will be proportionate to a hydraulic coefficient dependent on the angle of deflection from which it follows that, for the same velocity, the ratio of the two resistances will be as that of the two coefficients. The theoretical value of this ratio may be 200 or more, but must be taken as appreciably less although the surface friction too is greater in the direction of disturbed flow. In order to keep it as large as possible, sharp bends should be avoided, for these will add to both resistances and reduce the efficiency. When ever practicable, the piece should be straight; the next best is the circular form.

That the peculiar function of such a conduit is enhanced by increasing the number of buckets or elements and, consequently, cyclic processes in a given length is an obvious conclusion, but there is no direct proportionality because the successive actions diminish in intensity. Definite limits, however, are set constructively and otherwise to the number of elements per unit length of the channel, and the most economical design can only be evolved through long experience.

Quite apart from any mechanical features of the device the character of the impulses has a decided influence on its performance and the best results will be secured, when there are produced at **4**, sudden variations of pressure in relatively long intervals, while a constant pressure is maintained at **5**. Such is the case in one of its most valuable industrial applications which will be specifically described.

In order to conduce to a better understanding, reference may first be made to **Fig. 3** which illustrates another special use and in which **8** is a piston fixed to a shaft **9** and fitting freely in a cylinder **10**. The latter is closed at both ends by flanged heads **11** and **12** having sleeves or stuffing boxes **13** and **14** for the shaft. Connection between the two compartments, **15** and **16**, of the cylinder is established through a valvular conduit and each of the heads is similarly equipped. For the sake of simplicity these devices are diagrammatically shown, the solid arrows indicating the direction of undisturbed flow. An extension of the shaft **9** carries a second piston **17** accurately ground to and sliding easily in a cylinder **18** closed at the ends by plates and sleeves as usual. Both piston and cylinder are provided with inlet and outlet ports marked, respectively, **19** and **20**. This arrangement is familiar, being representative of a prime mover of my invention, termed **"mechanical oscillator"**, with which it is practicable to vibrate a system of considerable weight many thousand times per minute.

Suppose now that such rapid oscillations are imparted by this or other means to the piston **8**. Bearing in mind the proceeding, the operation of the apparatus will be understood at a glance. While moving in the direction of the solid arrow, from **12** to **11**, the piston **8** will compress the air or other medium in the compartment **16** and expel it from the same, the devices in the piston and head **11** acting, respectively, as closed and open valves. During the movement of the piston in the opposite direction, from **11** to **12**, the medium which has meanwhile filled the chamber **15** will be transferred to compartment **16**, egress being prevented by the device in head **12** and that in the piston allowing free passage. These processes will be repeated in very quick succession. If the nipples **4** and **5** are put in communication with independent reservoirs, the oscillations of the piston **8** will result in a compression of the air at **4** and rarefaction of the same at **5**. Obviously, the valvular channels being turned the other way, as indicated by dotted lines in the lower part of the figure, the opposite will take place. The devices in the piston have been shown merely by way of suggestion and can be dispensed with. Each of the chambers **15** and **16** being connected to two conduits as illustrated, the vibrations of a solid piston as **8** will have the same effect and the machine will then be a double acting pump or compressor.

It is likewise unessential that the medium should be admitted to the cylinder through such devices for in certain instances ports, alternately closed and opened by the piston, may serve the purpose. As a matter of course, this novel method of propelling fluids can be extended to multistage working in which case a number of pistons will be employed, preferably on the same shaft and of different diameters in conformity with well established principles of mechanical design. In this way any desired ratio of compression or degree of rarefaction may be attained.

Fig. 4 exemplifies a particularly valuable application of the invention to which reference has been made above. The drawing shows in vertical cross section a turbine which may be of any type but is in this instance one invented and described by me and supposed to be familiar to engineers. Suffice it to state that the rotor **21** of the same is composed of flat plates which are set in motion through the adhesive and viscous action of the working fluid, entering the system tangentially at the periphery and leaving it at the center. Such a machine is a thermodynamic transformer of an activity surpassing by far that of any other prime mover, it being demonstrated in practice that each single disk of the rotor is capable of performing as much work as a whole bucket-wheel. Besides, a number of other advantages, equally important, make it *especially adapted for operation as an internal combustion motor.* This may be done in many ways, but the simplest and most direct plan of which I am aware is the one illustrated here. Referring again to the drawing, the upper part of the turbine casing **22** has bolted to it a separate casting **23**, the central cavity **24** of which forms the combustion chamber.   To prevent injury through excessive heating a jacket **25** may be used, or else water injected, and when these means are objectionable recourse may be had to air cooling, this all the more readily as very high temperatures are practicable. The top of casting **23** is closed by a plate **26** with a sparking or hot wire plug **27** and in its sides are screwed two valvular conduits communicating with the central chamber **24**. One of these is, normally, open to the atmosphere while the other connects to a source of fuel supply as a gas main **28**. The bottom of the combustion chamber terminates in a suitable nozzle **29** which consists of a separate piece of heat resisting material.   To regulate the influx of the explosion constituents and secure the proper mixture of air and gas, conduits are equipped, respectively, with valves **30** and **31**. The exhaust openings **32** of the rotor should be in communication with a ventilator, preferably carried on the same shaft and of any suitable construction. Its use, however, while advantageous, is not indispensable the suction produced by the turbine rotor itself being, in some cases at least, sufficient to insure proper working. This detail is omitted from the drawing as unessential to the understanding.

But a few words will be needed to make clear the mode of operation. The air valve **30** being open and sparking established across terminals **27**, the gas is turned on slowly until the mixture in the chamber **24** reaches the critical state and is ignited. Both the conduits behaving, with respect to efflux, as closed valves, the products of combustion rush out through the nozzle **29** acquiring still greater velocity by expansion and, imparting their momentum to the rotor **21**, start it from rest. Upon the subsidence of the explosion the pressure in the chamber sinks below the atmosphere owing to the pumping action of the rotor or ventilator and new air and gas is permitted to enter, cleaning the cavity and channels and making up a fresh mixture which is detonated as before, and so on, the successive impulses of the working fluid producing an almost continuous rotary effort. After a short lapse of time the chamber becomes heated to such a degree that the ignition device may be shut off without disturbing the established regime. This manner of starting the turbine involves the employment of an unduly large combustion chamber which is not commendable from the economic point of view, for not only does it entail increased heat losses but the explosions cannot be made to follow one another with such rapidity as would be desirable to insure the best valvular action. When the chamber is small and auxiliary means for starting, as compressed air, may be resorted to and a very quick succession of explosions can then be obtained. The frequency will be the greater the stronger the suction, and may, under certain conditions, reach hundreds and even thousands per second. It scarcely need be stated that instead of one, several explosion chambers may be used for cooling purposes and also to increase the number of active pulses and the output of the machine.

Apparatus as illustrated in **Fig. 4** presents the advantages of extreme simplicity, cheapness and reliability, there being no compressor, buckets or troublesome valve mechanism. It also permits, with the addition of certain well known accessories, the use of any kind of fuel and thus meets the pressing necessity of *a self-contained, powerful, light and compact internal combustion motor for general work.* When the attainment of the highest efficiency is the chief object, as in machines of large size, the explosive constituents will be supplied under high pressure and provision made for maintaining a vacuum at the exhaust. Such arrangements are quite familiar and lend themselves so easily to this improvement that an enlargement on this subject is deemed unnecessary.

The foregoing description will readily suggest to experts modifications both as regards construction and application of the device and I do not wish to limit myself in these respects. The broad underlying idea of the invention is to permit the free passage of a fluid through a channel in the direction of the flow and to prevent its return through friction and mass resistance, thus enabling the performance of valve functions without any moving parts and thereby extending the scope and usefulness of an immense variety of mechanical appliances.

I do not claim the methods of an apparatus for the propulsion of fluids and thermodynamic transformation of energy herein disclosed, as these will be made subjects of separate applications.

I am aware that asymmetrical conduits have been constructed and their use proposed in connection with engines, but these have no similarity either in their construction or manner of employment with my valvular conduit. They were incapable of acting as valves proper, for the fluid was merely arrested in pockets and deflected through 90°, this result having at best only 25% of the efficiency attained in the construction herein described. In the conduit I have designed the fluid, as stated above, is deflected in each cycle through 360°, and a co-efficient approximating 200 can be obtained so that the device acts as a slightly leaking valve, and for that reason the term "valvular" has been given to it in contrast to asymmetrical conduits, as heretofore proposed, which were not valvular in action, but merely asymmetrical as to resistance.

Furthermore, the conduits heretofore constructed were intended to be used in connection with slowly reciprocating machines, in which case enormous conduit-length would be necessary, all this rendering them devoid of practical value. By the use of an effective valvular conduit, as herein described, and the employment of pulses of very high frequency, I am able to condense my apparatus and secure such perfect action as to dispense successfully with valves in numerous forms of reciprocating and rotary engines.

The high efficiency of the device, irrespective of the character of the pulses, is due to two causes: first, rapid reversal of direction of flow and, second, great relative velocity of the colliding fluid columns. As will be readily seen, each bucket causes a deviation through an angle of 180°, and another change of 180° occurs in each of the spaces between two adjacent buckets. That is to say, from the time the fluid enters or leaves one of the recesses to its passage into, or exit from, the one following a complete cycle, or deflection through 360°, is effected. Observe now that the velocity is but slightly reduced in the reversal so that the incoming and deflected fluid columns meet with a relative speed, twice that of the flow, and the energy of their impact is four times greater than with a deflection of only 90°, as might be obtained with pockets such as have been employed in asymmetrical conduits for various purposes. The fact is, however, that in these such deflection is not secured, the pockets remaining filled with comparatively quiescent fluid and the latter following a winding path of least resistance between the obstacles interposed. In such conduits the action cannot be characterized as "valvular" because some of the fluid can pass almost unimpeded in a direction opposite to the normal flow. In my construction, as above indicated, the resistance in the reverse may be 200 times that in the normal direction. Owing to this a comparatively very small number of buckets or elements is required for checking the fluid. To give a concrete idea, suppose that the leak from the first element is represented by the fraction $1/x$, then after the nth bucket is traversed, only a quantity $(1/x)^n$ will escape and it is evident that x need not be a large number to secure a nearly perfect valvular action.

What I claim is:

1. A valvular conduit having interior walls of such conformation as to permit the free passage of fluid through it in the direction of flow, but to subject it to rapid reversals of direction when impelled in the opposite sense and thereby to prevent its return by friction and mass resistance.

2. A valvular conduit composed of a closed passageway having recesses in its walls so formed as to permit a fluid to pass freely through it in the direction of flow, but to subject it to rapid reversals of direction when impelled in an opposite sense and thereby interpose friction and mass resistance to the return passage of the same.

3. A valvular conduit composed of a tube or passageway with rigid interior walls formed with a series of recesses or pockets with surfaces that reverse a fluid tending to flow in one direction therein and thereby check or prevent flow of the fluid in that direction.

4. A valvular conduit with rigid interior walls of such character as to offer substantially no obstacle to the passage through it of fluid impulses in one direction, but to subject the fluid to rapid reversals of direction and thereby oppose and check impulses in the opposite sense.

5. A valvular conduit with rigid interior walls formed to permit fluid impulses under pressure to pass freely through it in one direction, but to subject them to rapid reversals of direction through 360° and thereby check their progress when impelled in the opposite sense.

6. A valvular conduit with rigid interior walls which permit fluid impulses to flow through it freely in one direction, formed at a plurality of points to reverse such fluid impulses when impelled in the opposite direction and check their flow.

7. A valvular conduit with rigid interior walls having pockets or recesses, and transversely inclined intermediate baffles to permit the free passage of fluid impulses in one direction but to deflect and check them when impelled in the opposite direction.

In testimony whereof I affix my signature,

NIKOLA TESLA

N. TESLA.

FLOW METER.

APPLICATION FILED DEC. 18, 1916.

1,365,547.

Patented Jan. 11, 1921.

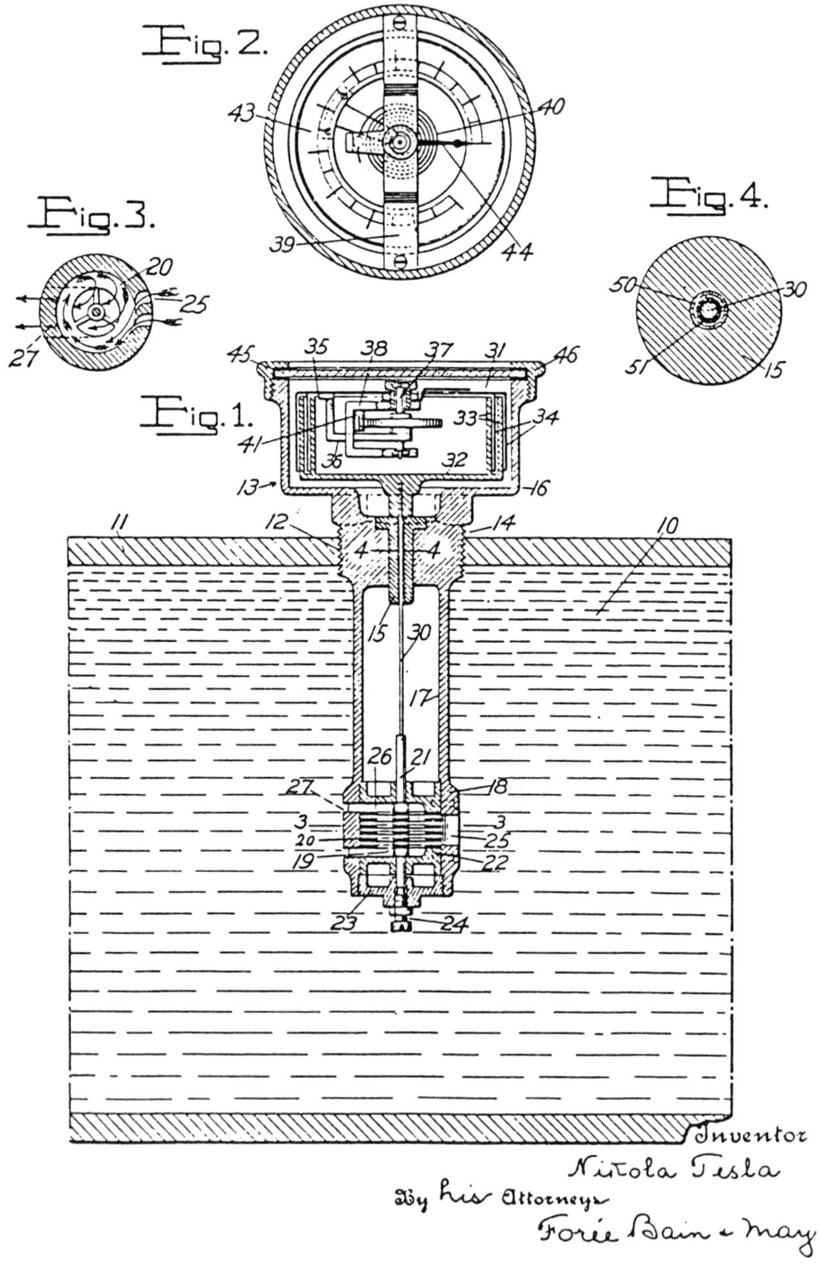

Fig. 2.

43   40

39   44

Fig. 3.

20
25
27

Fig. 4.

50   30
51   15

Fig. 1.

45   35   38   37   31   46
41   33   34
36   32
13   16
11   12   14   10
4   4
15   30
17
26   21
27   18
3   3
20   25
19   22
23   24

Inventor

Nikola Tesla

By his attorneys

Foree Bain & May

United States Patent   **January 11, 1921**

FLOW-METER

1,365,547

Application filed December 18, 1916.   Serial No. 137,688.

NIKOLA TESLA, OF NEW YORK, N. Y., ASSIGNOR TO WALTHAM
WATCH COMPANY, OF WALTHAM, MASSACHUSETTS,
A CORPORATION OF MASSACHUSETTS.

To all whom it may concern:

Be it known that I, NIKOLA TESLA, a citizen of the United States, residing at New York, in the county and State of New York, have invented certain new and useful Improvements in Flow-Meters, of which the following is a full, clear, and exact description.

My invention relates to meters for measurement of velocity or quantity of fluid flow. Its chief object is to provide a novel structure, simple, inexpensive and efficient, directly applicable to a conduit through which the fluid flows, and arranged to give instantaneous readings in terms of velocity, or quantity.

In the drawings I have shown a single embodiment of my invention in desirable form, and therein—

Figure 1 is a central, vertical section showing the device in use;

Fig. 2 is a plan detail of the indicating instrument with parts in section;

Fig. 3 is a horizontal section on line 3—3 of Fig. 1, and

Fig. 4 is an enlarged section on line 4—4 of Fig. 1.

Assuming that the flow of liquid **10** through a main **11** is to be measured as in gallons per hour, or feet per second, the main is tapped as at **12** and into the threaded orifice is screwed the body-casting of the flow-meter **13**. This casting has a threaded waist **14**, centrally apertured to receive the bearing bushing **15**, the upper portion of the casting being formed as a shell **16** for incasing the indicating mechanism, and its lower portion prolonged as a tube **17**, terminating in a head **18** to receive the flow driven element. The latter, I prefer, shall be a turbine of the type commonly identified by my name. Illustrating simply its essential elements, the rotor, **19**, is made up of centrally apertured parallel disks **20**, closely spaced and mounted on a shaft, **21**, extending through a shell **22** confined within the head **18** above the plug **23** that closes the bottom of the head and carries an adjustable step-bearing screw **24**. Inlet nozzles **25**, in the wall of head **18**, direct the liquid to the disks tangentially to set the latter in rotation and the water finds escape through the outlet passages **26** of the shell

22 and ports 27 of the head 18. Preferably the length of tube 17 should be such as to dispose the turbine rotor approximately at the center of the main, and of course the turbine will rotate at a rate linearly proportional to the velocity of the fluid at that point, according to a practically-determined constant.

Turbine shaft 21 connects with shaft 30 of the indicator, that preferably is of minimal diameter for the work to be done and that passes through the long bushing 15 for direct connection with the indicator 31. The primary element, 32, of this indicator, directly mounted on said shaft 30, preferably comprises a cup having multiple vertical walls 33 in concentric arrangement, these being interleaved with inverted cup walls 34 of a secondary element 35, that is pivoted and torsionally restrained and that bears a movable element of the reading scale. Specifically, the secondary element may have its inverted cup walls made of very thin aluminum mounted on arm 36, affixed to the spindle 37 that runs in jewel bearings carried by a yoke 38, supported on a bridge piece 39 spanning the casing 16. A coiled spring 40, at one end fast to the spindle 37 and its other end adjustably secured in split stud 41, on bracket 38, resists displacement of the secondary element which carries on its top a reading scale 43, graduated in terms of gallons per hour, feet per minute, or other units of measurement. This dial moves below the stationary pointer 44 that is visible through the sight-glass 45, carried by the cover cap 46 and tightly sealed. By constructing the indicator in accordance with principles fully explained in my Patent No. 1,209,359 the primary element, acting through the viscous or adhesive properties of air or other fluid medium filling the casing, is caused to displace the scale-bearing member against the tension of its spring substantially in linear proportion to the speed of rotation of the primary element, and by observing the conditions requisite to make the torque bear a rigorously linear proportion to the speed, and making the spring to permit deflections proportionate directly to the turning effort, the scale may be graduated uniformly without the employment of any compensating mechanism to this end.

The pressure or density of the gaseous fluid medium in the casing 60 should not be subject to change under varying conditions of pressure within the main, or the readings might be seriously inaccurate; nor, obviously, should escape of the liquid from the main into the indicator casing be permitted. To seal the running bearing of shaft 30 adequately to withstand very considerable pressures, I make what I term a "mercury-lock" by the following provision: the shaft 30 is made of fine steel of great and uniform density and the bushing 15 is preferably of hard copper, these having diameters leaving a clearance of only a few thousandths of an inch,—much to small for the capillary admission of mercury. These surfaces are treated for amalgamation with mercury. The bearing-portion of the shaft 30 is thinly copper plated, and then both bearing surfaces are coated, in a quickening solution, with mercury, after which the mercury-filmed parts are assembled. In this way, as sought graphically and exaggeratedly to be represented in **Fig.** 4, the mercury body **50** is introduced into the very narrow clearance, and although it is a unitary seal in its resistance to the passage of air or water, it may practically be regarded as forming two mirror-surfaced films between the bushing **15** and the copper plating **51** on shaft **30**. I have found such a mercury lock makes a very effective and enduring seal while permitting adequately free rotation of the shaft.

The combination of turbine rotor and air drag indicating mechanism as above described is especially advantageous in that the small turbine, developing a high shaft speed under even rather slow fluid flow, insures that the speeds of the primary element will be ample to result in high torque, so that the indicator may be of relatively rugged construction. Furthermore, the practical insensibility of the air drag instrument to temperature changes, without special compensating mechanism, makes a very simple construction available for many and variant uses. And since linear relationships exist between the rate of liquid flow, turbine-rotation and indicator-displacement, accurate marking of the scale in uniform graduations depends only upon the establishment of certain easily-ascertainable constants for any given conditions.

What I claim is:

1. A flow-meter comprising a body having a pipe engaging portion, a lower head of smaller diameter and an upper casing, a vertical shaft extending through said body, a disk-turbine in said head directly connected with said shaft, said head having inlet and outlet openings to the turbine disks, and indicating means comprising a rotatable primary element directly connected with said vertical shaft and a torsionally restrained secondary element displaceable by the first and equipped to show its displacement in desired terms.

2. In a device of the character described, the combination of a body fitting having an intermediate part for pipe engagement, a lower head, and an upper shell, a shaft passing vertically from said shell to said head, a pressure-resisting seal for said shaft adjacent said pipe engaging portion of the body, and indicator in said shell comprising a rotatable primary member having a vertical axis and directly connected with the upper end of said shaft, a torsionally-restrained secondary element displacable by the first, said secondary element associated with a scale for showing its defections in desired terms, and a horizontal disk-turbine rotor in said head, said rotor directly connected with the bottom of said shaft, said head having inlet and outlet openings to the rotor disk.

In testimony whereof I affix my signature.

NIKOLA TESLA

179,043 COMPLETE SPECIFICATION   *1 SHEET*

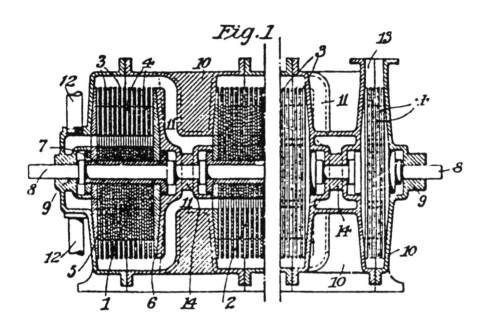

Fig. 1

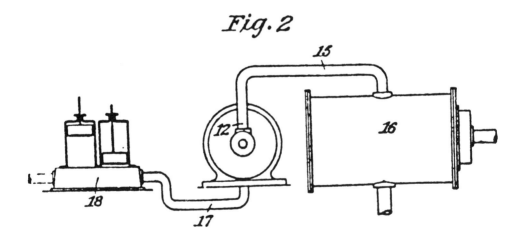

Fig. 2

Improved Process of and Apparatus for

Production of High Vacua.

BRITISH PATENT SPECIFICATION

179,043

COMPLETE SPECIFICATION:

Application Date: Mar. 24, 1921. No. 9098/21
Complete Left: Sept. 5 1921.
Complete Accepted: May 4, 1922.

I, Nikola Tesla, Mechanical and Electrical Engineer, citizen of the United States of America, of No. 8, West 40th Street, New York City, U.S.A., do hereby declare the nature of this invention and in what manner the same is to be performed, to be particularly described and ascertained in and by the following statement:

In the development of power by thermo-dynamic primemovers, as steam engines and turbines, a low back pressure is essential to good economy, the performance of the machine being increased from fifty to one hundred *percent*, by reducing the absolute pressure in the exhaust space from fifteen to about one pound per square inch. Turbines are particularly susceptible to such improvement and in their use for operation of power plants and manufacturing establishments the attainment and steady maintenance of high vacua has assumed great importance, every effort being made to better the conditions in this respect. The gain effected by this means is, in a large measure dependent on the initial pressure, characteristics of the primemover, temperature of the cooling medium, cost of the condensing apparatus and many other things which are all well-known to experts. The theoretical saving of from five to six *percent*, of fuel for each additional inch of vacuum is often closely approximated in modern installations, but the economic advantages are appreciably lessened when higher vacua are applied to existing machines purposely designed to operate with lower ones. More especially is this true of a turbine in which the reduction of back pressure merely increases the velocity of exit of the vapors without materially augmenting the speed of their impact against the vanes, buckets, or equivalent organs, when the loss of kinetic energy in the exhaust may offset a considerable portion of the useful work. In such cases some constructional changes in the turbine and auxiliaries may have to be made in order to secure the results here contemplated but the additional capital used for this purpose will be profitably invested. Summing up the situation it may be generally stated that a more or less substantial reduction of fuel cost can be made in most of the existing power plants by the adoption of proper pumping apparatus and establishment of working conditions nearly corresponding to those of an ideal condenser.

The chief difficulties which have thus far retarded advancement in this direction are encountered in the enormous volumes of the air and vapor at very low pressures as well as unavoidable leaks in the condenser, pipe joints, valves, glands and stuffing boxes. At present exhaustion is usually accomplished by reciprocating pumps and these, on account of the necessarily low speed of the pistons are large and, moreover, incapable of satisfactory performance in the presence of big leaks. As a direct result of this the condensing plant is both bulky and expensive and, worse still, its size and cost increase entirely in disproportion to the results attained. To illustrate - the outlay involved in the instalment of condensing apparatus for a twenty-eight inch vacuum is more than double that required for a vacuum of twenty-six inches and these draw-backs are still more emphasized with the further reduction of the back pressure. Rotary pumps and jets of water and steam are also used in the production of vacua, but without marked qualitative advantages.

Also to the possible employment of multi-stage centrifugal exhausters, engineers are still in doubt. Such machines have heretofore served only for purposes of compression and it is more than probable that they would prove unsuitable for very high rarefaction. The introduction of Sir Charles Parsons' "vacuum augmenter" and Weir's "dry air" pump was a decided progress towards the desired goal, nevertheless this important problem has only been partially solved and to this day the condensing apparatus is admittedly the most troublesome part of the whole power mechanism, to such an extent, indeed, that its duplication is often deemed advisable if not absolutely necessary to the safe and reliable working of the plant.

I have achieved better success in departing from the customary method of removing the air and entrained steam from the condenser by bodily carriers as jets, reciprocating pistons or rotating vanes, and availing myself of the properties of adhesion and viscosity which, according to experimental evidence, are retained by the gases and vapors even at very high degrees of attenuation. The new process which I have thus evolved is rendered practicable through a novel type of pump which I have invented and described in my British Patent No. 24,001 of 1910. This device, suitably modified in certain details of construction and run at the excessive peripheral speed of which an unloaded system is capable, exhibits two remarkable and valuable properties. One of these is to expel the rarefied fluids at such an immense rate that a hole of some size can be drilled in the condenser without much effect on the vacuum gauge. The other is to draw out the fluids until the exhaustion is almost complete. A machine of this kind, constructed in stages, is alone sufficient for the production of extremely high vacua and I believe this quality to be very valuable inasmuch as it is not possessed to such a degree by other types of commercial pumps which have come to my knowledge. However, in order to avoid undue complication and expense I make use of the ordinary exhausting apparatus and simply insert between it and the condenser my pump, which sucks out the highly attenuated media, compresses and delivers them to the "dry air" or other pump. This combination is especially advantageous from the practical point of view as good results can be secured with a single stage and the instalment of my device calls for but a slight change in the steam plant. The benefits derived are twofold: a higher vacuum is attained and, what is perhaps more important, the frequent and unavoidable impairments of the same, which seriously affect the economy, are virtually eliminated. My pump makes possible the maintenance of high vacua even when the percentage of air or other fluids carried with the steam is very great and on this account should prove particularly useful in the operation of mixed fluid turbines.

My invention will be more fully understood by reference to the accompanying drawings in which **Fig. 1** shows a multistage pump of this kind in sectional views, and **Fig. 2** illustrates its use in connection with a double-acting reciprocating pump.

In the first figure, **1, 2,** ... are rotors each of which, as **1**, comprises a number of relatively thin disks **3, 3** ... separated by starwashers **4, 4** ... and held together by rigid end-plates **5** and **6** on a sleeve **7** which is fitted and keyed to a shaft **8**, rotatably supported in bearings **9, 9**. The rotors are contained in separate chambers of a common structure **10** which surrounds them and is made up of parts held together by flange connections. Beginning with the first stage at **1**, the rotors diminish in width, each following being made narrower than the preceding, for obvious economic reasons. All the thin discs, as **3, 3** ..., and lefthand endplates, as **5**, are provided with the usual central openings, but the righthand endplates, as **6**, are blank. The individual chambers, containing the rotors, communicate with each other through channels, as **11**, extending from the peripheral region of one to the central part of the next, so that the fluids aspired at the intakes **12, 12** are compelled to pass through the whole series of rotors and are finally ejected at the flanged opening **13** of the last chamber. In order to reduce leakage along the shaft, close-fitting joints or locks, as **14**, are employed which may be of ordinary construction and need not be dwelled upon specifically. The number of stages will depend on the peripheral velocity and the degree of exhaustion which it is desired to secure, and in extreme cases a number of separate structures, with intermediate bearings for the shaft, may have to be provided. When found preferable the pump may be of the double-flow type, when there will be no appreciable side thrust, otherwise provision for taking it up should be made.

The modifications in details of construction, to which reference has been made, consist in the employment of smaller spaces between the discs than has hitherto been the case, and of close side-clearances. To give a practical example, I may state that spaces of $^3/_{64}$ of an inch will be effective in the production of very high vacua with discs of, say, 24 inches in diameter. I also make all discs tapering, when necessary, in order to operate safely at an extremely high peripheral velocity which is very desirable since it reflects both on the size of the machine and its effectiveness.

The arrangement represented diagrammatically in **Fig. 2** is especially suitable and advantageous in connection with existing steam plants operating with high vacuum and permits the carrying out of my improvements in a simple manner and at comparatively small cost. In this case my pump, which may have but one rotor of the above description, is connected with its intake **12**, through a pipe **15**, to the top of a condenser **16**, and with its discharge opening **13**, by pipe **17**, to the suction duct of a reciprocating dry air pump **18**. It goes without saying that in actual practice connections **15** and **17** will be short mains of very large section as the volume of fluids to be pumped may be enormous.

The operation will be readily understood from the foregoing. The intakes **12** (**Fig. 1**) being joined by an air-tight connection to the vessel to be exhausted and the system of discs run at very high peripheral velocity, the fluids, by reason of their properties of viscosity and adhesion, are drawn out of the vessel until the degree of rarefaction is attained for which the apparatus has been designed. In their passage through the series of rotors the fluids are compressed by stages and ejected through the opening **13** at a volume greatly reduced. The vacuum produced by this means may be extremely high because of the apparently unique properties of the device pointed out before, and as the fluids, irrespective of their density, are sucked out at an excessive speed, leaks through the glands, stuffing boxes and connections are of but slight effect.

In the arrangement shown in **Fig. 2** my pump serves to evacuate the condenser much more effectively and by compressing the fluids at the intake of the reciprocating pump improves the performance of the same. The instalment of the device in existing plants does not call for extensive alterations in the same and will result in a notable saving of fuel. My pump may also be advantageously employed in place of a steam jet in conjunction with a small condenser in which case it will be of insignificant dimensions and economical in steam consumption.

Having now particularly described and ascertained the nature of my said invention and in what manner the same is to be performed, I declare that what I claim is:

1. The improved process of rarefaction which consists in rotating a disc system communicating with a receptacle and continuously ejecting fluid adhering to said system, until a high vacuum is attained in the receptacle, as described.

2. The improved method of exhausting a vessel which consists in rotating a system of discs and continuously applying the frictional force, arising from the viscosity of the fluid and its adhesion to said system, to exhaust the vessel until a high vacuum is attained, substantially as described.

3. The improved process of rarefaction which consists in sucking out of a vessel attenuated fluids by the frictional force of a system of rotating discs, compressing them in the passage through the same, and discharging them into the intake duct of a positively acting pump, as described.

4. As a means for obtaining high vacua, the combination of apparatus, as illustrated and described.

Dated the 23rd day of August, 1921.

NIKOLA TESLA

Redhill: Printed for His Majesty's Stationery Office, by Love & Malcomson, Ltd. - 1922.

174,544 COMPLETE SPECIFICATION   *1 SHEET*

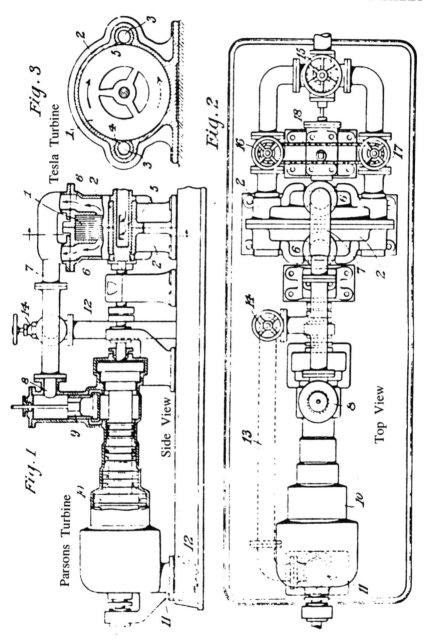

Fig. 3

Tesla Turbine

Fig. 2

Fig. 1

Parsons Turbine

Side View

Top View

Improvements in Methods of and Apparatus for the Generation of

Power by Elastic Fluid Turbines

BRITISH PATENT SPECIFICATION
174,544

COMPLETE SPECIFICATIONS:

Application Date: Apr. 1, 1921 No. 9729/21
Complete Left: Sept. 2, 1921.
Complete Accepted: Feb. 2, 1922.

I, NIKOLA TESLA, Electrical and Mechanical Engineer, citizen of the United States of America, of 8, West 40th Street, New York, N.Y., U.S.A., do hereby declare the nature of this invention and in what manner the same is to be performed, to be particularly described and ascertained in and by the following statement:

In the transformation of the heat of elastic media, by means of turbines, two methods are now extensively employed. In one, the working fluid is expanded through a stationary nozzle and the free jet, impinging against vanes or equivalent devices integral with the rotor, gives up to it velocity energy, thus setting it in motion by action. In the other, the fluid is admitted at full pressure to curved blades or channels in the rotor where it expands imparting energy to the same and causing it to turn by reaction. For well-known technical reasons turbines operating purely on either the first or the second principle are scarcely ever used, both processes being jointly applied in modern machines. Furthermore, almost invariably staging is resorted to with the object of subdividing the velocity and pressure-drop and improving thereby the performance in conformity with fundamental laws of propulsion.

As is obvious from theoretical considerations and heat diagrams, the reaction turbine with pressure stages is generally capable of a higher thermodynamic efficiency because it has a bigger "reheat factor" that is to say, it transforms into mechanical effort a considerable larger portion of friction heat than is recovered in the action turbine, with velocity stages. On the other hand, it will be equally apparent that the former is more limited in the temperature range and, in view of this handicap, its superiority would not be so pronounced were it not for the fact that usually the relative velocity of the fluid is greater in the latter turbine, this detracting still more from its efficiency.

These respective qualities and short-comings have long been fully recognized by engineers long ago and have gradually led to the employment of impulse and reaction-wheels merged into one unit which is thus better adapted for meeting the requirements and should be more economical. But although this idea seems sound, the temperature range has not been very much increased through its application and the gain, so far effected, is moderate indeed, to the point of being doubtful in many instances. Definite limits to progress in this direction have been reached in the existing commercial apparatus and the discovery of other ways and means for saving fuel and reducing the cost of installment and operation has become a problem rendered especially pressing throughout the world by the greatly increased cost of this commodity.

The economic advantages contemplated can be more completely realized through a process which constitutes my present invention and, briefly stated, consists in converting part of the heat energy of an elastic medium into mechanical work by friction, preferably at a high temperature, and a further part by action or reaction at a lower temperature. The best instrumentalities for the purpose, of which I am aware, are a friction turbine of the kind described in my British Patent No. 24,001 of 1910 and one of the reaction type, such as the Parsons, both being connected or worked independently. The fluid is admitted to my turbine through a suitable nozzle which may be expanding, straight or converging, and in traversing the spaces between the discs exercises a frictional drag, thus transforming a part of the available heat energy into mechanical work. Upon exhausting under proper temperature and pressure conditions it is passed through the reaction turbine in which another portion of its caloric energy is usefully converted by reaction.

In the accompanying drawings **Fig. 1** is intended to represent my improved turbine and one of the Parsons type operatively joined and with their shafts flexibly connected; **Fig. 2** is a plan view of the same with supply conduits and inlet valves, and **Fig. 3** a vertical cross-section of my turbine.

Referring to the figures, **1** illustrates the rotor of my turbine enclosed in a casing **2, 2**, provided with two inlets **3, 3**, for the working medium, nozzles **4** and **5** — one for normal operation and the other for reversal — and two exhaust openings **6, 6** which lead through a conduit **7** to the intake **8** and slide valve **9** of the Parsons turbine **10**. The exhaust **11** of the latter communicates through a conduit **12** with the condenser to which is also connected a by-pass **13**, branching out from exhaust pipe **7** and equipped with a valve **14**. A throttle valve **15** controls the admission of the elastic fluid to my turbine which has, besides, two suitable valves **16** and **17**, preferably joined by mechanical means as chain **18**, enabling them to be turned together so that one will be closed tight while the other is wide open.

In normal operation valves **17** and **14** are closed and the medium is admitted to my turbine through valves **15**, **16** and nozzle **4**, whence it passes through the rotor **1**, exhaust openings **6**, **6** and pipe **7** to the intake **8** and valve **9** of the Parsons turbine **10** and, after traversing the same, is discharged through exhaust **11** and conduit **12** into the condenser, under which conditions both the turbines are actuated in the same direction, rotation taking place in the sense of the solid arrow **Fig. 3**. When it is desired to operate in the reverse direction (indicated by the dotted arrow), valves **16** and **9** are closed and **17** and **14** opened wide, the medium entering my turbine through nozzle **5**, and after passing through the rotor **1**, exhaust openings **6**, **6**, pipe **7** and by-pass **13**, discharges into the condenser. The Parsons turbine is then driven in a direction opposite to its blading but offers a relatively small resistance owing to the vacuum therein; my turbine, on the other hand, develops an amount of power much greater than when working as first described on account of its direct connection with the condenser and correspondingly increased heat drop.

Careful scientific investigation, supported by experiment, has shown that important economic results can be secured by the new method and that this particular combination of apparatus possesses features of unusual merit.

In the first place my turbine is especially suited for very elevated temperatures and also high pressures, while the Parsons is particularly adapted to thermo-dynamic transformation at moderate temperatures and low pressures. Again, the former permits the fluid to be expanded either in the nozzle, the rotor or both, and this flexibility facilitates the establishment and maintenance of pressure and temperature conditions favorable to both turbines, thus enhancing economy. Their combination is, however, of quite exceptional value in cases when reversible units are indispensable, as on shipboard, where it provides a simpler and more effective apparatus for forward propulsion as well as backing, my turbine being much more dependable than the present forms with buckets and blades which are very liable to deterioration and easily damaged.

In the use of different types, as here contemplated, the individual heat drops in them may be considerably varied in magnitude, but to give a practical example I would say that very good results, when working with superheated steam alone, are obtainable by admitting the steam to the nozzle of the friction turbine at about 1100° F, and exhausting it at approximately 550° F. into a reaction turbine capable of operating safely at that temperature.

While my turbine in such combinations will yield the best results in co-operation with the Parsons, it is eminently qualified to serve as first stage, or stages, in conjunction with other types of turbines, of whatever kind; also with rotary and reciprocating engines, and in this broader sense my improved process may be defined as one in which the available heat energy of an elastic fluid is usefully transformed first by friction, as indicated, and then by action or reaction.

Having now particularly described and ascertained the nature of my said invention, and in what manner the same is to be performed, I declare that what I claim is:

1. The improved method of thermodynamic transformation which consists in converting a part of the heat energy of an elastic fluid by disc friction and a further part by blade action, substantially as described.

2. The hereinbefore described process of transforming the heat energy of an elastic fluid into rotary mechanical work which consists in converting a part of the energy of the fluid by friction at high temperature and a further part by action and or reaction at a lower temperature, substantially as described.

3. In the conversion of heat energy of elastic fluids the combination of the friction and reaction type of turbine, as described.

4. The combined use of a friction turbine of the kind described with an action and reaction engine in the transformation of the heat energy of elastic fluids into mechanical work.

5. The combination of a friction turbine of the type described with a turbine of the reaction type mounted on the same shaft or on connected shafts to form an operative unit for the transformation of the heat energy of elastic fluids into mechanical work.

6. The combination of a friction and a reaction turbine of the types described connected to form a power unit so that both may operate together in one direction or be driven in the opposite direction by the friction turbine, the reaction turbine running idle, as, described.

Dated the 23rd day of August, 1921.

NIKOLA TESLA

Redhill: Printed for His Majesty's Stationary Office,
by Love & Malcomson, Ltd. - 1922.

Jan. 3, 1928.   1,655,114

N. TESLA

APPARATUS FOR AERIAL TRANSPORTATION

Filed Oct. 4, 1927   2 Sheets—Sheet 1

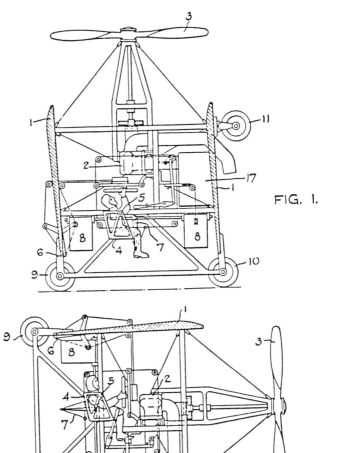

FIG. I.

FIG. 2.

INVENTOR.

NIKOLA TESLA.

BY

ATTORNEY.

THE ULTIMATE ULTRA-LIGHT

Jan. 3, 1928.   1,655,114

N. TESLA

APPARATUS FOR AERIAL TRANSPORTATION

Filed Oct. 4, 1927   2 Sheets—Sheet 2

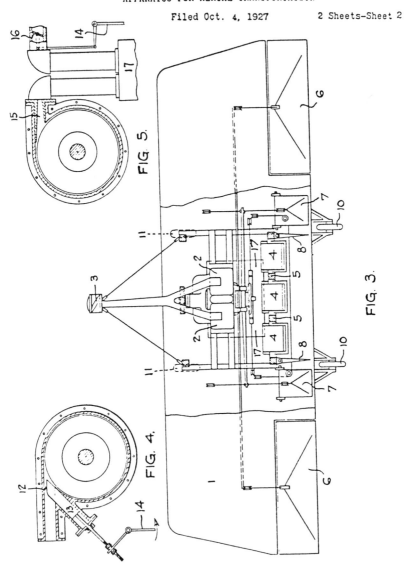

FIG. 5.

FIG. 3.

FIG. 4.

INVENTOR.

NIKOLA TESLA.

BY *John P. Tarbox*

ATTORNEY.

United States Patent *(Abridged)*   **January 3, 1928**

APPARATUS FOR

AERIAL TRANSPORTATION

1,655,114

Application filed October 4, 1927.   Serial No. 223,915.

This application is a continuation in part of my application Serial No. 499,518, filed September 9, 1921, and is made pursuant to the rules of the Patent Office, its purpose being to describe and claim apparatus which I have invented for carrying into practice the method therein disclosed. [Ed. Method of Aerial Transportation U.S. patent 1,655,113] . . .

I employ, preferably, a turbine described in my U. S. Patent 1,061,206 of May 6, 1913, which not only fulfills these requirements but lends itself especially to operation at very high temperatures. Two such turbines, designated **2, 2** together with other parts and accessories of the power plant, are bolted to the frame, being placed with due regard to the centers of gravity and pressure... Power is transmitted to the shaft from the turbines through gearing which may be of the single reduction type as illustrated, the turbines rotating in the same direction and neutralizing the gyroscopic moment of the screw. If, instead of one, two propellers are used, either coaxially or otherwise disposed, the motors should revolve in opposite directions... The turbine used is of great lightness and activity exceptionally qualified to perform such work for which the present aviation motors are unsuited. It is capable of carrying an extra-ordinarily great overload and running at excessive speed, and during the starting, landing and other relatively short operations, not only can the necessary power be easily developed, but this can be accomplished without incurring a serious loss of efficiency. Owing to its extreme simplicity the motive apparatus is very reliable, but should the power give out accidentally, landing can still be effected by volplaning...

The abnormal power requirements are met by supplying more of the working fluid to the motors and driving them faster, or running them at about the same speed and increasing the thrust by adjustment of the pitch of the propeller. On account of simplicity and much greater range it is preferable to resort to the first method...

In order to secure the best results I have found it indispensable to depart, in some respects, from the usual design of my turbines and embody in them certain constructive features and means for varying the power developed from the minimum necessary in horizontal flight to an amount exceeding by far their rated performance, as may be required in the operations of ascent and descent, or spurts of speed, or in combatting the fury of the elements.

Furthermore, I so proportion and coordinate the fluid pressure generator supplying the primary energy, the propelling and the controlling means, that for any attitude or working condition of the machine the requisite thrust may be almost instantly produced and accurately adjusted.

The understanding of these improvements will be facilitated by reference to **Fig. 4** and **Fig. 5**. In the first named the turbines are intended to operate as rotary engines, expanding the gases in the rotor as well as the inlet nozzle or port **12**, the depth of which can be varied by shifting a block **13**, fitting freely in a milled channel of the casing, through the medium of lever **14** controlled by the aviator. The orifice for the passage of the elastic fluid is straight or slightly converging, so that a much smaller velocity is obtained than with an expanding nozzle, this enabling the best relation between the peripheral speed of the rotor and that of the fluid to be readily attained. The performance of such an engine at constant pressure of supply is, within wide limits, proportionate to the quantity of the working medium passed through the inlet port and it is practicable to carry, for indefinite intervals of time, an exceedingly great overload, by which I mean up to three or even four times the normal. Exceptional strength and ruggedness of the motors being imperative in view of centrifugal stresses and critical speed, their weight need not be appreciably increased as would be the case in other forms of prime movers in which, as a rule, the weight is in nearly direct proportion to the power developed. To accomplish my purpose I further provide commensurately larger inlet and outlet openings. No serious disadvantage is thereby incurred because windage and other losses are virtually absent and most of the rotary effort is due to the peripheral parts of the discs. As shown in the figure, block **13** is in the position corresponding to minimum effort, the section of the inlet channel being about one-fifth of the whole which is obtained when the block is pulled in its extreme position indicated by the dotted line. Owing to the increase of the coefficient of contraction and counterpressure attendant the enlargement of the inlet, the same should be made of ample section.

Figure 5 shows a different means for attaining the same purpose. In this case the motors operate like true turbines, the working fluid being fully expanded, or nearly so, through divergent exchangeable nozzles as **15**, having a throat of sufficient section for the passage of fluid required during maximum performance. The exhaust opening is also correspondingly enlarged, though not necessarily to the extent indicated in **Figure 4**. The power is varied by means of a throttle valve **16**, as used in automobiles, located in the conduit supplying the air and carbureted fuel to the fluid pressure generator and mechanically connected to the controlling lever **14**. This apparatus is of a capacity adequate to the maximum demand by which I do not mean that it is necessarily much larger than required for normal performances, but is merely designed to supply the working fluid or, broadly stated, energy—whenever desired, at a rate greatly exceeding the normal. In **Figure 3** this apparatus is diagrammatically indicated by **17**, and may be any one of a number of well-known types, producing pressure by internal combustion of a suitable fuel or by external firing of a steam boiler. In the latter case, with constant pressure, the arrangement shown in **Figure 4** is best to employ, while the plan illustrated in **Figure 5** can be used to advantage when both pressure and quantity of fluid are varied...

I claim as my invention...

3. In an aeroplane adapted for vertical and horizontal propulsion and change from one to the other attitude, the combination of means for tilting the machine in the air, a fluid pressure generator capable of supplying fluid at a rate several time greater than required for horizontal flight, a prime mover consisting of a rotor of plane spaced discs with central openings and an enclosing casing with inlet and outlet orifices of a section much greater than required for normal performances respectively at the periphery and center of the same, and means for controlling the supply of the fluid to the motor in accordance with the inclination of the machine.

4. In an aeroplane adapted for vertical and horizontal propulsion and change from one to the other attitude, the combination of means for tilting the machine in the air, a thrust producing system having its principal energy producing elements designed for normal load in horizontal flight but support of the aeroplane in all attitudes, and means for controlling the energy produced in said system in accordance with the inclination of the machine...

In testimony whereof I hereunto affix my signature.   *NIKOLA TESLA*

NEW YORK TIMES, Feb. 22, 1928, p18:c4

TESLA GETS PATENTS ON HELICOPTER - PLANE

Wireless Experimenter Says His Invention is Ideal for Air Flivver.

Nikola Tesla, Pioneer wireless experimenter, has turned his attention to aviation. According to an announcement from Munn & Co., Patent attorneys, the 71-year-old inventor has received two patents from the United States Patent Office for a combined helicopter and airplane.

The plane has not been built, and according to the inventor he is not particularly interested in experimenting with the actual building.

Briefly, his helicopter-airplane takes off vertically as a helicopter and then by mechanical means is turned in the air until the lifting propeller is at right angles to its climbing position and draws the machine through the air laterally, or at any other angle the operator wishes it to go.

The inventor said yesterday that he conceives his plane as the ideal air flivver. It can be built with a wing spread of eight feet and a depth and length of the same dimensions. Its weight would be about 500 pounds, and a machine of this size would carry two people.

Mr. Tesla describes his power plant as a turbine engine which also combines some of the principles of the present-day internal combustion engine and aeronautical rotary motor.

A TRUE ENERGY AWARENESS

In closing, a short biography of a researcher is presented who was able to make the transition from closely held, though erroneous, ideas to a True Energy Awareness.

The discover of deuterium, or heavy water, Nobel prize laureate Professor Harold Urey (1893-1981), was one of the first and staunchest supporters of the use of nuclear power for electrical energy production. He was one of the prominent scientists to witness the hydrogen weapons test conducted at Bikini Atoll.

Professor Urey was dedicated to an effort that would exploit this power for the benefit of man and spearheaded a campaign devoted to the rapid establishment of nuclear power for electrical generation.

As one of the worlds most respected spokesman for the nuclear theme, it is significant to note that by the early 1970's, after a spiritual and intellectual awakening, he was totally convinced of the folly of his previous convictions.

Warning bells rang in professor Urey's psyche as he realized that the nuclear poisons could not and were not to be contained. He predicted that this demon, which he had once embraced, would devastate all human life on the planet without even a single detonation of a nuclear device.

Professor Urey began to sound the alarm bells in the scientific community with a fervor unknown to his previous nuclear promotions.

His message, however, was falling on deaf ears.

Professor Urey explained that environmentally derived energy production in unlimited quantities had been proven a reality, therefore negating any need for atomic power on earth.

He accused the scientific community of being blind to the true and simple facts of energy, stating that nuclear scientists are like children not knowing the true value of currency. Thinking they are richer with many pennies, rather than a single piece of highly numbered paper.

Tesla's Engine is one of these highly denominated but ignored devices professor Urey was making reference to.

Professor Urey was, like Tesla, a scientist of the highest integrity. In both of these men's lives, truth reigned supreme over ego.

Quoting Tesla:

The scientists, from Franklin to Morse were clear thinkers and did not produce erroneous theories. The scientists of today think deeply instead of clearly. One must be sane to think clearly, but one can think deeply and be
Quite Insane.

INDEX